Learning difficulties in primary classrooms

Under the Education Reform Act, 1988, all pupils, including those who have special educational needs, share the same statutory entitlement to a broad and balanced curriculum, including access to the national curriculum. It is thus the responsibility of all teachers to ensure that this requirement is translated into good practice. For many teachers this new challenge will necessitate the provision of appropriate guidance and support to help them to respond satisfactorily to these demands.

This book offers clear, practical guidelines to help ensure that the full breadth of the curriculum is made as available to children with special educational needs as the rest of their peers. Part I discusses the nature of learning difficulties and examines ways in which learning difficulties can be recognised during the early years of education. The contributors to Part II focus on the curriculum areas, discussing particular difficulties which children may experience in each area, and offering practical suggestions to help teachers in their efforts to maximise children's learning performance in the classroom. Part III examines ways in which pupils' learning can be supported within classrooms, schools and homes.

The book focuses on primary and middle schools and is directed towards the professional training needs and general interests of teachers and support staff, headteachers, governors and parents.

Kevin Jones is Head of the Department of Education at Cheltenham and Gloucester College of Higher Education.

Tony Charlton is a Research Fellow at Cheltenham and Gloucester College of Higher Education.

Learning difficulties in primary classrooms

Delivering the whole curriculum

Edited by
Kevin Jones and Tony Charlton

London and New York

First published 1992
by Routledge
11 New Fetter Lane, London EC4P 4EE

Simultaneously published in the USA and Canada
by Routledge
a division of Routledge, Chapman and Hall, Inc.
29 West 35th Street, New York, NY 10001

© 1992 Kevin Jones and Tony Charlton

Typeset in 10/12pt September by Leaper and Gard Ltd, Bristol
Printed in England by Clays Ltd, St Ives plc

British Library Cataloguing in Publication Data

A catalogue reference for this book is available
from the British Library.

ISBN 0–415–08389–3
0–415–08388–5

*Library of Congress Cataloging in Publication Data
has been applied for.*

Contents

Contributors   vii

Introduction   1

Part I Recognising special educational needs within the primary classroom   3

1 Recognising successes and difficulties in learning   5
   Kevin Jones

2 Giving access to the national curriculum 'by working on the "self"'   24
   Tony Charlton

3 Providing for special educational needs within the primary curriculum   41
   Bill Brown

Part II Providing for special educational needs within an appropriate educational context   59

4 The primacy of talk   61
   Diana Hutchcroft

5 A real context for reading   73
   Helen Arnold

6 Providing for pupils' writing needs   88
   Stuart Dyke

7 Meeting the special needs of mathematical low attainers in the primary school   103
   Derek Haylock

8 Investigating science and technology   115
   Caroline Dray and Kevin Jones

9 Providing for movement learning needs   126
   Barbara Brown

10 Access to humanities   145
    Tim Copeland

11 Art – a special form of provision   156
    Nigel Furness

12 Religious education – finding a way   167
    Ted Huddleston

13 A classroom plan for personal and social education in primary
    schools   174
    Kenneth David

    Part III Support for learning within the classroom   187

14 Special educational provision: a shared responsibility   189
    Kevin Jones and Tony Charlton

15 Collaborative enquiry-based learning and training   201
    Susan Jones

16 Accessing the curriculum with microtechnology   212
    Marie Buckland

    Index   218

Contributors

Helen Arnold is a part-time Senior Lecturer in reading and language at Homerton College, Cambridge, an educational consultant and writer. After extensive teaching experience, she became a College of Education lecturer at All Saints, Tottenham and then at Homerton College. She was seconded from Homerton from 1973 to 1977 to work as research associate with Vera Southgate (Director) on the Extending Beginning Reading Project (Schools Council, Manchester University). Helen was County English Adviser, Suffolk County Council from 1977 to 1982.

Her research interests and publications have resulted in an unpublished M.A. thesis, University of London, 'Children's Talk, 7–9' and the following publications; *Extending Beginning Reading* (co-author) Heinemann, 1981: *Making Sense of It, Texts for Miscue Analysis*, Hodder and Stoughton, 1984; *Wordcraft, A Primary Language Course*, Collins, 1985; *Reading Together, for Parents and Children*, Pan/Macmillan. She has also made numerous contributions to journals and contributory chapters to books.

Bill Brown is Headteacher of a special school for children who experience difficulties in learning, which is situated in Wiltshire. Besides writing articles on special education he has also published a number of books on outdoor pursuits.

Barbara Brown is a Senior Lecturer in education in the Faculty of Education and Health at the Cheltenham and Gloucester College of Higher Education. Her particular expertise rests in the area of children's movement learning difficulties.

Marie Buckland is a Deputy Headteacher in a primary school and was formerly Assistant Manager at Bristol SEMERC with a responsibility for INSET and the development of training materials, particularly in mathematics. Her research into the use of the floor turtle with children with special educational needs has resulted in an unpublished M.Phil.

Tony Charlton has taught in primary, secondary and special schools and he is tutor to the in-service course at University College, Cardiff. Formerly a Principal Lecturer and Head of the Special Needs Department, he is currently a Research

Fellow at Cheltenham and Gloucester College of Higher Education. He has published on counselling in Britain and America.

Tim Copeland is Vice Chairperson of the education committee of the British Archaeological Society and a Senior Lecturer in Education. He was previously Head of a primary school in Oxfordshire and still resides close to Oxford. He has published widely in the area of Heritage Education.

Kenneth David has for some years been a freelance lecturer and writer, with publications in the field of health education, personal and social education and pastoral care. In a variety of early careers he has been a soldier, primary school teacher, colonial service principal, secondary Head of English, and an adviser in Gloucestershire and Lancashire. He has published widely in the area of Personal and Social Education.

Caroline Dray is a teaching Head in a primary school on the borders of Gloucestershire and Hereford and Worcester. Caroline has undertaken advanced study in Science Education and Learning difficulties and shares her understanding and experiences of those areas in this book.

Stuart Dyke is a Staff Development Officer with Service Children's Schools in North-West Europe. Previously he held the post of Language Development Officer for the same authority. His teaching was with primary-aged pupils in the United States and middle school children on the Isle of Wight. His Masters Degree in Education was from Southampton University. He has been involved in the National Writing and Oracy projects and is currently undertaking a research study into the development of children's writing at the University of East Anglia.

Nigel Furness is a primary school Headteacher in Devon. His interests in art education and the special educational needs of primary-aged pupils have led to the development of work which is of interest to all teachers who strive to provide rich curricular experiences for all pupils.

Derek Haylock is a Lecturer in mathematics education at the University of East Anglia. He has published widely in mathematics education journals. His main research interests have been in mathematical creativity in schoolchildren and in the problems of low-attainers in mathematics in the age range 9–12 years. He was director of the UCAN (Using Calculators to Aid Numeracy) project, 1985–7, based at the University of East Anglia. He has recently published two significant texts in the area of mathematics education: *Understanding Early Years Mathematics* (Chapman, 1989) and *Teaching Mathematics to Low-Attainers, 8–12* (Chapman, 1991).

Ted Huddleston has had ten years' practical experience teaching Religious Education in schools. He was Saint Luke's College Foundation Fellow, from 1985–8, School of Education, University of Exeter, researching the whole area of Religious Education for children with special educational needs. The work of the

Saint Luke's project has already resulted in 'Practical Approaches: Religious Education for Children with Special Educational Needs' (Devon Education Dept and St. Luke's Foundation, 1988) and it is hoped to publish a more general report on the findings of the project. He is currently writing a Ph.D on Religous Education and the needs of children with learning difficulties.

Diana Hutchcroft has had wide and varied experience in schools, more latterly as a Headteacher of a large primary school in Avon. Her book 'Making Language Work' was particularly well received in educational circles, especially in the light of her work on the Bullock Committee.

Kevin Jones is Head of the Department of Education at the Cheltenham and Gloucester College of Higher Education. His teaching experience spans primary, secondary and special schools and he has also served in an advisory capacity and support role. He has published a range of articles relating to special educational needs in primary schools and has contributed a chapter entitled 'Working with Parents' to T. Charlton and K. David (eds) *Managing Misbehaviour* (Macmillan, 1989). His research interests include the assessment/recognition of learning diffi-culties, special educational provision in mathematics and co-operative teaching approaches. He has carried out research into the special oral language needs of low-attaining mathematicians which has led to an unpublished Ph.D thesis (University of East Anglia).

Susan Jones worked in scientific research before undertaking a further degree in philosophy. Between 1978 and 1985 she lectured in Social Studies and Computer Literacy at the Gloucestershire College of Arts and Technology. Since then she has worked as a freelance lecturer, consultant, and writer in the areas of teacher and management training. Her research work and writings span a wide area, including teacher training, health education and training, special needs education and management training. She ardently believes that the problem of the special needs pupil is, essentially, part of the wider problem of poor educational and industrial performance, and that this can only be effectively tackled by changing the non-democratic, hierarchical relations which predominate between teacher and pupil, teacher and parent, teacher and teacher, manager and employee. She has recently published a book which identifies the core collaborative skills that need to be developed by all practitioners in education, health and industry, as a basis for achieving human motivation, personal development and organisational success.

Introduction

Teachers work within a climate of constant change. At times, these changes and their associated demands, generate considerable anxieties and concerns within members of the profession. The Education Reform Act (1988), and the implementation of the national curriculum in particular, are currently placing burgeoning demands upon staff in schools, whose energies are already being challenged by other innovation.

The new legislation states that all pupils, including those who have special educational needs, share the same statutory entitlement to a broad and balanced curriculum, including access to the national curriculum. Consequently, it is the responsibility of all teachers to ensure that this entitlement is translated into good practice. For many teachers this new challenge will necessitate the provision of appropriate guidance and support to help them to respond satisfactorily to these demands.

This book focuses upon primary and middle schools and is directed towards the professional training needs and/or general interests of:

- classteachers
- special educational needs' support teachers
- headteachers and senior staff
- governors
- parents
- members of support services
- teachers on pre- and in-service courses
- educational psychologists
- others involved with, or otherwise concerned for, pupils with special educational needs.

The contents offer clear, practical guidelines to help ensure that the full breadth of the curriculum is made as available to children with special educational needs as the rest of their peers.

Part I discusses the nature of learning difficulties and – with reference to research carried out by the editors – examines ways in which learning difficulties can be recognised during the early years of education. Having addressed concerns about the appraisal of special educational needs, the book continues by examining ways in which education should be provided in 'special' ways within the context of the wider curriculum.

In Part II, contributors focus upon key curriculum areas. First, they discuss particular difficulties which children may experience in each area. Second, they offer practical suggestions to help teachers in their efforts to maximise children's learning performance in the classroom.

Part III examines ways in which pupils' learning can be supported within classrooms, schools and homes. Within these chapters the writers discuss – and stress the importance of – the need to develop 'partnerships with pupils, parents and professionals' and make appropriate use of 'microtechnology'.

Part I

Recognising special educational needs within the primary classroom

In Chapter 1, Kevin Jones discusses how, over a number of years, teachers, parents and other professionals, have been presented with a variety of explanations for children's learning difficulties. He explains that whilst some of these accounts have located the 'source' of difficulties within the child, others have identified problems within the curriculum which is presented to the child. He then examines the shortcomings of these explanations and considers the range of factors which must be taken into account when describing the learning difficulties which are experienced by children. As a conclusion, he presents a model for the recognition of learning difficulties in primary classrooms.

The question of access to the national curriculum is the subject of Chapter 2, where Tony Charlton discusses ways in which aspects of children's emotional (mal)functioning can 'block' their ability to profit from the mainstream curriculum. He then focuses upon the association between learning difficulties and emotional problems before exploring ways in which emotional problems can generate learning difficulties (such as reading problems) which may then impede access to the mainstream curriculum. To conclude, attention is drawn to the crucial role of the classteacher in identifying, and making appropriate provisions to meet, children's emotional needs. By ensuring that such provision is appropriate, teachers may 'unblock' the 'block' that impeded meaningful access to the national curriculum.

Finally, in Chapter 3, Bill Brown explores and develops arguments for a broad-based primary curriculum that serves the interests of all children, irrespective of their special educational needs. With reference to the Educational Reform Act (1988), DES Circulars and LEA guidelines, he discusses ways in which teachers can make the breadth of the national curriculum accessible to their pupils.

Chapter 1

Recognising successes and difficulties in learning

Kevin Jones

Very few of us would wish to marginalise children who experience difficulties in learning by excluding them from the full range of educational opportunities which are available to the majority of children of their age. This spirit is echoed in statements which suggest that: *all* children should have access to a broad, balanced, coherent and relevant curriculum (National Curriculum Council, 1989).

The making of statements is relatively easy. Similarly, the majority of us feel comfortable with the notion that *all* children, including those who are experiencing learning difficulties, should enjoy equality of access to the breadth of educational experiences which are enjoyed by their peers. Translating those rights into reality, however, is much more difficult.

Many children will require special consideration and support (ILEA, 1985) if the above aims are to be achieved. These requirements will present teachers, parents and associated professionals with a considerable, but not insurmountable, challenge. In our attempts to provide for children with special educational needs, we are likely to encounter a variety of obstacles (e.g. lack of time, resources, knowledge) which may impede our efforts to help the children concerned. Those obstacles must not be brushed aside. Like all other factors which help or hinder access to learning, they must be assessed and responded to. If we are serious in our attempts to open up the breadth and depth of the curriculum for all children, we must attempt to recognise and attend to all factors which facilitate or hinder such access. This book aims to provide guidance for those who are engaged in that task.

The particular focus of the first two chapters is upon ways in which teachers, pupils, parents and other professionals can join together to:

(a) seek out those factors which help or hinder access to the breadth of the curriculum;
(b) use that information to describe a pupil's special educational needs;
(c) give appropriate consideration and support to that child, in order that s/he gains access to the breadth and depth of the curriculum.

CHOOSING THE BEST APPROACH

There are many different ways in which children's special educational needs can be appraised. Tests abound, as do checklists, rating scales and advice on observation and recording procedures. In choosing the best approach we must ensure that our overall strategy is the one which leads to the most accurate description of the child's special educational needs and the most appropriate form of provision.

A QUESTION OF BALANCE

At this juncture, it is important to clarify what we mean when we refer to the special educational needs of children who experience difficulties in learning. There are many different ways of interpreting the word 'special', each having considerable impact upon the kind of provision which is made for the children concerned. This can be illustrated by comparing two different interpretations.

First, let us consider the word 'special' when it is applied to the needs of children in an educational context. In 1988, Jones and Charlton conducted a questionnaire survey, to which 35 primary school teachers from three local education authorities responded. Teachers were asked, amongst other things, to describe the special educational needs of children in their classes. The completed questionnaires revealed a number of descriptions of 'special' educational needs. For example, teachers suggested that particular children had a special need for:

- programmes of work to help with visual perception
- listening activities
- activities to help with sequencing in written language
- speech therapy
- pencil control activities
- phonic development
- intensive input to develop pre-writing skills
- computer programmes for spelling
- precise objectives in number
- structured handwriting programmes

Without exception, the children were said to have a special need for additional provision which focused on the difficulties which they encountered.

The descriptions of special educational needs which emerged from the completed questionnaires produced very few surprises given the fact that teachers, parents and other professionals have been encouraged to conceptualise 'special educational needs' in a particular way. Under the terms of the 1981 Education Act (DES, 1981) a child is considered to have special educational needs if s/he has learning difficulties which are greater than those encountered by the majority of pupils of the same age, which require special educational provision to be made. Thus, in relation to educational needs, the word 'special' is often directly associated with the need for extra provision which responds to a child's difficulties in learning.

Now let us consider a different interpretation of the word 'special', within the context of our own all-round needs. When groups of adults are asked to produce descriptions of their 'special' needs the resultant list, of which the following is typical, has quite a different flavour. Adults often suggest that they have a special need for:

- love
- health
- happiness
- concern for others
- a nice place to live
- time to spend with their family
- reading
- opportunities to walk in the countryside
- money
- nice clothes
- opportunities to play tennis or go sailing

This list consists of a lot of pleasant things (and there are many others which could be added); things which those people enjoy, are interested in, concerned about, or within which they have already experienced some success. Whilst some adults consider that they have a special need to learn to do something which they find difficult, often they tend to relegate it to the bottom of their list.

So why is the interpretation of the term 'special needs', in an educational context, so different for children? Why do so many 'statements' of special educational need refer only to those things which children cannot do? Are not their special educational needs similar in flavour to our all-round needs?

Special educational provision can easily get 'out of balance' by 'focusing upon those things which the child cannot do, rather than building upon those things which the child is interested in, enjoys doing and within which some success has already been experienced' (see Figure 1.1).

There are two aspects of special educational need. Firstly there are: (a) those special needs which relate to the child's interests, concerns and successes; and secondly there are: (b) those special needs which relate to the difficulties which a child encounters.

In our desire to help particular children we often focus heavily upon the latter of the two aspects, thereby creating an unbalanced form of provision. 'Special' means building upon successes as well as responding to difficulties.

Fortunately, there is a simple way to redress the balance. Turn the term 'special educational needs' around, so that it reads, 'needs educational special' and analyse a particular child's special educational needs in that order:

1. *Needs*   What are the child's all-round needs?

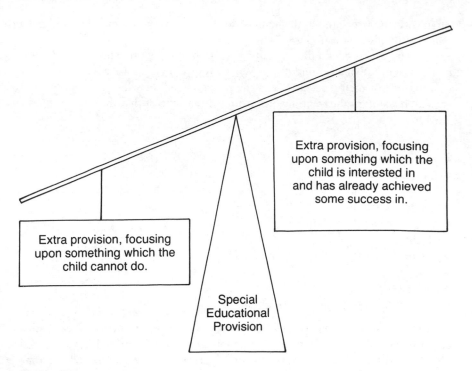

Figure 1.1

2. *Educational*   What are the child's educational needs?
3. *Special*   What factors cause the child to experience successes and diffi-
                    culties in learning? How can that information be used to give
                    the child access to the breadth of educational needs outlined in
                    2 and to the fulfilment of their all-round needs in 1?

The following text illustrates how a consideration of the above components, in the suggested order, can lead to a more balanced picture of a child's 'special educational needs'.

All-round needs

If we were to ask children to describe their own special educational needs (as indeed we should as part of a comprehensive appraisal of their needs) they would be likely to come up with a list which is quite different from that drawn up by their teachers. Their list would probably contain items similar to those chosen by adults. Children typically suggest that they have a special need for:

● activities which are of particular interest or concern to them
● opportunities to pursue areas of the curriculum within which they have already experienced success

- activities in which they can gain approval
- learning which involves them actively

Some children realise that they need to develop skills and understanding in areas within which they encounter difficulties, but such 'special' needs are not high on their list.

Thus, our first task in planning appropriate provision for children who experience difficulties in learning is to ensure that the overall pattern of the school day feels 'special' to them. If we respond to their all-round needs, the resultant learning experiences will provide a motivating context within which we can begin to help them to overcome specific difficulties. This view has been previously expressed by Rowland (1987) who suggests that:

> if our concern leads us to concentrate primarily upon devising a machinery for diagnosing children and preparing detailed packages for learning according to clearly defined objectives, I fear we shall be missing out on the heart of what these children, and indeed all learners, need from their teachers. The need is for teaching- and learning-relationships in which the children's interests, abilities and concerns are seen to be at the centre of their curriculum, and in which their expressions – whether in writing, painting, speech or other symbols – are taken as being serious endeavours to communicate something of significance.
>
> The challenge with which children who experience learning difficulties present us is to listen more carefully, and take bolder steps towards understanding their world, as reflected in the choices they make and the interpretations they form of their environment. Such a challenge is not easily met in the classroom.

The importance of providing a learning context which involves children actively in purposeful and interesting activities is a recurrent theme throughout this book.

The process of matching teaching and learning experiences to the all-round needs of children can be refined even further by probing the particular interests and concerns of individual pupils. This process, which often leads to successful learning outcomes, was clearly evident in the case of Mark, a nine-year-old pupil who had experienced considerable difficulties in learning to read over the four years of his formal schooling. A discussion, at which Mark and his parents were present, revealed that he had a particular interest in farming and farm-machinery, interests which had emerged from several visits to his uncle's farm. On the basis of this information the context within which the teaching of reading was based was changed. 'Fiction' from reading-schemes was replaced with 'factual texts' related to farming. This change of context, coupled with other factors (e.g. the introduction of paired-reading) helped Mark to develop an interest in books, a desire to develop his reading skills and experience considerable success.

When the child's all-round needs have been considered in detail, the focus of our attention can shift towards an examination of the breadth of their educational needs.

Educational needs

Special educational provision has often been criticised for being narrow in focus; for concentrating upon the 'basics' at the expense of other educational needs.

Over recent years many statements have appeared (see Chapter 3) which affirm that:

> All pupils share the right to a broad and balanced curriculum, including the national curriculum. The right extends to every registered pupil of compulsory school age attending a maintained, or grant maintained school, whether or not he or she has a statement of special educational needs.
>
> (National Curriculum Council, 1989)

This right is implicit in the Education Reform Act (1988) which entitles every pupil in maintained schools to a curriculum which is balanced and broadly-based and which: (a) promotes the spiritual, moral, cultural, mental and physical development of pupils, and (b) prepares such pupils for the opportunities, responsibilities and experiences of adult life.

The Act also sets out certain key elements which must figure in every pupil's curriculum. They include:

- religious education for all pupils at county and voluntary schools, except those in nursery classes
- the national curriculum for those of compulsory school age in maintained schools. All pupils in primary schools should have access to: the core subjects of English, Mathematics and Science; and the foundation subjects of Technology (including design), History, Geography, Music, Art and Physical Education.

Thus, it is no longer appropriate to confine those children who experience difficulties in learning to an unbalanced diet of reading, spelling and arithmetic. Like all other children they are entitled to the breadth of educational experiences outlined above.

There are two senses in which the breadth of a child's educational needs should be considered. Firstly, we must ensure their participation across key aspects of learning (i.e. the core and foundation areas, religious education, and other important cross-curricular areas such as Health Education and Education for Citizenship). Secondly, we should ensure that children are able to gain access to the breadth of learning within each of the core and foundation areas. For example, in mathematics children should not be confined to 'number'. They should be given the opportunity to participate in other areas of the mathematics curriculum such as: 'using number, algebra and measures in practical tasks to solve real-life problems', and 'selecting, interpreting and using appropriate data'

(DES 1985: National Curriculum Council, 1989a). Likewise, in English, children should not be restricted to a diet of 'phonics'. We must ensure, amongst other things, that they: 'are able to understand the spoken word, express themselves effectively,' and 'develop information-retrieval skills' (National Curriculum Council, 1989b).

Children can be introduced to all these areas of learning from the earliest stages of their education. For example, it is a fallacy to suggest that children need to 'know their sounds' before they can become involved in information-retrieval, which can be achieved through the use of pictures and home-made 'factual' books in the first instance.

Special educational needs

Finally, we must turn our attention to the special consideration and support which children will require if they are to fulfil their all-round needs and gain access to the breadth of their educational needs.

Basically, there are two different ways of determining the special consideration or support which a particular child will require. On the one hand, we could attempt to:

(a)   identify and describe the child's successes in learning;
(b)   recognise factors which lead to those successes;
(c)   use that information to design similar learning experiences in areas of the curriculum within which that child is encountering difficulties.

On the other hand, we could try to:

(d)   identify and describe the difficulties which are being experienced by the child;
(e)   recognise factors which cause those difficulties;
(f)   modify the learning environment so that those factors are less likely to cause difficulties in the future.

Unfortunately, many professionals rely on the latter perspective. That is a pity, because the information which emerges from a recognition of factors which cause the pupil to experience success in learning is often equally (or even more) valuable. Since both perspectives have the potential for yielding relevant information they will both be discussed in the final parts of this chapter.

RECOGNISING FACTORS WHICH LEAD TO SUCCESSFUL LEARNING

A number of writers (e.g. Lindsay and Galloway, 1988) have claimed that it is only possible to identify and describe a child's special educational needs by appraising the reasons for their successes as well as their difficulties.

We can begin this process by using a procedure which has been referred to as ecological mapping (Laten and Katz, 1975). This procedure is designed to estimate the 'fit' of a pupil into various aspects of the learning environment. A teacher or associated professional can create an ecological map in the following way:

First   Note the settings in which the pupil operates (see Figure 1.2).
Second   Note those areas in which the child is experiencing both success and difficulty. On the ecological map, areas of success are indicated by solid lines between the child's name and the relevant area. Similarly, areas of difficulty are shown by broken lines (see Figure 1.3).

   Note: In some areas (e.g. Maths) a child might experience success in, for example, 'measure', whilst encountering difficulties in others, such as 'number'. The ecological map can easily be adapted to accommodate this additional information (see Figure 1.3, in which Maths is now split into the two areas of number and measure).

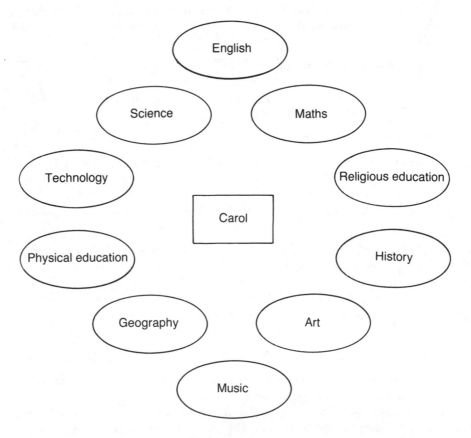

Figure 1.2

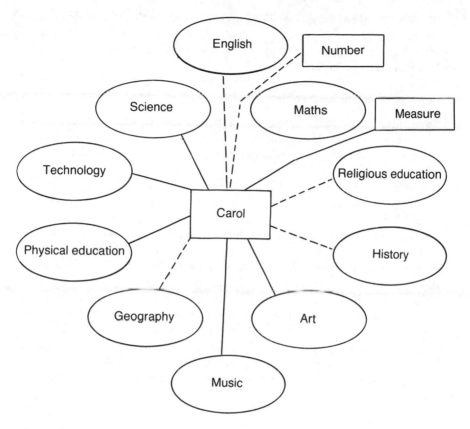

Figure 1.3

Third Examine factors within those settings which appear to be contributing to those successes. This stage of analysis revealed that Carol was achieving success in those areas of the curriculum which typically involved:

- hands-on, active approaches to learning
- a balance between paired/group work and class teaching
- a variety of methods of recording (e.g. diagrams, photographs, models, discussion, written, graphical)

The structure of lessons in which Carol appeared to achieve the most success comprised:

- a short introduction in which the teacher conveyed the purpose of the whole lesson to the class, or to a group of children
- a period of time in which the children, in pairs or small groups, were allowed to explore the materials/resources which the teacher had prepared for them
- an instructional period during which the teacher gave some background infor-

mation and then set the task/investigation upon which the children were about to embark

- paired/group work supported by the teacher if/when appropriate
- a verbal summary of findings
- the recording of findings in a format agreed by the pair/group and deemed appropriate by the teacher/class

Within this type of lesson structure Carol was able to keep on task for the majority of time, was able to participate with other children in the group, had the opportunity to discuss difficult concepts in her own language and record her findings in a format which did not present her with any undue difficulties. This contrasted most markedly with her experiences in other subjects (e.g. Geography, History) which were largely teacher-led and involved a considerable amount of written work.

A closer examination of Carol's performance within particular subjects might reveal other reasons for her successes (e.g. the use of a wordbank to help with the recording of information, the collection of information from less traditional sources such as a simplified computer database).

Having established some of the main reasons for Carol's success in certain areas of the curriculum, attempts can now be made to develop similar 'learning contexts' in those areas within which she is encountering difficulties. For example, many of the difficulties which she is experiencing in Geography and History could be prevented. In Chapter 10, Tim Copeland describes ways in which both subjects can be made accessible to many more children if more opportunities are given for:

- active, hands-on learning
- a balance between class and group work
- a variety of methods for recording findings

Given our understanding of contexts within which Carol does learn we could now be fairly confident that the approach advocated in Chapter 10 would help to prevent many of the difficulties which she is currently experiencing in Geography and History, and lead eventually to much success and enjoyment.

RECOGNISING FACTORS WHICH CAUSE PUPILS TO EXPERIENCE DIFFICULTIES IN LEARNING

Research undertaken by Croll and Moses (1985) showed that many primary school teachers believe that learning difficulties are caused by:

- factors innate to the child (e.g. IQ/ability)
- the child's attitude or concentration
- home circumstances

The first are presumed to be responsible for learning difficulties, whilst the last are considered to lead to emotional and behaviour problems.

These beliefs are also reflected in the types of assessment which teachers undertake when they attempt to clarify the reasons for a particular child's difficulties. Croll and Moses (op. cit.) showed that the majority of teachers use norm-referenced tests (e.g. word recognition and number tests), which simply compare children of the same chronological age on measures of reading, spelling performance and achievement in mathematics.

This process results in little more than a crude form of 'labelling' (e.g. child A has a Chronological Age of 9.3 years and a Reading Age of 7.1 years) which tells us very little about the child's special educational needs. On the basis of such tests, children are often attached to a special group of children who appear to be 'similar'. Recommendations about the action which should be taken on behalf of such similarly 'special' pupils are often stated in the following ways:

- James should join the special reading group.
- John requires placement in a mainstream classroom, with support.
- Rachel needs small group language exercises on a daily basis.

Dissatisfaction with vague statements of special educational need, which stem from this form of assessment, has led to a demand for more detailed information about the difficulties which children encounter. This has resulted in the emergence of a number of different types of assessment, each of which is designed to produce information upon which the teaching and learning needs of children can be determined.

Three different models of assessment, described by Jones and Charlton (1989), are discussed below. These are the:

- diagnostic-prescriptive model
- analytical model
- recognition model

Whilst all three models have something to offer, if used in isolation the first two can lead to narrowly conceived, and often inappropriate, types of provision. Children who experience difficulties in learning will only receive appropriate educational provision if it takes account of, and responds to, the whole range of factors which contribute to the child's learning difficulties and successes.

The diagnostic-prescriptive model   examines factors 'within the child' (e.g. vision, auditory memory, visual discrimination) which might be causing him/her to experience difficulties in learning. The most obvious 'within-child' factors which can cause learning difficulties are poor hearing and poor vision. Teachers can identify the occurrence of such barriers to learning by watching out for indicators as children work in the classroom. The following indicators (Ainscow and Muncey, 1981) are particularly helpful in this respect.

Indicators of hearing loss. As the child works, watch out for the following symptoms which may be indicators of possible hearing loss:

1 Tilts head at an angle to hear sound.
2 Shows frequent lack of attention during oral lessons.
3 Fails to respond when questioned.
4 Has difficulty in following directions.
5 Has peculiar voice qualities, often high pitched.
6 Tends to rush words together.
7 Depends on classmates for instructions.
8 Watches the faces (especially mouth and lips) of speakers.
9 Shows defects in speech.
10 Frequent use of 'pardon', 'Eh?', 'Uh?'

Other possible indicators include recurring abnormalities of the ears (e.g. earache, running ears). If there is any doubt about a child's hearing it should be discussed with the child's doctor.

Indicators of poor vision. Difficulties of vision may be indicated by the following symptoms when working in the classroom:

1 Rubs eyes excessively.
2 Shuts or covers one eye.
3 Is sensitive to light.
4 Squints, blinks, or frowns when doing close work.
5 Holds reading material too close or too far.
6 Complains of pains, itching or aches in the eyes.
7 Complains of blurred or double vision.
8 Reverses letters, syllables or words.
9 Confuses letters or similar shapes.

Other, less obvious, 'within-child' factors can also contribute to difficulties in learning. For example, some children will encounter difficulties because they have a specific problem with processing information through the auditory channel. For example, Liz finds it particularly difficult to: (a) remember a sequence of sounds (she can remember up to four numbers in sequence); and (b) differentiate between certain sounds (e.g. tap, tip, top). Liz encounters particular difficulties in spelling. This is hardly surprising since she has been taught by a phonic 'sound-it-out' method, which relies almost entirely upon the auditory channel!

Various instruments such as the Aston Index and Aston Portfolio (Newton and Thomas, 1976) have been developed to help teachers and other professionals to assess factors which appear to cause particular children to encounter difficulties in learning. These instruments help teachers and other professionals to plot a profile of the child's performance in areas such as:

• auditory discrimination

- auditory memory
- auditory sequencing
- visual discrimination
- visual memory

The information derived from this kind of approach can be used in one of two ways: (a) to plan activities to remediate areas of weakness, or (b) to plan learning approaches which make use of strong channels.

In Liz's case the first option would have resulted in the development of a programme which involved a lot of exercises designed to improve her auditory discrimination and her auditory memory (see Aston Portfolio). Whilst some small improvement could have been made in those areas, the second option might have led to a much more dramatic improvement in her spelling performance. If the teacher had utilised her strong channels and developed an approach to the teaching of spelling which relied more heavily upon the visual (see Cripps, 1986) or visual and kinaesthetic (see Cripps and Cox, 1989) channels, Liz would not have been handicapped by inherent auditory difficulties. It is highly likely that she would have achieved considerable success in learning to spell if her strong channels had been utilised.

Whilst the above approach can help teachers to open up the breadth and depth of the curriculum for *some* children, it only addresses a few of the factors which cause children to encounter difficulties in learning. To presume that this kind of analysis will give a comprehensive picture of a child's special educational needs is to ignore a whole range of other factors, discussed below, which might be causing him/her to experience learning difficulties.

The analytical model of assessment comprises a number of different methods which have been used to examine the 'match' of the curriculum to the needs of the child, in the belief that mismatch will cause the child to experience difficulties in learning. These methods vary in the degree of precision which they bring to that process.

At a fairly general level the match of the curriculum to the needs of a child can be compared by:

(a) appraising the performance of a child against statements of attainment, and
(b) evaluating the appropriateness of the curriculum to that child's levels of attainment. Such comparisons are often made by using checklists such as those developed by Wolfendale and Bryans (1978), Conibear (1984), and more recently the National Curriculum Council (1989a); or, more informally, through the teacher's own methods of recording attainment in the classroom.

The following extract (Wolfendale and Bryans, 1978) illustrates the kind of criteria which teachers use when appraising children's attainment in oral language. Statements of attainment are listed under the two main headings of Receptive/Listening Skills and Expression. The teacher observes the children's performance on each criteria over time and in a number of different settings, before answering yes or no to the following questions:

Receptive and listening skills   Is it the case that the child:

1 Cannot follow simple instructions (does not seem to hear or listen to them)?
2 Is restless and inattentive in story time?
3 Is unable to answer questions about a story which s/he has just heard?
4 Cannot interpret the content of pictures?
5 Seems unable to retain information?

Expression   Is it the case that the child:

6 Is reticent in verbalising?
7 Speaks in short sentences or monosyllables?
8 Has difficulty in conveying his/her thoughts?
9 Does not initiate conversation with adults?
10 Has difficulty in describing his immediate setting?
11 Still uses infantile words (e.g. doggie, gee-gee)?
12 Cannot enact simple stories, even when they are familiar?

This kind of 'criterion-based' assessment serves to focus upon those particular areas (e.g. interpretation of pictures) within which children may be experiencing difficulties, in order that some form of suitable provision can be made for them.

There is little doubt that this kind of assessment is more closely related to children's teaching and learning needs than norm-referenced tests. If, however, the process of needs' analysis does not proceed beyond the 'broad' areas of analysis listed above the resultant provision is likely to be similarly wide in scope (this was not intended by Wolfendale and Bryans). Whether or not that provision (e.g. the use of language 'kits') meets the particular needs of a child will be a matter of luck.

The above example illustrates how broad-brush assessments can lead to inaccurate attempts to provide for special educational needs. Other means of assessment have been developed in an attempt to specify special educational needs more precisely. Influenced by the work of writers such as Brennan (1979) a number of approaches, such as task analysis, precision teaching and the use of behavioural objectives, have come to the fore.

The behavioural objectives approach, described in detail by Ainscow and Tweddle (1979), is one example of an approach which sets out to describe the special educational needs of pupils in precise, observable terms. This approach seeks to give a detailed description of the end product of the proposed learning which contains details of:

- what a child is expected to do
- under what conditions s/he is expected to do it
- the level of success required.

Cameron (1981) gives the following example of a behavioural objective:

> When asked to add two numbers totalling less than ten (e.g. what is three add five?) the answer is stated correctly without hesitation and without using concrete materials on at least nine out of ten trials.

Once objectives have been clearly defined in this way it is then possible (through observation) to determine the child's present level of performance. By comparing the base-line of present performance with the listed objectives it is possible to design an appropriate form of provision. This normally involves the design of a number of incremental teaching objectives which take the child from the existing base line to the desired stage of development (see Figure 1.4). Special educational provision based entirely on this approach (which was not intended by Ainscow and Tweddle, op. cit.) often results in learning being broken down into a number of small, achievable steps, through which pupils can reach desired long term objectives. When success is achieved in this way it can be shown that pupils are making 'measurable progress'.

Whilst the behavioural objectives approach can help children to develop certain skills, the approach should be used with caution. Firstly, experience suggests that the emphasis on incremental and measurable progress focuses attention upon the teaching of 'skills' (e.g. phonics – initial sounds), thereby

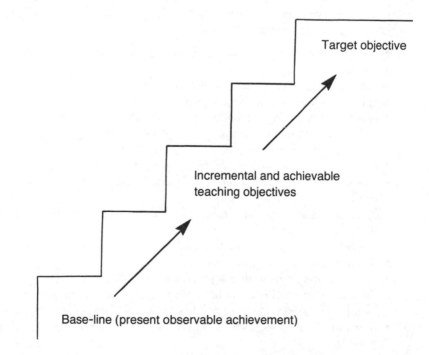

Target objective

Incremental and achievable
teaching objectives

Base-line (present observable achievement)

Figure 1.4

relegating the importance of comprehension and conceptual understanding. Secondly, by focusing upon the child's observable progress within the curriculum, the approach might deflect attention away from other significant factors which could be contributing to the child's difficulties in learning. These additional factors are incorporated within the recognition model.

The recognition model

Earlier in this chapter, it was proposed that special educational provision should respond to the whole range of factors which might cause a child to experience difficulties in learning. This requires the foundation of a process which sets out to recognise and describe those factors accurately. The spotlight in this approach shifts from a narrow focus on the child towards a wider beamed examination of the total learning context, of which the child is only one part.

The writer proposes that teachers, parents and other professionals, through the process of 'needs' recognition', should seek to determine the breadth of factors, including those within the child's environment (e.g. curriculum presentation, management of learning, grouping strategies) which may be causing him/her to experience difficulties in learning.

This approach is supported by evidence from the Scottish Education Department (1978) which suggests that the main causes of learning difficulties are connected with the design and presentation of the school curriculum. The Report suggests that pupils experience difficulties:

1   due to a failure to master the first basic skills in language, reading and number;
2   in coming to terms with concepts and processes;
3   with reading skills beyond the first stage of decoding;
4   arising from terminology and other specialised language demands;
5   due to the adoption of inappropriate methodology e.g.
    • lack of appropriate pacing
    • lack of chances for revising and reinforcement
    • lack of time for genuine pupil–teacher discussion to explore learning difficulties
    • difficulties due to absence, broken education or having too many teachers during the session
    • difficulties due to the cumulative load of work
    • difficulties arising from the work having an image for
    • pupils inappropriate to their age and stage of development
    • difficulties due to the failure of pupils to grasp the relevance of the work being undertaken to their needs, life style and social background
    • difficulties due to the instruction not being in the native tongue of the pupil.

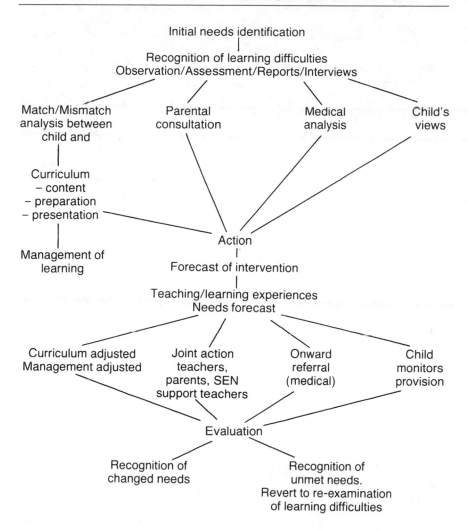

Figure 1.5 Model for the recognition of special educational needs

By highlighting factors, such as those above which are causing a child to experience difficulties in learning, the recognition process leads to a conceptualisation of special educational needs as 'unmet needs' (Booth *et al.* 1987).

Another example of unmet needs is given by Tony Charlton (Chapter 2) who suggests that many pupils perform less well academically because they are not encouraged to take more personal responsibility for their own learning outcomes. Subsequent studies demonstrate that if such needs are recognised, they can be met via counselling (David and Charlton, 1988) and other techniques which often lead to significant academic gains. This view is borne out by Torgesen (1980) who views learning-disabled students as inactive learners and attributes poor problem-solving to difficulty in applying task-appropriate strategies rather than to specific psychological processing deficits. This production deficiency may be partially responsible for poor mathematical problem-solving. In essence, then, the recognition process involves a wide-beamed search for all those factors within the pupil and the learning environment which (separately or in combination) might be causing him/her to experience difficulties in learning.

The special educational provision which results from the recognition process is somewhat different from that which resulted from other procedures (e.g. the diagnostic and analytical models of assessment) which have been discussed above. The emphasis within the recognition model is upon change inside a number of areas of the curriculum which would otherwise cause the pupil to continue to experience difficulties in learning. If this process is carried out successfully the pupil is more likely to be given access to the whole breadth of educational experiences which are offered throughout the curriculum.

From the above comments it will be appreciated that the most appropriate forms of special educational provision will only emerge from a consideration of all these factors. It is for this reason that the writer suggests that the model for the recognition of special educational needs (Figure 1.5) should be used by teachers and other professionals when they attempt to provide for the special educational needs of their pupils.

REFERENCES

Ainscow, M. and Muncey, J. (1981) *Small Steps: A Workshop Guide about Teaching Children with Learning Difficulties*, Coventry: LEA publication.

Ainscow, M. and Tweddle, D.A. (1978) *Preventing Classroom Failure: An Objectives Approach*, Chichester: John Wiley.

Booth, T. *et al.* (1987) *Preventing Difficulties in Learning*, Oxford: Blackwell.

Brennan, W. (1979) *The curricular needs of slow learners*, Evans/Methuen.

Cameron, R.J. (1981) 'Curriculum development 1: clarifying and planning curriculum objectives', *Remedial Education*, 16(4), 163–70.

Conibear, V. (1984) 'A study in the development of a simplified criterion reference checklist in language', *Remedial Education*, 19(3), 125–28.

Cripps, C. and Cox, R. (1989) *Joining the ABC*, Wisbech: LDA.

Croll, P. and Moses, D. (1985) *One in Five*, London: Routledge & Kegan Paul.

David, K. and Charlton, T. (1988) *The Caring Role of the Primary School*, Basingstoke: Macmillan Education.

Department of Education and Science (1981) *The 1981 Education Act*, London: HMSO.

Department of Education and Science (1985) *Mathematics 5–16: Curriculum Matters*, London: HMSO.

Department of Education and Science (1988) *Education Reform Act 1988*, London: HMSO.

ILEA (1985) *Educational Opportunities for All*, London: Inner London Education Authority.

Jones, K. and Charlton, T. 'Appropriate educational experiences', *Support for Learning*, vol. 4(1) 53–58.

Laten, S. and Katz, G. (1975) *A Theoretical Model for Assessment of Adolescents: the ecological/behavioural approach*, Madison, Wisconsin: Madison Public Schools.

Lindsay and Galloway, D. (1988) 'Identifying and meeting special needs in the primary school', *Education Section Review*, vol. 12(2) 27–38.

National Curriculum Council (1989) *Curriculum Guidance 2: A Curriculum for All*, York: National Curriculum Council.

National Curriculum Council (1989a) *Mathematics in the National Curriculum*, York: National Curriculum Council.

National Curriculum Council (1989b) *English in the National Curriculum*, York: National Curriculum Council.

Newton, M. and Thompson, M. (1976) *The Aston Index*, Wisbech: LDA.

Rowland, S. (1987) 'Ian and the shoe factory', in Booth, T., Potts, P., and Swann, W. (eds) *Preventing Difficulties in Learning*, Oxford: Blackwell.

Scottish Education Department (1978) *The Education of Pupils with Learning Difficulties in Primary and Secondary Schools in Scotland: a progress report*, Edinburgh: HMSO.

Wolfendale, S. and Bryans, T. (1978) *Identification of Learning Difficulties: A model for intervention*, Stafford: NARE Publications.

Chapter 2

Giving access to the national curriculum 'by working on the "self"'

Tony Charlton

Much school time is given to working on literacy and oracy skills. However, whether or not time is allocated to work on children's affective functioning too often depends on adventitious encounters with teachers who have been converted to the need to address such areas. It is time – as a profession – that we all recognized, for example, the need to give adequate time to 'working on the self'.

It is inequitous for us not to undertake this task. As educators, are we called upon to help educate the 'whole' child? If not, who looks after the neglected parts?

(Charlton, Jones and Brown, 1990)

INTRODUCTION

In common with others in this book, this chapter directs attention upon the national curriculum. However, it differs from other chapters in that it is less concerned with the actual *content* of the curriculum and more preoccupied with its *delivery*, particularly in situations where pupils experiencing learning difficulties (reading difficulties in particular) may have their access to it restricted unnecessarily.

The chapter commences by drawing attention to ways in which access to the national curriculum may be restricted to primary school pupils who are experiencing reading difficulties. Secondly, it highlights the nature/extent, and some causes, of the reading problems which pupils may encounter, before focusing upon the association between reading and emotional problems. Thirdly, the chapter discusses findings from a sample of research studies which have indicated directions within which teachers may provide better for the needs of children encountering difficulties learning to read. Finally, the view is stressed that by meeting these needs successfully, teachers can help children to maximise their access to the national curriculum.

READING: A KEY FACTOR IN ACCESSING THE NATIONAL CURRICULUM

The degree to which satisfactory progress is achieved by each pupil within the core and foundation subjects of the national curriculum is influenced to a large extent by the individual pupil's reading ability (the older the pupil the more crucial the skill becomes). It is hardly surprising, therefore, that an important area of educational research is that which focuses upon pupils' reading progress (or lack of it). Whilst the results from such enquiries are unequivocal in stressing that the majority of children are making satisfactory progress in this key area, they suggest a significant number of pupils whose progress is far from satisfactory.

This unsatisfactory progress (and the difficulties often associated with this 'failure') often permeate into, and become manifest within most (if not all) of their academic work in school. Proficiency in reading is a key academic skill which – in one way or another – expedites access to, and underpins, much of the work within the national curriculum. For those primary school pupils who fail to acquire basic reading skills there is the distinct likelihood that the difficulties they have experienced already will generate even more extensive and pervasive ones elsewhere within the national curriculum. Furthermore, it is widely accepted that the longer these reading difficulties remain unresolved the more dismal becomes the prognosis for improvement.

Understandably, the remediation of reading difficulties has been (and remains) a priority for teachers and the varied services which support teachers in what can be often an exacting and frustrating task. This task is often made even more demanding by the considerable number of children who experience these types of difficulties.

READING DIFFICULTIES: ANOTHER 10–20 PER CENT?

The large number of teenagers who leave school each year having failed to attain satisfactory standards in reading, is a major concern of teachers, associated professionals, employers, parents and – at times – the youngsters themselves. Nielson and Long's (1981) article, for example, refers to 22 per cent of American adults who possess inadequate reading skills as well as 13 per cent of high-school graduates who remain unqualified for occupations requiring minimal standards of literacy. In this country Southgate (1972) showed that one in ten of her sample of fifteen-year-olds were at least four years retarded in their reading, and The National Child Development Study (ALBSU, 1983) revealed that 10 per cent of school leavers reported significant problems in reading. In a broader context Carr *et al.* (1991) make reference to studies suggesting prevalence figures on underachievement ranging up to 50 per cent. Earlier, Kedney (1975) mentioned estimates of between one and three million adults who were not functionally literate. From a school rather than pupil perspective, a recent study by HMI (DES, 1990)

– requested by the Secretary of State in view of 'recent and widespread expressions of concern about reading standards and teaching methods in primary schools' – revealed that whilst reading standards were satisfactory, or better, in 80 per cent of schools, standards were poor in 20 per cent of the schools surveyed.

Sundry explanations have attempted to account for these dismal figures. Some, for example, have blamed progressive primary schools for directing too much time, emphasis and attention away from the teaching of reading, whilst others have suggested inadequacies in teacher training, contending that many teachers 'have been trained neither to teach reading to those of their pupils who have failed to master initial reading skills nor to consolidate and extend the reading skills of average and above average readers' (Southgate, 1972).

From a more sanguine perspective HMI (DES, 1990) suggested a range of factors likely to have 'positive influences' upon reading standards including:

- an enthusiastic and committed staff
- experienced and well-informed co-ordinators
- good parental support
- good quality of reading-related resources
- a sound policy for reading linked to clear guidelines
- a balanced approach to the teaching of reading
- sound monitoring of pupils' progress

The report infers that the more a school is bereft of these *positive* influences the greater the chances become of its pupils encountering reading failure.

However plausible these and other contentions may appear, available evidence suggests that schools do not always respond competently to the needs of a significant proportion of their clientele. This is not an indictment of schools and their teachers. No one should doubt that the majority of teachers are both highly skilled and motivated. Unmet needs of this nature may have more to do with the complexity of the problem some children are experiencing, the extreme demands they make upon teachers and the failure of teacher training to equip students with the appropriate skills and strategies.

Learning, as is well known, is a complex process influenced by a plethora of intra- (e.g. cognition, learning styles, affective states) and extra-child factors (e.g. quality of home background/school instruction) which can interact in ways which are often confusing and unclear (see Kevin Jones' comments on this matter, in Chapter 1). One particular 'interaction' which schools are increasingly becoming aware of, and placing a long overdue emphasis upon, is concerned with ways in which children's emotional states affect (and are affected by) their reading performance.

EMOTIONAL PROBLEMS AND READING PROBLEMS

Published reports (e.g. Lawrence, 1971; 1972; Coles 1975; Charlton and

Brown, 1982) have suggested that considerations of children's emotional states are seldom in evidence in schools. More specifically, where reading difficulties are in evidence, the child's emotional functioning is rarely taken into account. In many ways this neglect is surprising. For example, concern has often been expressed about the limited efficacy of traditional remedial help made available to children encountering reading difficulties (Cashdan and Pumfrey, 1969; Lawrence, 1971; Charlton and Terrell, 1986). Too frequently, it appears, this type of help has focused exclusively upon the identification and remediation of mechanical skills (e.g. phonics) and sub-skills deficits (e.g. perceptual) and neglected any meaningful considerations of children's feelings, or affective, emotional states (e.g. self-esteem, anxiety, locus of control beliefs), towards the tasks where their difficulties have become manifest. From a parallel (though more practical) perspective, Lawrence (1985) is critical of teaching practices where:

> despite their implicit acknowledgement of the need to focus on both aspects there is still explicit concentration on methods of skill instruction, with self-esteem enhancement relegated to an incidental 'framework of teaching'.

This omission has been remarkable given the well-documented association between academic and affective variables (e.g. Bryan and Pearl, 1981; Burns 1982; Charlton, 1985).

Whilst some controversy exists regarding the direction of the causal ordering within the association, the connection is not disputed. Some maintain that emotional problems, by interfering with the cognitive/motivational processes necessary for healthy learning, give rise to learning problems (see Stott, 1981); others share the opinion that learning problems cause unhealthy affective states (see Wilson, 1985). However, the consonant view often prevails that affective

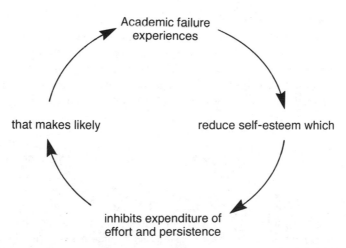

Figure 2.1 Model showing cause and effect association between failure experiences and affective problems

problems may both precipitate, and be a consequence of, learning problems. McMurray (1990) reaffirms this thinking and suggests that the two areas should not be viewed 'as discrete entities but as part of an interactional process with each affecting, and reinforcing, the effect of the other'. An indication of this type of interactional process is included in Figure 2.1 which shows a simplistic cyclical model illustrating possible cause-and-effect association between failure experiences (i.e. academic failure) and affective problems (i.e. low self-esteem).

A brief reference to two primary school pupils may help translate the above model into practice from two different perspectives.

James

James was an eight year old who suffered frequent asthmatic attacks. Despite sound advice from the local GP that he should be allowed to 'live a normal life', both parents countenanced James' frequent absences from school. In three years James was absent from school on average for over one and a half days a week. These absences militated against satisfactory reading progress. Consequently, problems in reading and other academic areas became evident, to the extent that the school requested help from the Schools Psychological Service. Eventually, when the educational psychologist's help was enlisted, her report stated that James' 'problems' were considerable. His reading failure had shaped a low self-esteem; consequently he was convinced that he was not very 'bright'. In James' case, persistent and frequent academic failure seemed to have generated a low self-esteem; and the low self-esteem convinced him that it was pointless trying to succeed (so why try?). By not trying, further failure became inevitable.

Susan

Susan came from what can only be described as a deprived home. Her upbringing in a fragmented and disrupted family (mother had left home when Susan was four; father then invited a series of 'aunts' into the home) left her deprived of adequate care, and love. Expelled from her primary school because of her disruptive behaviour she was placed in a residential school for maladjusted children. At the age of eleven she had a reading age of under seven. The psychologist's report stated that:

> In view of her early home experiences, and the consequent emotional/behavioural problems they generated, it is unsurprising that her academic performance in general – and her reading in particular – is so poor. I suggest that academic improvements are unlikely to take place until her emotional problems are resolved, or at least minimised. Undoubtedly, she has a low opinion of herself, as a pupil, as a daughter, a member of a family, and – in very general terms – as a person. This area may be one upon which the school can direct its work.

In contrast to James, Susan's problems seem likely to have commenced with the low self-esteem which constructed a block to learning (whilst her body was at school, perhaps her mind was elsewhere?); in turn this block appeared to hinder the achievement-striving which was so necessary for successful learning to take place.

Whichever the direction of cause-and-effect, for some children it may be imperative that therapeutic help is directed towards the restoration of emotional well-being within the child (e.g. raising self-esteem levels/reducing anxiety levels), in addition to arranging opportunities for them to acquire the skills and sub-skills necessary for efficient reading. This notion seems sound, for as Lawrence (1975) comments with particular reference to the self-image 'the child with poor self-esteem is not likely to be motivated towards learning'. One plausible explanation of this demotivation is offered by Good and Brophy (1977). They discuss the possible impact of failure experiences upon children's self-image, when confronted by the task where they have failed repeatedly, where they convince themselves that they can't, and never will, succeed. The writers continue by contending that:

> Task concentration will be interrupted by defeatest self-talk (I can't do this, I'm going to fail, everyone is laughing at me, I look foolish), often to the point where giving up and accepting another failure becomes easier than prolonged further anxiety and pain.

James *et al.* (1991a, 1991b) suggest the following model as an aid to understanding the relationship between aspects of a pupil's feelings (e.g. the self-image) and his/her academic performance (see Figure 2.2).

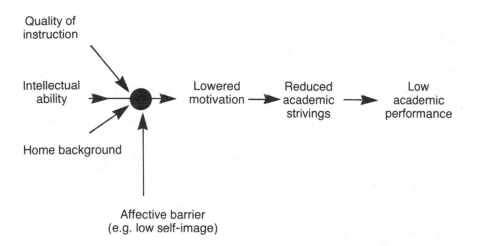

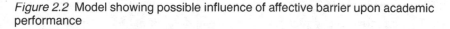

Figure 2.2 Model showing possible influence of affective barrier upon academic performance

FOCUSING ON THE SELF

In instances where children experience reading difficulties, the attention of teachers/researchers has been directed increasingly towards what are often referred to as the emotional 'blocks', perceptional 'binds' (Somerville and Leach, 1988) and dysfunctional motivational and affective states (Carr *et al.* 1991) that often present barriers to successful classroom learning. This chapter is now concerned with an examination of the theoretical underpinning of the 'emotional block' perspective on learning difficulties; and a discussion of associated ways of encouraging healthy learning through the employment of therapeutic strategies designed to remove such 'blocks', 'binds' and/or 'states'. Linked with this examination/discussion is the contention that the removal of these blocks, and the subsequent amelioration of related reading difficulties, is likely to heighten access opportunities to the mainstream curriculum.

Central to this perspective is the notion of the individual's self-image (in the literature the terms 'self-concept', 'self-image' and 'self-esteem' are often used interchangeably: erroneously on occasions). The self-image is comprised of the images/pictures, and associated evaluations, we hold about our 'whole' person; our physical, academic, social and emotional make-up. These images are constructed through experiences, experiences which include the individual's perception of feedback (s)he receives from significant others (e.g. parents, teachers, friends) on his/her performance and appearance in school, in the home and elsewhere. (Carl Rogers (1969) stresses that it is not events which affect the self, but interpretations of them.) More succinctly, Coopersmith (1967) claims that self-esteem 'expresses an attitude of approval or disapproval and indicates the extent to which an individual believes himself to be capable, significant, successful and worthy'.

During recent years we have become more aware of the self-image as a mediating variable that affects pupils' academic performance in school. Few now refuse to accept that the self-image is not only influenced by this type of performance but is also an influential determinant of it (Charlton and David, 1989; Charlton and Leo, (in press)). The importance of the self-image – the personal feelings an individual holds which are associated with it, and their mediating role upon academic achievement – are encapsulated within Lawrence's (1987) contention that 'one of the most exciting discoveries in educational psychology in recent times has been the finding that people's levels of achievement are influenced by how they feel about themselves.' However, discoveries of this type remain unproductive, unless they are used to good effect in classrooms and schools.

A QUESTION OF ACCESS

The advent of the national curriculum has been welcomed by many, regarded with scepticism by some, and viewed with disdain by others. Nevertheless, the national curriculum is now becoming 'part and parcel' of school life. Schools and teachers are now legally required (with exemptions in particular instances), as they have been for some years, to make the curriculum accessible to all their pupils. With some children this access will become practicable – in any real sense – only when appropriate regard is given to their emotional states in general, and their concept of self in particular.

Arguably the self-concept (and the locus of control, which will be discussed later) is a powerful determinant of pupil behaviour. Every classroom is populated by at least some pupils who don't succeed at their academic tasks because their 'self' is telling them persistently and consistently 'you can't succeed', 'you are going to fail' and/or 'you can't improve'. Where messages like this are despatched continually it becomes only too easy for the pupil to become convinced of his/her own inadequacy, incompetency and inability. These types of self-convictions often block any meaningful attempt by the pupil to succeed, to avoid failure, and to improve; beliefs become translated into practices (or as John Lilly wrote in *The Centre of the Cyclone*: 'Whatever one believes to be true, either is true or becomes true in one's mind'). Consequently, the pupil becomes convinced in his/ her mind that 'little is to be gained by trying, and nothing to be lost by not trying' (Craske, 1988). In a similar manner Widlake (1984) talks of pupils who 'can not learn effectively if they have poor views of themselves as learners' and Burns (1982) contends that 'children whose self-concepts do not include the view that they can achieve academically tend to fulfill that prediction'.

At times we may all need a salient reminder that during their time at school our pupils carry much more around with them than their bags, books and coats. More importantly they carry a 'self' around with them each day; from home to school, lesson to lesson, and school to home. Whilst our endeavours in school unquestionably 'work on the self' of each pupil, we delude ourselves if we believe that the effects of these labours are always positive and desirable. Good teaching maximises opportunities for each 'self' to become a facilitator of learning; unhealthy influences 'weight the "self" down' so that it becomes a burden to the pupil and likely to impede satisfactory learning. Experience tells us that some children arrive at school with a 'self' already adversely affected by experiences at home. Dragging a 'damaged self' to, and around, school each day is hardly an experience conducive to healthy and successful learning!

IMPROVED READING THROUGH 'WORKING ON THE SELF'

Attempts to translate the notion of therapeutic help into educational practice (e.g. Lawrence, 1971; 1972; 1985; Cant and Spackman, 1985; James *et al.* 1991a; 1991b) have added significant increments to existing knowledge concerning the effects of classroom psychotherapy (designed to enhance the self-image) upon children's reading accomplishments. The first two studies examined the differential effects of three treatments (remedial reading, counselling, and counselling plus remedial reading) upon reading performances of remedial readers in junior schools. Whilst remedial reading concentrated upon improving the children's mechanical skills, the counselling intent was to improve their self-concepts. (Lawrence reasoned that at least some of the pupils in his study were failing to read because their low self-concepts were creating barriers – or emotional blocks – to reading.) After a six-month intervention period it was reported that the 'counselled' group evidenced significantly greater gains in reading scores than either of the other two treatment groups. Similar results were revealed in a later study (Lawrence, 1985) where it was reported that skills teaching, supported by a therapeutic input (either counselling or drama) designed to enhance self-concepts, produced greater reading score gains than those evidenced after 'skills teaching' in isolation.

In all studies the counselling was uncomplicated. Lawrence stressed that:

> the techniques involved do not require so much a training as a briefing. Given first a personality which is sympathetic, warm, intelligent, lively, and of sound mental health, all that is required is a brief instruction in principle, which can be learned fairly quickly.

> (Lawrence, 1973)

The counselling techniques were based on self-concept theory and required adults (lay professionals were used in one of Lawrence's studies: indeed grand-mothers were used to great effect in another, as yet unpublished, enquiry) to establish relationships with pupils, of a kind which were non-judgemental and accepting. Central to the counselling content were three cardinal counselling qualities:

Acceptance   This involves an acceptance of a pupil no matter how disruptive or disappointing her/his behaviour is. One way to accomplish this is to separate the child from the behaviour; the behaviour may be criticised but the child remains accepted. Arguably this is not a task that everyone can undertake, perhaps no-one can undertake it with all children. Nevertheless it is a quality that all successful counsellors have, and one to which teachers need to give their professional consideration.

Genuineness   Requires a person to be her/himself, and not to hide behind a persona. The 'outer' person reflects truly the 'inner' one. People who are genuine seem to offer a sense of security and trust to those with whom they work.

Empathy   Indicates an ability to truly understand how another person feels; it is as if one person is 'in tune' with the other. Leo (1991) describes this attribute as one where the teacher 'listens to the thoughts and feelings of the pupil'. The extent to which individuals possess empathic skills varies greatly, and to some extent the skill depends upon the ability to 'read' correctly verbal and non-verbal messages. What seems indisputable is that good counsellors/teachers tend to have well developed empathy skills (Charlton and Hoye, 1988).

Together, these three cardinal skills appeared to provide a therapeutic environment which helped the pupils to discard the emotional barriers which were impeding satisfactory learning progress (Lawrence contended that the counselling's success derived from its focus upon children's improved feelings.) For these children, repeated failure in the educational settings appeared to have depressed their self-concepts to a level where their 'natural curiosity and enthusiasm for learning remained inhibited' (Lawrence, 1971) and their motivation for learning was poor.

James *et al.* (1991a; 1991b) utilised intervention techniques not dissimilar to those employed by Lawrence to successfully enhance young secondary school pupils' spelling and reading performances. However, from more than one aspect, the counselling strategies reported by James and colleagues were innovatory; they adopted the concept of peer counselling to favourably affect the academic performance of the counsellees (all of whom were experiencing learning difficulties). Counsellees comprised twelve second-year pupils who were in receipt of special educational support. A control group was formed by twelve other second-year pupils (from the same special educational needs' classes) who were cross matched on spelling and reading attainments.

The twelve counsellors were selected from fifth- and seventh-year pupils (on the advice of teaching staff who saw those chosen as possessing – amongst other attributes – the ability to build and sustain healthy relationships with their peers). Training was administered to prospective counsellors over a period of three weeks (four sessions of approximately one hour), and included instruction to:

(a) improve their listening skills (they were encouraged to act as 'sounding boards' for counsellees' comments);
(b) enhance their empathy skills (to assist them to understand, for example, counsellees' fears and concerns, particularly where they related to poor academic performance).

After training, each counsellor was required to befriend one of the younger pupils (counsellees). This befriending took place, on a weekly basis, on occasions when the younger pupils were timetabled for English and the counsellors were undertaking 'Service to the School and Community' sessions. Another important diversion from Lawrence's techniques was the directive nature that the counselling sometimes assumed. Whilst the central thrust of the intervention was to effect academic improvements through self-image enhancement, the treatment also made use of locus of control theory (which is discussed later). Where pupils admitted their poor academic performance ('I'm no good at reading') the counsellors were asked to stress the effort-outcome association from locus of control theory. For example, in response to a comment that the counsellee was 'poor at reading' the counsellor might respond, 'I know what you mean. I used to be poor at maths, but I kept trying – and I'm quite good at it now.'

During the weekly periods, spanning some twenty weeks, when each of the counsellor/counsellee pairs met, the emphases (on the counsellor's part) were to:

(a) listen attentively and sympathetically, and try to understand comments from the younger pupils' perspective;
(b) try and build up the younger pupils' self-image by, for example, praising achievements, effort, persistence and appearance; and

(c) link outcomes such as academic achievement to effort.

As already mentioned the strategies employed in the above study proved successful in terms of enhancing pupils' academic performance and may offer useful concepts/practices for others to experiment with.

Interestingly, in a much earlier report, Rogers (1969) discussed a research enquiry undertaken in the USA and elsewhere, where attempts were made to correlate particular teacher behaviours with specific learning outcomes. From a list of teacher behaviours three were identified as being closely correlated with fewer discipline problems, higher pupil self-images, more favourable attendance rates and greater learning initiatives on the pupils' part. These teacher behaviours were identified as:

1   The ability to understand the meaning that the classroom experience is having for each pupil.
2   The demonstration of respect and positive regard for each pupil as an individual.
3   The ability to engage in a genuine relationship with each child.

These three desirable teacher traits are almost indistinguishable from those counselling skills deemed so important by Lawrence.

Supporting Lawrence's findings were those from a later enquiry undertaken by Cant and Spackman (1985). They reported improved reading in their sample of children who received counselling help designed to enhance the self-image. The investigators maintained that their results:

> suggest that considerable gains in pupil self-esteem can be achieved through a programme of systematic but fairly basic counselling provided by a class teacher. It also seems likely that the parallel and distinctive gains made by the experimental group in reading ability and English quotient scores are related to their enhanced self-esteem.

Within recent years academic achievement (particularly in the context of 'learning difficulties') has also been examined within the conceptual framework of Rotter's (1966) social learning paradigm where, for example, children's levels of goal-directed behaviour (i.e. achievement-striving) are viewed as being determined by reinforcement and expectancy variables. Central to this paradigm is the locus of control expectancy construct which refers to the degree to which people expect their performance/outcomes to be dependent upon their own behaviour (an internal locus of control) or under the control of external forces such as fate, luck or chance (external locus of control). Pupils' strivings become maximal (and, therefore, their opportunities for success) when, simultaneously, they desire success because they value consequent reinforcements (e.g. high marks in a test) and believe or expect that it is practicable (i.e. they can succeed through their own efforts). It is unsatisfactory for only one of these states to exist for, as Charlton (1985) emphasised:

by itself a belief that you can do well does not necessarily mean that you will do well; because without the desire to do well, you may not try. Similarly, a desire to do well may only become translated into approach tendencies if you believe you can.

Although pupils' expectancies (beliefs) for success/failure are affected by a range of factors, the beliefs which they hold regarding the influence their behaviour has upon outcomes (i.e. locus of control) are crucial determinants. Internal locus control beliefs characterise pupils who believe that academic outcomes are dependent upon their personal behaviour; where they desire success they believe it is attainable through their own efforts. Conversely, those who espouse external locus of control beliefs perceive academic outcomes being independent of their expenditure of time and energy, and controlled by extrinsic forces such as fate, luck or chance. On occasions when they desire success they remain unconvinced that they are 'masters of their own destiny'. Beliefs of this type often preclude achievement-striving and serve only to help guarantee failure.

Understandably, the notion has developed that an internal locus of control belief is an attractive personality characteristic conducive to achievement strivings likely to enhance opportunities for academic success. Research reports have tended to support this reasoning; an abundance of findings have shown internality to be associated with high academic grades and test scores, whilst externality has been linked with inferior grades/scores (Bar-Tal *et al.* 1980; Walden and Ramey, 1983; Charlton, 1985). More specific to the area of special education needs, Finchem and Barling (1978), Rich (1981) and Mindingall *et al.* (1981) have indicated that low achievers are frequently characterised by their external locus of control beliefs.

These findings imply that where children experience learning difficulties and hold external control beliefs, the locus on control construct promotes an additional understanding of the nature of the problems these children experience, and gives an indication of the type of classroom help required if improved learning is to take place. It may be the case that where learning difficulties are evident, the problems are not merely confined to limited competencies in the areas of reading skills. The children may also evidence poor levels of motivation which prohibit them responding successfully to skills' teaching alone. Carr *et al.* (1991) make reference to these unsatisfactory motivational levels as 'dysfunctional motivational and affective states'. Persistent failure – despite some measure of effort on their part – may have reinforced feelings that their efforts do not control outcomes and, to them, it appears rational and expedient to cease meaningful efforts to improve. In their minds (as with the self-image) they have convinced their 'selfs' that to persist with achievement-striving serves only to confirm their 'failure' label; it seems more acceptable not to strive, and fail anyway. Consequently, teacher intervention is likely to require a therapeutic input to promote children's internal beliefs to a level where feelings re-emerge that academic failure can be avoided, and success opportunities maximised through the employment of effort and persistence.

To test this thinking, Charlton (1988) used a group counselling programme which was directed towards the enhancement of pupils' locus of control beliefs (i.e. to increase internal beliefs). The programme had been used successfully, in an earlier enquiry, to effect improvements in children's internal locus of control beliefs. The reasoning underpinning the use of the programme in the second study was that enhancing locus of control beliefs could motivate the pupils to spend greater periods of time on-task which, in turn, would lead to improved reading test scores. The counselling programme was administered to a group of primary school pupils over a pre-post test period of thirteen weeks. Pupils were drawn from second-year, junior classes (N=2) located in two inner-city primary schools, serving similar catchment areas (i.e. in terms of parents' social-economic backgrounds). One class (N=32) served as a control group whilst the treatment group (N=29) received 11 forty-minute group counselling sessions from the class teacher spread out over a period of nine weeks. An examination of pre/post reading test scores showed significant differences between the groups' post intervention reading scores as well as the groups' mean gain reading scores (i.e. differences between pre/post reading test scores). In both instances the group receiving the counselling intervention made the greater improvements in their reading.

Conclusions drawn from this study suggest 'teaching' strategies which can be used in classrooms to help at least some children to improve their reading performance. Generally speaking these techniques have much in common with those utilised in Lawrence's studies (1971; 1972; 1985). They include recommendations that:

- *positive reinforcements* (praise, attention, smiles) be distributed regularly, yet judiciously, among all children for desired behaviour (e.g. effort, persistence, achievement, prosocial behaviour). Whenever practicable, teachers to make clear what behaviours are being rewarded. ('Good' may not always be adequate. It may be more helpful to say, 'Your work is tidy. You must have taken a great deal of care with it.') The award of reinforcements in this manner helps demonstrate to pupils how their own behaviour has achieved rewarded outcomes.
- *listening facilities* be made available to pupils. 'Real' listening offers opportunities for children to experience from their teachers a genuine concern for, as well as an understanding of (or a wish to understand), what they are saying. By listening in this manner, teachers become more aware of children's feelings. This awareness derives more from an understanding of, than a knowledge about, children.
- *pupils to practise analysing problem situations.* Like adults, children learn, and derive benefit, from analysing the problems they and others have encountered or are encountering. Through these analyses they can become more aware of the influence of people's behaviour upon their outcomes/experiences (e.g. John had to stay in because he was rude to his father). By providing

children with stories, plays, audio-tapes and videos depicting 'failure' climates the teacher can encourage them to analyse and discuss behaviour-outcome links. The subsequent stage is for pupils to suggest (and role-play) alternative behaviours likely to change the failure climate to one of success.

The above strategies – and others referred to earlier in studies focusing upon the self-image – appeared to have effected improved academic/intellectual perform-ance via working on aspects of pupils' affective functioning (feelings and expec-tancies). However, the root or source of this work seemed to derive from subtle changes in teacher behaviour. Rosenthal and Jacobsen (1968), discussing find-ings from a similar research enquiry, capture the essence of these changes when they suggest that:

> by what she said, by how and when she said it, by her facial expressions, postures, and perhaps her touch, the teacher may have communicated to the children of the experimental group that she expected improved intellectual performance. Such communications together with possible changes in teacher techniques may have helped the child learn by changing his self-concept, his expectations of his own behaviour, and his motivation, as well as his cognitive style and skills.

CONCLUSION

Increasingly (though this trend is long overdue), teachers are recognising the need for the work undertaken in schools and classrooms to become more proactive, and effective, in enhancing each individual's self-image and internal locus of control beliefs. There are at least two separate, though related, arguments underpinning this recognition. Firstly, the notion is compelling that individuals in school (and elsewhere) should be provided with appropriate opportunities and experiences to enable them to feel good about their 'selfs'. The enhancement of each person's 'self' should be an explicit educational goal. The age, and society, in which we live often make burgeoning demands upon its members. It has become too commonplace, and too easy, for individuals to feel isolated, unloved, uncared for and unrecognised. Feelings such as these, and the conditions they derive from, can easily expedite a depressed regard for, and by, the person's 'self'. Reflections upon our life experiences can inform us of, and confirm, the impact of experi-ences upon our own feelings. There is much that we can learn from these self-reflections. Recollections of experiences, for example, which made us feel inferior, unwanted or inadequate can help rekindle within us memories of a miserable and inadequate self. We can remember too, the ways in which these feelings affected our behaviour. How many of us failed in school because teachers/parents/peers communicated to us expectations that we would fail. How many withdrew – for varying periods of time – from attempts to build relationships with peers because they felt unwanted. These feelings are unwanted as well as unhelpful.

Clearly, there is much need for schools not only to assist children to maximise the development of healthy concepts of 'self', but also to help them to 'protect' their 'self' from external forces which threaten it.

Secondly, the association between self-image and educational achievement is now well established; similarly there is an increasing recognition of a causal relationship between the two variables. With particular reference to the findings from a number of his own research enquiries Lawrence (1988) suggests that:

> It is clear from these experiments, conducted over the past decade and a half, that teachers can be more effective in their teaching if they pay attention to the child's self-esteem.

However, in a more despondent manner, he comments that 'it is depressing to observe that teachers have not been helped to appreciate this' (Lawrence, 1988). I share this pessimism. Discussions and conversations with teachers over the last ten years or so all too often indicate a sad neglect of any meaningful consideration of the educational import of the self-image within initial teacher training courses.

If we accept that a healthy self-image is important to our pupils' affective well-being, and if we recognise that a positive self-image can exercise favourable impact upon the pupils' educational performance it becomes inequitous where schools fail to make satisfactory arrangements to influence healthily their pupils' images of 'self'. In a like-minded manner Bond (1987) writes:

> Unless schools can provide some means of giving pupils a feeling of dignity and a sense of their own worth they will have failed in their task of contributing to the well-being and actualization of their pupils.

The national curriculum is now with us; our colleagues working in primary schools are particularly conscious of its arrival. However there are considerable semantic differences between the arrival of the curriculum and the condition of its being made available satisfactorily to all pupils. As Bill Brown mentions in Chapter 3 the word and spirit of the Education Reform Act advocates the right of all pupils (whether or not they have learning difficulties) to have access to a broad and balanced curriculum which includes the national curriculum. This access may be denied to some children unless schools become more adept at providing appropriate help to their children who are experiencing difficulties mastering skills in reading. 'Unblocking the blocks' to successful learning is one approach (a curative strategy); another – 'stopping the blocks' – is more preventive and concerned with stopping such blocks occurring in the first place. Both of these strategies are likely to demand meaningful attention to the affective domain.

The self-image and locus of control constructs discussed in this chapter offer explanations for some children's difficulties in acquiring reading skills. More importantly they also offer directions for teacher interventions in both a curative and preventive contact; help likely to enable pupils to derive maximal benefit from the national curriculum. However, it is unlikely that the notion of therapeutic intervention will permeate satisfactorily into classroom practices until

LEAs and teacher training institutions become more proactive in drawing attention to the considerable body of research which is highlighting the values of such intervention strategies. Similarly, the practice of whole-school approaches to 'working on the self' will be a priority with all schools seeking to improve the quality of their offering to their pupil-clients. Gurney (1987) forcefully argues that:

> It is important to plan for intervention on pupils' self-esteem over a school-wide basis. Only in this way can consistent, positive support be given to children who are at risk in terms of low self-esteem.

REFERENCES

ALBSU (1983) *Literacy and Numeracy* Evidence from the National Child Development Study, (Adult Literacy and Basic Skills Unit).

Bar-Tal, D. Kfir, D., Chen, M. and Somerville, D.E. (1980) 'The relationship between locus of control and academic achievement, anxiety and level of aspiration', *British Journal of Educational Psychology*, 31, 482–90.

Bryan, T.H. and Pearl, R.A. (1981) 'Self-concepts and locus of control of learning disabled children', *Journal of Clinical Psychology*, 8, 223–6.

Burns, R. (1979) *The Self-concept Theory, Measurement, Development and Behaviour*, Harlow: Longman.

Burns, R. (1982) *Self-concept Development and Education*, Eastbourne: Holt, Rinehart & Winston.

Cant, R. and Spackman, P. (1985) 'Self-esteem, counselling and educational achievement', *Educational Research*, 27, 1, 68–70.

Carr, M., Borkowski, J.G. and Maxwell, S.E. (1991) 'Motivational components of underachievement', *Developmental Psychology*, 27, 1, 108–16.

Cashdan, A. and Pumpfrey, P. (1969) 'Some effects of the remedial teaching of reading', *Educational Research*, 11, 7, 138–147.

Charlton, T. (1985) 'Locus of control as a therapeutic strategy for helping children with behaviour and learning problems', *Maladjustment and Therapeutic Education*, 3, 1, 26–32.

Charlton, T. (1986) 'Differential effects of counselling and operant conditioning interventions upon children's locus of control beliefs', *Psychological Reports*, 59, 137–138.

Charlton, T. (1988) 'Using counselling skills to enhance children's personal, social and academic functioning', in Lang, P. (ed.) *Thinking about ... Personal and Social Education in the Primary School*, Oxford: Basil Blackwell.

Charlton, T. and Brown, B. (1982) 'Locus of control and children's academic behaviours: implications for the special class setting', *Links*, 7, 1, 11–15.

Charlton, T. and David, K. (1989) *Managing Misbehaviour*, Basingstoke: Macmillan Education.

Charlton, T. and Hoye, L. (1988) 'Counselling in primary schools', in David, K. and Charlton, T. (eds) *The Caring Role of the Primary School*, Basingstoke: Macmillan Education.

Charlton, T. and Jones, K. (1990) *Working on the Self*, College of St Paul and St Mary Press, Cheltenham.

Charlton, T. and Leo, E. (in press) *Surveying the Self: In School*, Edgerley Publications, Marshfield.

Charlton, T. and Tenell, C. (1987) 'Enhancing Internal Locus of Control Beliefs through Group Counselling: Effects upon Children's Reading Performance', *Psychological Reports*, 60, 928–30.

Coles, C. (1975) 'Counselling and reading retardation', *Therapeutic Education*, 5, 1, 10–18.

Craske, M. (1988) 'Learned helplessness, self-worth motivation and attribution retraining for primary school children', *British Journal of Educational Psychology*, 58, 152–164.

Fincham, F. and Barling, J. (1978) 'Locus of control and generosity in learning disabled, normal achieving and gifted children', *Child Development*, 49, 530–3.

Good, T.L. and Brophy, J.E. (1977) *Educational Psychology – A Realistic Approach*, Eastbourne: Holt, Rinehart & Winston.

Gurney, P. (1987) 'Self-esteem enhancement in children: a review of findings', *Educational Research*, 29, pp. 130–6.

James, J., Charlton, T., Leo, E. and Indoe, D. (1991a) 'Using peer counsellors to improve secondary pupils' spelling performance', *Maladjustment and Therapeutic Education*, 9, 1, 33–40.

James, J., Charlton, T., Leo, E. and Indoe, D. (1991b) 'A peer to listen', *Support For Learning*, 6, 4, 165–70.

Kedney, R. (1975) 'Adult literacy and the numbers game', in Moyle, D. (ed.) *Perspectives on Adult Literacy* (UKRA).

Lawrence, D. (1971) 'The effects of counselling on retarded readers', *Educational Research*, 13, 2, 119–24.

Lawrence, D. (1975) 'Counselling of retarded readers by non-professionals', *Educational Research*, 15, 1, 48–54.

Lawrence, D. (1975) 'Remedial reading and counselling', *Reading*, 9, 1, 12–17.

Lawrence, D. (1985) 'Improving self-esteem and reading', *Educational Research*, 27, 3, 194–9.

Lawrence, D. (1988) *Enhancing Self-Esteem in the Classroom*, Paul Chapman Publishing Ltd.

Leo, E. (in press) 'Understanding the self', in Charlton, T. and Leo, E. (eds) *Surveying the Self: In School*, Edgerley Publications, Marshfield.

Marsh, H.W. (1990) 'A multi-dimensional, hierarchical model of self-concept: theoretical and empirical justification', *Educational Psychology*, 2, 2, 77–172.

McMurray, P. (1990) 'The self-concept and the teacher', in Charlton, T., Jones, K. and Brown, B. (eds) *Working on the Self*, Cheltenham: College of St Paul and St Mary Press.

Mindingall, A., Wesley Libb, J. and Welsh, M. (1981) 'Locus of control and personality functioning of learning disabled children', *Journal of Clinical Psychology*, 36, 1, 137–42.

Nielson, L. and Long, M. (1981) 'Why adolescents can't read; locus of control, gender and reading abilities', *Reading Improvements*, 18, 4, 339–45.

Rosenthal, R.R. and Jacobson, L.L. (1968) *Pygmalion in the Classroom*, Eastbourne: Holt, Rinehart & Winston.

Somerville, D.E. and Leach, D.J. (1988) 'Direct or indirect instruction?: an evaluation of three types of intervention programme for assisting children with specific reading difficulties', *Educational Research*, 30, 1, 46–53.

Rich, H.L. (1981) 'Educationally handicapped children's locus of control and reading achievement', *Exceptional Children*, 244–8.

Rogers, C. (1969) *Freedom to Learn*, Charles Merrill.

Stott, D.H. (1981) 'Behaviour disturbance and failure to learn: A study of cause and effect', *Educational Research*, 23, 3, 163–72.

Walden, T.A. and Ramey, C.T. (1983) 'Locus of control and academic achievement: Results from a pre-school programme', *Journal of Educational Psychology*, 75, 3, 347–58.

Widlake, P. (1984) *How to Reach the Hard to Teach*, OUP.

Wilson, M. (1984) 'Why don't they learn? Some thoughts on the relationship between maladjustment and learning difficulties', *Maladjustment and Therapeutic Education*, 2, 2, 4–11.

Chapter 3

Providing for special educational needs within the primary curriculum

Bill Brown

At the heart of the educational process lies the child. No advances in policy, no acquisitions of new equipment have their desired effect unless they are in harmony with the child. We know little about what happens to the child who is deprived of the stimuli of pictures, books and spoken words; we know much less about what happens to the child who is exposed to stimuli which are perceptually, intellectually or emotionally inappropriate to his age, his stage of development, or the sort of individual he is. We are still far from knowing how best to identify in an individual child the first flicker of a new set of concepts or enter into new relationships.

(Plowden Report, 1967).

There is nothing new in the commitment by primary schools to meet the needs of children who encounter learning difficulties. The Plowden Report, with its far reaching and significant influence on primary education, has provided the hall-mark from which many other educational initiatives have sprung. Chapter 21 of the report is concerned with what were then termed as handicapped children in ordinary schools.

An analysis of their recommendations makes interesting reading. Recommendations suggest:

1 a recognition that the fundamental educational needs of ordinary and handicapped children are similar but that there will be differences in the way in which they are satisfied;
2 classes should be small;
3 in-service training is essential if children with learning difficulties are going to benefit from being integrated into primary schools;
4 children should receive individual attention;
5 the needs of children with learning difficulties have to be addressed;
6 support for Circular 276 (1954) whereby no handicapped child should be sent to a special school who could be satisfactorily educated in an ordinary school;
7 strong support for the concept of integration;
8 a need for the early and accurate identification of special needs;

 9 opportunities for children to reach their full potential in ordinary schools;
10 the development of pre-school provision;
11 an emphasis on the involvement of parents;
12 the need for a multi-disciplinary approach in providing for children with handicaps;
13 the need for an advisory and counselling service for the parents of handicapped children;
14 an extension of both the initial and in-service training of teachers for children with special needs;
15 an emphasis on the climate and ethos of the school;
16 the importance of the school providing for all its members;
17 an understanding that not every teacher can overcome the emotional and psychological reactions which some handicapped children arouse;
18 an acceptance that handicapped children add greatly to the responsibilities of a busy teacher of a large class;
19 the importance of ancillary help;
20 the success of some severely physically handicapped children being integrated into primary schools;
21 the development of special classes for the partially hearing and partially sighted;
22 an acceptance that 'special classes' often serve a wider geographical area than the school's usual catchment area;
23 an acceptance that children with emotional and behavioural disabilities are rarely placed in special classes attached to primary schools;
24 an understanding that the vast majority of children with learning difficulties will remain in the primary school.

The backcloth of concern was therefore already set up when Margaret Thatcher (then Secretary of State for Education) established in 1974 what was to become known as the 'Warnock Committee'. The Report was published in 1978 and after some hesitation a White Paper entitled 'Special Needs in Education' was introduced to Parliament in 1980. The main thrust of this White Paper was to remove the restrictive classifications of handicaps and introduce a broader definition of special educational needs. In reality the appropriate placement for young children with learning difficulties would continue to be in their primary school with, hopefully, more effective and consistent support from the LEA. The Warnock Committee estimated that about twenty per cent of the school population had special educational needs at some time during their school career.

The Warnock Committee influenced the move towards integration and indirectly affected the attitude of those responsible for implementing the Education Act (1981). Many LEAs have a well established policy of integration for children with learning difficulties. Integration is, however, a matter of attitude. It is recognised that special educational needs are on a continuum and that they are extremely variable in their intensity. The Warnock Report (op. cit.) distinguished three forms of integration: locational, social and functional. Functional integration involves pupils learning with their peers for all or most of the time; social integration brings pupils together during certain lessons, breaktimes, meal-times etc; whilst locational integration involves the physical siting of special schools or units on the same campus as an ordinary school.

The Warnock Committee further identified the conditions for effective provision of special education in ordinary schools, emphasising that children with special needs in the ordinary school must have the maximum possible opportunity to share experience of both curricular and extra-curricular activities. It was realised that this would make new and considerable demands of teachers and would require additional facilities, on-the-spot support services and INSET. Chapters 7 and 11 of Warnock underline the conditions required for effective integration.

Although the precise beginnings of the movement towards integration cannot be clearly defined, stemming as it does from a multiplicity of sources, the Report on Education Number 77 (DES, 1973) was a direct response to increasing integration. Although it never appeared on the statute book, expansion of this policy was reinforced by Section 10 of the 1976 Education Act. In some areas of the country, children with learning difficulties continued to be retained in primary schools and fewer children were transferred to special schools.

During the past fifteen years, primary schools have experienced a period of considerable change in terms of the ways in which they meet the needs of children who experience learning difficulties. The period since the NAHT surveys of 1974 and 1978 has seen the introduction of the Committee of Enquiry into the Education of Handicapped Children and Young People (DES, 1978), the Education Act (DES, 1981), the implementation of the Circulars and Statutory Instruments associated with the Act, the Education Reform Act (DES, 1988) and the process of implementing the national curriculum. Many commentators have used the Warnock Report (DES, 1978) and subsequent legislation (DES, 1981) as a means of highlighting the need for a more positive approach towards learning difficulties being met within the purview of mainstream education (Brennan, 1982; Hegarty *et al.* 1981 and 1982).

The Education Act (1981) stated that a child has special educational needs if s/he has a learning difficulty which calls for special educational provision to be made. The definition of the terms used in the Act, such as 'learning difficulties', 'special educational needs' and 'special educational provision' are somewhat vague and open to a variety of interpretations (see Chapter 1).

In essence the new legislation has required LEAs to extend to a larger group of children the help which it already offered to children who would have been 'ascertained' as handicapped under previous legislation. LEAs are required to provide active support to ordinary schools and simultaneously they have to identify, assess and review the needs of those children who have complex and severe needs. This requirement is now reflected in a far more comprehensive and formal way than previously envisaged. There is also a much greater involvement by parents. The LEA has a mandatory responsibility to identify all children with special educational needs and to assess those needs in order to determine and make arrangements for the appropriate educational provision.

The assessment procedures do not necessarily result in the child having the protection of a formal statement. Increasingly pupils who have been assessed as having special educational needs are retained in the primary school. Assessment is often perceived as a means of arriving at a clearer understanding of a child's learning difficulties. In theory, since the implementation of the 1981 Act the child's progress has to be monitored through the annual reviews and statutory reassessment. For some primary schools the introduction of Records of Achievement and the Annual Report will further enhance the quality of reviewing the child's progress.

Implicit in the 1988 Education Reform Act is the right of all pupils, whether or not they have a statement of special educational need, to participate in a broad and balanced curriculum which includes the national curriculum. The 1981 Education Act with its integration aims has encouraged the retention of more children with learning difficulties in primary schools. Undoubtedly, where this type of change takes place, the demands of children with learning difficulties will challenge the professional skills of teachers, support agencies, parents and governors.

Circular Number 5 (NCC, 1988) 'Implementing the national curriculum – Participation by Pupils with Special Educational Needs' strongly recommends that all children with special needs should have maximum participation in the national curriculum. Existing good practice is the criteria on which the programmes of study and attainment targets will need to be built. NCC Curriculum Guidance 2 (1989) emphasises that in those schools where all the staff are committed to the same aims concerning a broad, balanced, relevant and differentiated curriculum, which includes raising standards for all the children whom they teach, there are enhanced opportunities for children with learning difficulties being educated in ordinary school. This will require that the school has a united policy on special educational needs; that this policy is constructed by the staff working closely with parents, the local education authority, other agencies and the wider community. Within this context pupils' individual needs have to be identified and assessed. The full range of pupils' abilities and needs have to be considered in planning and implementing schemes of work. There are also implications for a unified approach regarding pupil behaviour, setting standards of work, recognising achievement and recording progress.

A strong foundation for widening areas of whole-school agreement will be based on the development of programmes of study, and attainment targets provided through the national curriculum via the school's development plan, (e.g. its schemes of work and consideration given to the learning environment). These elements, when brought together, will enable pupils with special educational needs to have access to the balanced and broadly based curriculum of Section 1 of the Education Reform Act.

The school's development plan will be concerned with meeting future require-ments by making any necessary organisational changes, identifying priorities for change and targeting resources. A curriculum audit similar to that described in 'Curriculum Guidance 1 – A framework for the Primary Curriculum' (NCC, 1989) will lend support to this process. Such an audit is clearly outlined in 'Curr-iculum Guidance 2 – A Curriculum for All' (NCC, 1989) and will review short-falls in existing provision, INSET needs, staffing implications, resources (availability and allocation) and, of course, the existing curriculum including subject areas, cross curricular themes and so on. The combination of the statu-tory requirements of the Education Reform Act concerning record keeping and reporting, combined with the implementation of the national curriculum may well include a further emphasis on monitoring, evaluation procedures, school policies for continuous assessment, the development of Records of Achievement, the management of time, revising existing schemes of work, recruitment policies, and the management of resources. Additionally, the translation of policy into practice in schools will need to be regularly reviewed.

Many primary school teachers have previously enjoyed a considerable measure of autonomy but have had little effect on whole-school policies (Taylor *et al.* 1974). This autonomy rested on the belief that decisions concerning school policy and those concerning practice in the classroom were not necessarily a shared process. Boyd (1984) claims that:

> the uniqueness of each classroom setting implies that any approval – even at school level – needs to be tested and verified and adapted by each teacher in his/her classroom. The ideal is that the curricular specification should feed a teacher's personal research and development programme through which s/he is progressively increasing his/her understanding of his/her own work and hence bettering his/her teaching. To summarise the implications of this position, all well founded curriculum research and development, whether the work of an individual teacher, of a group working in a teachers' centre or of a group working within the co-ordinating framework of a national project, is based on the study of classrooms. It thus rests on the work of teachers.

The impetus for curriculum development emphasised by Wilson (1981), Hughes (1983) and Brennan (1985) has been encouraged by an increase in the psycholog-ical developments associated with learning difficulties. Issues concerning the caring role of the primary school, supporting schools, and managing children's difficulties are under the spotlight of professional scrutiny. Such commentators, together with Charlton and David (1990) are making a significant contribution to this area of education. Defining teaching objectives, behavioural approaches, task analysis and criterion-based approaches are some of the skills which need to be developed by the teacher of children with learning difficulties so that they become regular features in planning and implementing the educational programme.

It may be necessary for some schools to further enhance, and consolidate, established practices in recording the individual child's progress. Criteria for keeping records must be that they are available as professional documents, provide essential information, are functional, easy to complete, easy to use and flow naturally from the teaching activities. An analysis of the needs of children who experience learning difficulties requires explicit guidelines being drawn up with regard to the policies, aims and practices of the school. Well defined guidelines for each area of the curriculum enable staff to plan their own work and relate it to that of colleagues. Alongside the broad curriculum development must be clearly defined short-term goals within individual learning programmes. Consultation, co-ordination, monitoring and evaluation are supportive to these processes.

For children who experience learning difficulties, curriculum programmes need to emerge which have something special in design and implementation (see Kevin Jones' comments on this matter in Chapter 1). Teachers need to evaluate carefully the effectiveness of the programmes which they offer and the resources which they use. Children need to be assessed in respect of their functioning levels, vis-a-vis direct curriculum areas such as language competence, understanding in numeracy, level of social skills, gross and fine motor efficiency and so on; rather than in terms of quantifiable data. Children need to be assessed in terms of both their strengths and weaknesses. Systematic procedures are required to provide an effective entry into the educational programme. Judgements need to be made with regard to the suitability of the programmes' range and intensity, in respect of the individual child (see Chapter 1).

A more explicit monitoring of the child's performance and progress may have to be established. Communicating the child's current programme and needs to external agencies, such as professional support services and parents, will need to become more meaningful.

By investigating the teacher/pupil relationship, discipline and emotional climate (see Chapter 2), preparation and arrangement of materials, and sequences of learning, attempts can be made to overcome mild, moderate and specific learning difficulties. Teachers must also be concerned with assessing strengths and weaknesses, effecting and evaluating individual learning programmes, the implementation of prescriptive programmes within a teaching situation, and making efficient use of resources. Activities need to be designed which produce the exact situation required to enable the children to think independently. Situations need to arise which have to be assessed; a judgement has to be made on that assessment; a decision has to be made on how to act on that judgement; and finally the action itself has to be implemented.

The national curriculum will make new curricular demands on pupils who have learning difficulties. With additional support these pupils can be stimulated, with their learning being extended into new areas. Many pupils with learning difficulties have not previously been provided with access to such areas as science and design and technology. It is expected that the national curriculum will do much to redress this neglect.

In many ways the national curriculum has met with both professional and political approval. The establishment of a clear curricular entitlement for all children along with continuity both between and within schools is to be welcomed. In framing the national curriculum the Secretary of State used his powers to appoint members of both the National Curriculum Council (NCC) and also individual members of the subject working parties. Even so a wide range of experts have been included in the various subject working parties.

If they are to gain the maximum possible benefit from the national curriculum, children who experience learning difficulties require positive attitudes from staff. This partnership will further encourage the pupils whenever possible to not only evaluate their own learning programmes, but also to encourage them to be actively involved in building and planning their activities. This necessitates an educational climate whereby children may risk making mistakes without the fear of criticism. The resultant increase in children's 'images of self' can encourage them to develop feelings of personal adequacy, social competence and increasing independence (Tony Charlton explores these areas more fully in Chapter 2).

The question arises 'Will the national curriculum requirements need to be modified or lifted for individual pupils or groups?' Curriculum Guidance 2 (NCC, 1989) makes it quite clear that this will rarely be the case and that 'exceptional arrangements' for modifications and exceptions will probably be kept to a minimum. It also makes clear that ordinary schools must not be tempted to use the statementing procedures for obtaining placement in special schools or units, just because some pupils will probably not perform well on the national assessments. Such an approach would be in conflict with the 1981 Education Act with its emphasis on integration. This has not been superseded by the Education Reform Act.

Coulby and Ward (1990) give an overview of the composition of the national curriculum working groups, including the constraints under which these groups operated and the immediate effect of their recommendations. They further indicate that, at times, the Secretary of State used his powers to direct the working groups with regard to the way in which they should modify and rethink their reports. The Secretary of State has not necessarily accepted the initial recommendation of the working groups. A recent example of this (February, 1991) is the Secretary of State's response to the recommendations made by the working group on physical education.

Coulby and Ward's (1990) interpretation of the core national curriculum in an integrated context shows a high level of understanding concerning the current challenges facing this aspect of education. They argue that the Secretaries of State have ensured that teachers are required to translate a subject-orientated framework into an appropriate primary national curriculum. They argue that the well-accepted approach towards effective primary practice is based on the criteria that children have the greatest success within a negotiated and topic-based curriculum.

The modification of some of the Programmes of Study and Attainment Targets is a direct result of the subject-based nature of the working groups. Being committed to their own particular subjects, and working in isolation, the working groups have attempted to include as many areas of knowledge as possible in their recommendations. This is due to the uncertainty that other groups would include them. It must also be emphasised that the members of the working groups had very heavy professional schedules and were required to slot in their involvement with the national curriculum in their own time and within the constraints of a tight schedule.

The same broad pattern was used for the construction of the three core areas of the national curriculum. Even so, there were subtle and important differences. Coulby and Ward (1990) are critical of this overall structure of the national curriculum into separate subject working groups and are concerned with the lack of systematic consultation between the groups. They say that:

> to assume that content can be dissociated from method is fallacious and it will show that the core national curriculum, at the level of detail in which it has been drawn up, can be properly taught only in an integrated context. The primary curriculum should be responsive to children, their experiences and their initiatives. An integrated curriculum is desirable, not simply because it exercises teachers in weaving clever topic webs which cover all possible areas of the curriculum, but because the starting points should be what children and teachers are able to initiate collaboratively.

Their view that the core national curriculum, because of the considerable detail in which it has been devised and presented, can only be properly taught in an integrated context will find considerable support in the profession.

'A Framework for the Primary Curriculum' (NCC, 1989) also lends support to the continued development of cross curricular approaches. Coulby and Ward (1990) cite Rowland's (1984) model of 'interactive teaching' whereby teaching and learning are seen as a dynamic interaction between teacher and pupils in which either the teacher or the child might provide the initiative or stimulus. The child responds and then proceeds to some inventive activity, while the teacher acts as a reflective agent, responding to the child's actions and providing direct instruction where necessary and where requested by the child.

The HMI Survey (DES, 1978) criticises 'topic work'. Unfortunately some practitioners have interpreted this as a criticism of the philosophy and practice of integrated work and may well be indicative of a detrimental attitude towards thematic or integrated approaches. The HMI criticism, whilst being concerned with a specific aspect of the pedagogy, was not integral to the breadth and balance embodied in a fully integrated curriculum. It should be noted that the subject-based national curriculum documents are in support of a cross-curricular approach at the primary stage. The Non-Statutory Guidance (NSG) also lends its support to à cross-curricular approach.

The national curriculum should not hinder the development of integrated topic work derived from the children's initiative. Ownership of activities increases the commitment. Practical Issues in Primary Education (PIPE), Issue Number 5 (1991), strongly supports the principles of Active Learning, illustrating how High/Scope, which had its origins in British Primary Practice in the 1960s and was then developed by the High/Scope Foundation in America, can be used as a means to create wider interest in the context of the national curriculum. In summarising the principles of Active Learning PIPE states that children need:

1   the opportunity to make informed choices that directly affect their learning;
2   appropriate, well organised and freely available resources;
3   a predictable daily schedule which provides a framework for planning;
4   to be encouraged to reflect on their activities and discuss these with both adults and other children;
5   a teacher who facilitates learning through careful observation and appropriate support.

This last principle is also embodied in much of the thinking behind the introduction of Records of Achievement, through which teachers are encouraged to observe and build upon the existing strengths and interests of their pupils. The indication is that:

> the Government sees Records of Achievement as integrally linked with the National Curriculum. The underlying principles of recognising positive achievement in all pupils are common to both the National Curriculum and Records of Achievement. Record of Achievement schemes have often served to bring together schools' policies and practices on assessment, recording and reporting into a coherent whole. The Secretary of State applauds such developments, which are very much in the spirit of the National Curriculum. For the future he sees Records of Achievement as the means by which achievement across the National Curriculum and beyond can be most effectively reported to a range of audiences.
>
> (DES Circular 8/90)

The Record of Achievement provides a brief and clear summary of the work covered by the pupil. For children who experience learning difficulties the use of the Record of Achievement have the following potential benefits:

1   improvement in self concept;
2   pride in recording and in celebrating personal success;
3   making specific suggestions as to how the pupil may improve;
4   talking points to highlight personal interests and thus encouraging communication skills;
5   recognising achievements outside the core and foundation subjects of the national curriculum;
6   providing a basis for discussion at the annual review;

7   reporting on subjects and profile component levels in the national cur-
     riculum;
8   encouraging even stronger links with the pupil's home.

Records of Achievement make a real impact in enabling children to build up feelings of personal adequacy, social competence and independence. The process
enable the pupils to have documents which are not only of personal value with
real meaning for them, but which can also be shared with others. It celebrates the
individual pupil's achievements within and beyond the national curriculum.
Records of Achievement are part of a school's clearly defined process for the
transfer of information. Whilst teachers have a pastoral role the children also
have an active role in their annual review. Their perception of themselves is
important.

    In attempting to illustrate the contribution which Records of Achievement can
make in enabling teachers to respond more adequately to learning difficulties in
the classroom, the governors of Allington School, Chippenham, consider that the
pupils' involvement in the Record of Achievement process is fundamental. The
school does not differentiate between recording activities and experiences from
outside the school compared with those in the school. All activities and events,
depending on the view of the pupil concerned, can form part of the Record of
Achievement. A home/school diary also encourages the pupils to include events
during the weekends and holidays in their personal profile.

    The SEAC publication 'Records of Achievement in Primary Schools' (SEAC
11/90) in conjunction with DES Circular 8/90 provides valuable information in
encouraging the development of whole school policies on reporting. It also aims
to offer guidance which is both practical and manageable. This exceptionally
well presented document supports the introduction of Records of Achievement in
primary schools. The guidance which it offers is straightforward, unambiguous
and welcome. In so many ways it reinforces the existing good practice established
in many schools. Records of Achievement are especially relevant to children with
learning difficulties.

    In recent times Her Majesty's Inspectorate, the National Curriculum Council
and the Schools Examination and Assessment Council have made considerable
efforts to inform and update the profession through the publication of a wide
range of documents. The Aspects of Primary Education Series (DES, 1989)
combined with Curriculum Guidance Series (NCC, 1990) and the Teacher
Assessment Packs (SEAC, 1990) are supportive to the demands currently being
made on primary schools. Strategies are being successfully implemented to translate the theory of the national curriculum into practice by providing a whole
primary school framework using themes and topics. Bell (1990) in the series
'Practical Topics for the Primary School' cogently argues the need to further
encourage and develop such approaches whilst being aware of the criticisms
which have been levelled at such an approach within the eduational press,
including for example its lack of rigour, over-prescribed work, lack of quality in
planning with no clearly stated objectives.

Bell argues (contrary to the view expressed by some) that with the introduction of the national curriculum themes and topics the change in emphasis from 'what should I teach next' to 'how am I going to teach this' will solve may of the practical issues involved in implementing effectively a successful whole school project approach. Bell is optimistic to the extent that he believes that the educational promises of the 1960s may well be fulfilled in the 1990s.

With the introduction of further programmes of study and attainment targets there will be the need to revise regularly the school development plan. Such exercises will continually need to take into consideration the way in which the school can best meet the needs of pupils who experience learning difficulties. This emphasis on ensuring that the development plan takes into consideration the needs of all children must ensure that the effects of the national curriculum can be monitored and evaluated. Any member of staff designated as responsible for special needs within the school will support this process. All staff must know which pupils have special educational needs, the nature of those needs and how best to meet them. Such requirements, of course, have implications for staff development and the provision of adequate resources.

In devising and revising schemes of work, consideration must be given to differentiated teaching strategies, planning progression and ensuring that special educational needs are integral to this process. Such schemes of work are defined in the Non Statutory Guidance – Science (NCC, 1989) as 'a written statement which describes the work plan for pupils within a class or group over a specific period'. Curriculum Guidance 2 (NCC, 1989) recommends that schools analyse their programmes of study into a series of tasks and activities related to attainment targets. This implies that schools will need to both decide upon methods for presenting the work and setting out their aims and objectives. It may well be that schools need to consider the following:

1   How best to deploy staff?
2   What is the financial implications with regard to material resources?
3   Recording, reviewing and evaluating pupils' progress needs to be defined in a whole school procedure.
4   For pupils with language difficulties various communication methods will need to be considered.
5   Integral to the programmes of study in foundation subjects are areas of personal and social education and cross curricular schemes.
6   Pupils with learning difficulties need to understand what is required of them.
7   They will need to know the purpose of activities and how these purposes are to be achieved.
8   These activities need to be broken down into a series of small and achievable steps.
9   Strategies will need to be devised which will enable children with learning difficulties to experience success.

The above has implications for activities at any of the attainment levels.

Curriculum Guidance 2 (NCC, 1989) emphasises the importance of the learning environment of the school as a whole and also that of the classroom. The classroom environment must be concerned with arousing pupils' curiosity and in providing the extra stimulus and encouragement to overcome learning difficulties. The quality of this environment will be a reflection of the policies and provisions of the school. This has implications for the staff, governing body and local education authority. The same document states that the characteristics of a good learning environment will include:

- an atmosphere of encouragement, acceptance, respect for achievements and sensitivity to individual needs, in which all pupils thrive
- classroom layout and appearance which will stimulate pupil/teacher interaction and adjustment to changing curricular needs
- easy access to resources including IT
- flexible grouping of children
- management of pupil behaviour through a whole school approach to behaviour
- co-operative learning among pupils
- communication and co-operation among staff and with governors, in order to create a forum for discussing how pupils' needs can be met within the national curriculum
- effective management of SEN support staff, such as classroom assistants, parents, volunteers, and so on through clear definition of roles and use of room management
- one-to-one tutoring and other strategies
- access to specialist advice through SEN advisory staff and support services, school psychological services, speech therapy, health and social services and other sources
- co-operation between special and ordinary schools in providing the national curriculum
- relevant and well researched in-service training, both school and centre based
- continuous communication with parents and mutual parent-teacher support.

Achievement of the above is made more effective by a whole school approach. The objectives related to children with learning difficulties need to be informed by careful analysis of what is to be learned. This more consciously planned approach towards teaching and learning is given an impetus by the growth of monitoring and evaluation. A differentiated curriculum is more likely to include children's strengths. Children with learning difficulties operate more effectively where the curriculum embraces different skills' levels. The principle of inclusion strengthens the concept of breadth and balance within a more flexible approach. It could be argued that working within a narrow ability range deskills the teacher. Teachers need to be sensitive to the child's rate of learning and to the areas where there needs to be a structured approach related to specific difficulties.

Teachers may well need to ask themselves the following questions when considering improving the quality of education for children with learning difficulties:

1   Does the implementation of the national curriculum promote change and development?
2   How does the school generate processes which can be realised?
3   How are more democratic approaches developed in planning school development?
4   How do we involve children in their own learning?
5   How do we seek pupils' opinions?
6   How do we enable children to undertake independent learning, thus releasing the teacher to give others more individual attention?
7   How do we encourage parental involvement with the whole curriculum?

Working with children who experience learning difficulties also requires the school to have a clear and coherent assessment policy which is dependent upon agreed and commonly held principles that reflect the aims and objectives of the school. Hanson (1990) advocates that such policies are only philosophically sound if they are achievable. He further considers that 'good assessment practice':

1   is based on clear curriculum intentions;
2   plays an integral part in classroom activities;
3   is appropriate to the task;
4   focuses on learning processes as well as learning outcomes;
5   allows for unexpected, as well as expected, learning outcomes;
6   draws upon a wide range of evidence;
7   places achievement in context;
8   indicates strengths and identifies weaknesses;
9   involves pupils in reflection and review;
10 informs about individual progress.

Experience of working with children who have learning difficulties in Allington School (1990) supports the above view and begs a consideration of the following questions and comments:

1   What is the school all about?
    (a) philosophy
    (b) aims
    (c) objectives
2   What do we want the children to learn?
3   What activities and experiences promote these intentions?
4   How is the evidence of this learning revealed?
5   A close relationship is required between:
    (a) the curriculum offered
    (b) the learning strategies

(c) the learning outcomes
6 There is a fitness for purpose and the same teaching strategies do not apply to all situations.
7 What children learn is not what is taught. It is what the children take away from the learning situation.
8 Activities and events sometimes only become valuable when they are not available.
9 There is an argument that schools should audit the talents of staff and fit these into the curriculum.
10 Assessment is about how children learn.
11 Assessment is concerned with the insights which we gain from the learning process.

Central to the educational programme for children with learning difficulties is the need for staff to be able to work with other professionals and parents, and to understand and minimise those factors which impede progress in any aspect of the child's life. The special needs of each child are to be reviewed annually and the Record of Achievement makes an essential contribution to this process.

Teachers need to continually examine their roles in the light of change and to re-align themselves with fresh ideas. For some this may mean re-defining their own part in the community in which they are working as members of a multi-skilled team. Planned programmes need to be carried out, covering wide aspects of a child's life, and where the whole child is a subject for concern. By investigating the teacher-pupil relationship, discipline and emotional climate, preparation and arrangements of materials, and sequences of learning, attempts can be made to devise strategies to overcome mild, moderate and specific learning difficulties.

Children with learning difficulties often have major problems so challenging that it can be difficult to see a way forward. This necessitates a structure wherein the children can find the maximum amount of care. There is a need to ensure that this care is always combined with reason, in order that staff avoid the various emotional problems that can arise in wrong relationships.

Maximum encouragement needs to be given to the children by steady and supportive care. This needs to be within the framework of a structured and disciplined climate. Small group work and some individual tuition and monitoring enable the children to work at their own rate, responding to the challenge of appropriate targets. Starting at their own level children should be encouraged to work towards specific competences.

For children who experience difficulties in learning, this needs to include:

the formal programme of lessons in the timetable, the so-called extra curricular and out-of-school activities, deliberately promoted or supported by the school climate of relationships, attitudes, styles of behaviour and the general quality of life established in the school community as a whole.

(HMI A View of the Curriculum, 1990)

The curriculum needs to extend beyond the classroom door, making full use of the facilities on the school campus and the community at large.

Children experiencing learning difficulties need to develop such positive attitudes as a respect for truth, a respect for reason, respect for self and others, responsibility towards self and society, for hard work and commitment and perseverance, for tolerance, compassion, integrity and honesty. These values must permeate the total life of the school. The quality of interpersonal relationships not only between staff and children but amongst members of staff and pupils themselves are of prime importance.

Children need to be able to consider the treatment of values and attitudes which increasingly arise from a consideration of alternatives. Consequently the school needs to develop strategies for dealing with attitudes and values in this way. The ethos of a school can significantly alter the incidence of pupils' problems. The atmosphere and climate of a school has a strong influence on the performance and behaviour of the children. Personal qualities on the part of those who work with children are of the utmost importance. Amongst these qualities must be the skill to understand the needs of the children in a truly caring and positive way.

The Annual Report of HM Senior Chief Inspector of Schools, concerning standards in education for 1989 to 1990 (DES, 1991) provides encouraging signs that primary schools have made a tremendous effort in implementing the national curriculum in line with the Statutory Orders. The purpose of the report is to comment on the state of the education service in England on the basis of the inspections and related work of HMI in 1989-90 and the reports published and prepared during that year. HMI do not see all that there is to be seen and the annual report does not claim to be all-seeing. But, if that which HMI have seen is more or less typical of what exists, then what the report has to say reflects the strengths and weaknesses of the system as a whole, and its findings will be of value to the work of policy-makers, administrators, managers and teachers.

The 1991 annual report compliments the schools in the improvement of their management, the quality of planning at class, department and school levels and also in the universal presence of physical science and technology. The report accepts that the concern which is expressed in the previous year (whereby teachers' morale and job satisfaction could be undermined due to the implementation of the national curriculum) has proved unfounded. The report further indicates that the improved morale of teachers is partly due to the competences and confidence which they have gained in implementing the National Curriculum Attainment Targets and Programmes of Study. It would appear that the response made by many pupils has further enthused teachers in their willingness to bring these recent initiatives to a worthwhile realisation. The report also recognises that the national curriculum, with its related assessments and recording, makes severe demands on primary schools. There is also a concern for the lack of non-teaching time for the majority of primary teachers. This would appear to be an obstacle to the effective planning and preparation of work in many primary schools.

There are, however, some criticisms of primary education and it is stated that some schools are not making enough demands on the older and more able pupils. This criticism is particularly relevant to technology, history, geography, art, history and drama. There is also concern over the superficial work carried out in Religious Education. By comparison it is claimed that the national curriculum is having a beneficial effect on topic work. The report commends those schools whose preparation and planning for topic work involves selecting more unified elements from one subject rather than a scant selection from many subjects.

The Annual Report also concedes that the future roles of some special schools are uncertain with an increasing number of children with special educational needs being accommodated in ordinary schools. The matching of attainment targets and programmes of study to pupils' different levels of ability has still to be addressed. If children with special needs in the ordinary school are to have full access to the national curriculum there must be a continued emphasis on in-service training, including specialist subject training.

The demands of the national curriculum for challenging and differentiated learning, involving effective organisation, presents complex problems. It would appear that efforts to provide extensive individual work does not compensate for this situation with much of the work lacking depth and being fragmented. It would appear that in most primary schools assessing children's learning is not yet well established. There would appear to be a need for teachers to develop a greater understanding of how to determine if the schemes of work and methods of teaching used are effective.

The education of those children who experience difficulties in learning in the primary school will need to become a partnership between staff, parents, governors, the LEA and other professional agencies if the high ideals expressed in the Warnock Report (1978) are to become a reality. Primary schools will need to uphold the Warnock view that:

> Education has certain long-term goals, that it has a general point and purpose, which can be definitely, though generally stated. The goals are twofold, different from each other, but by no means incompatible. They are first, to enlarge a child's knowledge, experience and imaginative understanding, and thus his awareness of moral values and capacity for enjoyment; and secondly to enable him to enter the world after formal education is over as an active participant in society and a responsible contributor to it, capable of achieving as much independence as possible.
>
> (Warnock Report, 1978)

In upholding the Warnock view, working with children in the primary classroom who experience difficulties in learning will demand teachers of a high level of professional skill, knowledge and experience, combined with the dedication and commitment which is a hallmark of this aspect of education.

REFERENCES

Ainscow, M. and Tweddle, D. (1984) *Early Learning Skills Analysis*, Chichester: Wiley.

Avon County Council (1991) 'Practical issues in primary education', Issue No. 5. *Active Learning*, Bristol: Avon County Council.

Bell, P. (1990) *Practical Topics for the Primary School*, Preston: Topical Resources.

Boyd, J. (1984) *Understanding the Primary Curriculum*, London: Hutchinson.

Brennan, W.K. (1979) 'School Council Working Paper 63' *Curricular Needs of Slow Learners*, London: Evans/Methuen Educational.

Brennan, W.K. (1985) *Curriculum for Special Needs*, Milton Keynes: Open University Press.

Bryant, P. (1974) *Perception and Understanding in Young Children*, London: Methuen.

Charlton, T. and David, K. (1989) *Managing Misbehaviour*, Basingstoke: Macmillan Education.

Charlton, T. and David, K. (1990) *Supportive Schools: Case studies for teachers and other professionals working in schools*, Basingstoke: Macmillan Education.

Cox, B. (1985) *The Law of Special Educational Needs*, London: Croom Helm.

Coulby, D. and Ward, S. (1990) *The Primary Core National Curriculum*, London: Cassell Educational Ltd.

Craig, I. (ed.) (1987) *Primary School Management in Action*, Harlow: Longman Group Ltd.

Cornall, J.N. (1986) 'The small school: achievements and problems', *Education Today*, vol. 36, no. 1, pp. 25–36.

David, K. and Charlton, T. (1987) *The Caring Role of the Primary School*, Basingstoke: Macmillan Education.

DES (1973) *Reports on Special Education. No. 77. Special Education: A Fresh Look*, London: HMSO.

DES (1981) *Education Act 1981*, London: HMSO.

DES (1988) *Education Reform Act*, London: HMSO.

DES (1989) *Aspects of Primary Education: The Teaching and Learning of Language and Literacy*, London: HMSO.

DES (1989) *Aspects of Primary Education: The Teaching and Learning of Mathematics*, London: HMSO.

DES (1989) *Aspects of Primary Education: The Teaching and Learning of Science*, London: HMSO.

DES (1989) *Aspects of Primary Education: The Teaching and Learning of History and Geography*, London: HMSO.

DES (1989) *Aspects of Primary Education: The Education of Children under Five*, London: HMSO.

DES (1989) *Education Reform Act. Circular 5/89*, London: HMSO.

DES (1989) *Education Reform Act. Circular 7/89*, London: HMSO.

DES (1989) *Records of Achievement, Report of the National Curriculum Steering Committee*, London: HMSO.

DES (1990) *National Curriculum, Secretary of State Speech, 25th January 1990*, London: HMSO.

DES (1990) *Education Reform Act. Circular 8/90*, London: HMSO.

DES (1991) *Standards in Education 1989–90. The Annual Report of HM Senior Chief Inspector of Schools*, London: HMSO.

Emerson, C. and Goddard, I (1989) *All about the National Curriculum*, Oxford: Heinemann Educational Ltd.

Hampshire LEA: Hampshire Assessment Development Centre (1989) *National Curriculum Attainment Summaries Resource Pack*, Winchester: Hampshire County Council.

Hampshire LEA: Hampshire Assessment and Recording Achievement Resource Pack

(1990) *Recording Achievement Resource Pack*, Winchester: Hampshire County Council.

Hanson, D. (1990) *Guidance Notes for Assessment*, Trowbridge: Wiltshire LEA.

Hegarty, S., Pocklington, K. and Lucas, D. (1981) *Educating Pupils with Special Needs in the Ordinary School*, Windsor: NFER-Nelson Publishing Co.

Hegarty, S., Pocklington, K. and Lucas, D. (1982) *Integration in Action*, Windsor: NFER-Nelson Publishing Co.

Hinson, M. and Hughes, M. (1982) *Planning Effective Progress*, Amersham: Hulton and NARE.

National Curriculum Council (1989) *Curriculum Guidance 1: A Framework for the Primary Curriculum*, York: National Curriculum Council.

National Curriculum Council (1989) *Curriculum Guidance 2: A Curriculum for All*, York: National Curriculum Council.

National Curriculum Council (1990) *Curriculum Guidance 3: The Whole Curriculum*, York: National Curriculum Council.

National Curriculum Council (1990) *Curriculum Guidance 4: Education for Economic and Industrial Understanding*, York: National Curriculum Council.

National Curriculum Council (1990) *Curriculum Guidance 5: Health Education*, York: National Curriculum Council.

Mitler, P (ed.) (1970) *The Psychological Assessment of Mental and Physical Handicaps*, London: Methuen.

Plowden, B. (1967) *Children and their Primary Schools: A Report of the Central Advisory Council for Education (England) Vol. 1*, London: HMSO.

Ridley, K.I. (1990) 'Mixed ability teaching in the primary school', in Brophy, J. (ed.) *Methods of Teaching*, London: College of Preceptors.

Rutter, M., Tizard, J. and Whitmore, K. (1970) *Education, Health and Behaviour*, London: Longman.

SEAC (1990) *Children's Work Assessed*, London: SEAC.

SEAC (1990) *A Guide to Teacher Assessment. Pack C. A Sourcebook of Teacher Assessment*, London: Heinemann Educational.

SEAC (1990) *Records of Achievement in Primary Schools*, London: SEAC.

Tomlinson, S. (1982) *A Sociology of Special Education*, London: Routledge & Kegan Paul.

Warnock Report (1978) *Special Educational Needs: Report of the Committee of Enquiry into the Education of Handicapped Children and Young People*, London: HMSO.

Wiltshire County Council (1989) *County Curriculum Policy Document*, Trowbridge: Wiltshire County Council.

Wiltshire County Council (1990) *Self Evaluation in the Primary School*, Trowbridge: Wiltshire County Council.

Wiltshire County Council (1990) *Quality through Partnership – The Monitoring and Evaluation of Schools*, Trowbridge: Wiltshire County Council.

Wiltshire County Council (1991) *Assessment in Wiltshire – Reporting Pupil Achievement – School based Inservice Guidelines*, Trowbridge: Wiltshire County Council.

Part II

Providing for special educational needs within an appropriate educational context

Part II discusses first particular difficulties which children may experience in primary classrooms in the areas of:

- spoken language
- reading
- writing
- mathematics
- science and technology
- movement learning
- humanities
- art
- religious education

Second, the writers focus upon a wide range of strategies which teachers can use in classrooms both to maximise pupils' performance in the above key areas and help them derive optimal benefit from their access to the mainstream curriculum. These strategies are discussed in ways which make their value easily recognised and understood.

Chapter 4

The primacy of talk

Diana Hutchcroft

TALK IS VITAL

Language deprivation is one of the most serious ills that can beset a human being. Children lacking in language skills are handicapped right across the board academically in history, science, mathematics or whatever; they are handicapped socially for they can lack the means of forming easy friendships and, perhaps most importantly, they are handicapped emotionally for the inner monologue of thought will not be theirs to command.

The Bullock committee (DES, 1975) stated:

> It is a confusion of everyday thought that we tend to regard 'knowledge' as something that exists independently of someone who knows. 'What is known' must in fact be brought to life afresh within every 'knower' by his/her own efforts. To bring knowledge into being is a formulating process, and language is its ordinary means, whether in speaking or writing or the inner monologue of thought.

It is therefore of paramount importance that teachers aim to develop the language skills of every child to his/her full potential and, to do this, oracy must take precedence. Wells (1985) says:

> it is through the power of language to symbolize 'possible worlds' that have not yet been directly experienced, that parents and, later, teachers can enable children to encounter new knowledge and skills and to make them their own ... the relationship between teacher and learner must, at every stage of development, be collaborative. Teaching, thus seen, is not a didactic transmission of pre-formed knowledge, but an attempt to negotiate shared meanings and understandings.

How can anyone negotiate meaning if they lack the language skills with which to pursue their desire for knowledge? Children who experience difficulties in learning, possibly more than any of their peers, need both time and opportunity for the interpersonal exchange of ideas, for discussion, for questioning. For every child, lack of these essential occasions can lead to anything from partial error to gross misconception, but for some children their omission is disastrous and may lead to total alienation. All new knowledge must be fitted into one's own framework of experience, so the problem is 'how can the teacher help these children who encounter difficulties in learning'. The solution, in the first instance, is to develop the child's power to talk.

This talk must take place both with the adult and within the peer group which, of course, has important implications for class organisation. Discussion with an adult depends largely upon the ability of the teacher to organise both her/his own time and that of the children so that for some part of the day s/he is free to sit with a group in a tutorial manner, uninterrupted by children's other demands. S/he must learn to listen. This is a difficult task for many teachers and a skill which is often neglected in teacher training courses (see Charlton and Hoye, 1987). How can teachers ensure that the learner has understood the message unless they discuss the subject on a one-to-one basis with their pupil? Many books of 'Howlers' have been published; howlers often committed because children do not know a particular word and therefore substitute the nearest one in their own vocabulary. For instance, one ten-year-old girl introduced a lesson to her peer group on the topic of 'obstacle illusions'! When challenged she replied, 'Oh! I thought they were called that because they get in the way of your understanding.'

Possibly the greater danger for a child who has failed to follow a teacher's instructions, or been lost in the verbiage of the teacher's monologue is that s/he may retire from the fray. The communicative child can ask for clarification, the child lacking in language ability is usually poor at interactive dialogue, and so resorts to guessing what was said rather than asking directly.

The teacher must frequently guide discussion with open-ended questions which will stimulate thought and provoke answers which are neither monosyllabic nor limited to short, regurgitated phrases. And s/he must record, and later diagnose and plan, future strategies.

Classroom discourse

All children have a great deal to learn about classroom discourse. Those from healthy and stimulating homes, where conversation with parents or other adults is usual, will have realised that it takes two to play, each must respond to the other, taking turns. This is reinforced by such verbal games as 'I Spy', 'Peep Bo', 'Where's Baby Gone?' or the question-and-answer sessions where parents help their offspring to recognise objects, colours, people and so on. This is frequently the type of learning which is continued in the reception class, so these children are well-prepared and most make the change from home to school without too much difficulty. Even so, when they first start school, they will have to conform to a very different pattern of discourse. As Tizard and Hughes (1984) state:

> our study suggests that the kind of dialogue that seems to help the child is not

the one currently favoured by many teachers in which the adult poses a series of questions. It is rather one in which the adult listens to the child's questions and comments, helps to clarify his/her ideas, and feeds him/her the information she asks for.

Even those children who attend a nursery school before entering the reception class of the primary school will not find the change-over a simple matter.

But for some children the huge gulf between home and school is traumatic. In Britain nowadays some children have to cope with a complete change of language, but this is such an obvious hurdle that it is recognised and, at best, catered for. There are other children who meet barriers which are not always so apparent, and are therefore more difficult to recognise and to remove. No teacher speaks exactly in the pattern the child has learnt at home, but when the pupil's linguistic experience is far removed from that of the school s/he will be bound to find the going hard.

Thus, the unfamiliar environment and the unfamiliar style of the spoken language are hurdles which every teacher must be aware of and have strategies available to assist those children who stumble. One essential is to enlist parental help wherever possible (see Chapter 14).

Promoting talk in classrooms

There are many ploys that can be usefully undertaken to help children develop their spoken language.

Games are very useful and can be simply constructed with cardboard and wrapping paper or commercially produced 'stickers'. 'Bingo', for instance, needs a base card for each player and a set of matching cards for the 'caller'. Well thought out, games can enable the teacher to help the children learn the names of colours or mathematical shapes, or to recognise descriptions of objects or pictures, or they may be specially prepared so that the participants gather the words used for orientation. At the outset the 'caller' should be the teacher or another trained adult, but it is of obvious benefit to the children if they can take over such roles as soon as they are capable.

Classroom experiences should also be used (see National Curriculum Council, 1989, Para 2.3). For example, when individual children (or a group of children) have completed a model – be it the large junk building of the reception class child, or the precise scientific model of the older primary student – they should be asked to explain the method of construction, with the listening adult ensuring that the sequence is correct, and questioning whenever the explanation is unclear or lacking in precision.

Another useful ploy is to provide a group of children with a large sheet of card with a 'map' of a winding road crossing it, and then ask them to create a neighbourhood or a townscape, with houses, shops, supermarket, bus station; or an area of countryside with farms, outbuildings, fields, paths and animals. When the sketches are complete the children must be asked to talk about their ideas, to fill in all imaginary detail. This forms an ideal opportunity for the teacher to go beyond the concrete to those worlds created by words alone. All children need help in disembedding their thoughts from the immediate contexts, so in this illustration, one might ask the group to enlarge upon what they think is happening beyond the confines of the sketch. The teacher might challenge them to explore outside the 'here and now' with questions about the area in the past, for example, why it has developed as they imagined it, and what may happen in the future.

This type of extension of the children's thinking should also be employed when discussing a child's own drawings with him. Where the pupil says, 'This is me playing with my dog', possible lines of thought to pursue may be triggered by such questions as:

- Are you indoors or out of doors?
- What sort of game are you playing with him?
- Have you any friends with you?
- What were you doing before you began to play with the dog?
- When you have finished playing this game what do you mean to do next?

Many children who experience difficulties in learning avoid the use of the past tense; maybe they see little use for it if demand for recall has not been a part of their conversation. Similarly if their work in school is very repetitive and their home life uninspiring they will have little reason to ponder or speak of coming events. A lively programme is essential for these children, and discussion with an adult about this should form an integral part of their day.

Past- and future-related questions are particularly useful when children are engaged in project work. They often need help to recall facts that they really know about. 'Brainstorming' is an essential technique for the planning of any sort of written work; it enables all children to realise that their brain is indeed a very powerful asset for carrying memories and bringing forth ideas. Memory-related questions should be paralleled with future-related topics also; for instance:

- How are you going to use your information?
- When will you be ready to start writing about it?
- Will you need to do any further research?
- Who will you need to interview?
- Who will you need to write to?
- Do you need to make any outside visits? Where to?
- What materials shall you require?
- Will you want any help from me during the next hour?

This sort of assistance given to the child during the planning and drafting stages is vital (see Chapter 6).

Fantasy-related drama also provides a starting point for much oral work. Properties may be used as triggers; or themes, or role-play may be suggested to the child who then has to be encouraged to think out ways to expand the ideas (see also National Curriculum Council, 1989, Para 4.8).

A number of different approaches can be brought together to help children develop particular aspects of their spoken language. The development of the skill of 'sequencing', which is discussed below, provides a good example.

Sequencing is a most necessary skill, playing a key role in reasoning and logical thinking, and it is one in which children who experience difficulties in learning need a great deal of practice. There are two strands to consider; the sequencing of one's own ideas, and the sequencing of the ideas of others. The latter is the more simple matter for the teacher to cater for; some kinds of activities that spring to mind to help in its development are:

(a) Practice in following chains of instructions, starting with easy, short chains but gradually increasing the difficulty and the length.
(b) Use a deck of cards and ask children to select a card on demand. For example, 'Hold up a card that is black and has a king on it.' 'Hold up a card that is neither a spade, nor a club, nor a heart.'
(c) Sound sequences recorded on tape: these can be used for plain recall of order but, better still, can be used as stimuli for story making.
(d) Sequencing of pictures.
(e) Sequencing of a known story; retelling it orally, paying particular attention to the story-line.

The sequencing of one's own ideas proves a more challenging task for many children because they are confronted with the necessity of providing the material to sequence. Plots for stories, themes for topics and characters do not always come easily into the children's mind. The literary style of the written word and the component parts of the story are often absorbed by children who have had the advantage of listening to tales from their early childhood. For other children the holding of the story-line can be a great problem needing much help and practice. If the teacher is reading aloud a long story, with instalments heard daily, it is an excellent idea to ask for a very brief precis of every session, each to be written out on card and pinned to the wall underneath the previous one, and linked to it by an arrow showing the growth of the plot. The advantages are threefold:

(a) The author's skill in the development of the plot stands out clearly.
(b) The teacher is able to read more difficult books to the children because they are better able to follow any intricacies.
(c) Children who have been absent from any session can immediately inform themselves of the parts they missed.

Further good practice can be introduced by the telling of 'Fortunately-unfortunately' stories; for example, one child might start by saying: 'All the family set out to take the dog for a walk. Fortunately it was a lovely fine day.' This statement must now be followed by a further development of the same theme, following semantically on the first one but beginning with the word 'unfortunately'. ('Unfortunately the wind slammed the door behind us and no-one had a key'.) This ploy is most useful when used in small groups or in twos. When one listens to certain children retelling stories, or composing their own, their speech is often lacking in fluency, is jerky, and lacks links between the sentences. These children can gain valuable support by working in small groups or in pairs.

Another useful spur to invention is to use a picture (or wrapping paper) on which there are drawings of various characters and a dice. These can be turned into a game for two participants: the first child throws the dice, counts along the line of subjects, and starts a story about the person. The second child then throws, counts along, and has to continue the story started by his/her partner but now involving the character on whom his/her dice landed.

Involving all children in classroom talk

Factors which cause potential difficulties

There are really three main modes of classroom organisation – whole class tuition, individual teaching and work in small groups. The whole class method is the least suitable for children who experience difficulties in the development of their spoken language. They are frequently non-participants in ordinary class-room discussions because putting forward an idea or answering a question can be daunting, particularly when unsure of their ground, or dubious about the recep-tion of their contribution. The teacher, very conscious of the need to involve these children in the debate, often poses closed factual questions for them to answer, questions requiring answers in monosyllables or in short regurgitated phrases which stimulate neither speech nor thought.

Children who experience learning difficulties are frequently confused by instructions because they need clearer, slower, and more specific information in order to understand the task required. Some children will seek clarification or explanation from their friends. However, this source of assistance is frequently not available to those children who will need sympathetic, systematic and profes-sional help to establish their place within the peer group.

It is worth considering why these children so often find themselves as 'out-siders', and rejected from the 'in' society of the classroom.

When any number of adults are talking together, many are listening, but also are waiting for a break in the flow of conversation to enable them to forward their own ideas; some interrupt, such is their keenness. This is equally true of groups of children. In situations of this type some children will rarely be able to gain a hearing.

Observation shows that they are rejected as partners not usually by deliberate unkindness but because they are less than thrilling conversationalists. Indeed, dialogue with some children can be hard work, and so unrewarding that it is often sub-consciously regarded by their peers as not worth the effort required to involve them actively in the group.

In the past, teachers and speech therapists have often believed that speech impediments and poor enunciation have been prime factors in debarring children from active membership of a group. The following examples suggest that other factors might be worthy of equal or even greater consideration. Anna Mary, an eight-year-old who has cerebral palsy, is speech impaired through lack of control of the requisite muscles. Her phrasing is made erratic by trouble with breath control and it requires considerable effort and patience on the part of her hearers to comprehend her. But she is 'sparky', full of bright ideas, amusing, out-going, and academically able. Despite the speech defects she has no trouble in forming friendships, in participating in groups, and is frequently the leader in areas which do not demand physical prowess.

By way of contrast Brenda is beautifully spoken, but slow of thought and lacking in the ability to hold a satisfactory conversation. She offers little, or nothing, in the way of originality and her replies to questions are monosyllabic. She is usually neglected by her classmates.

It would appear to be more profitable for the teacher or speech therapist to concentrate less upon surface detail and actual voice production and more upon the development of ideas, concentration and continuity – language is for com munication.

The importance of group dynamics

When one listens to a group of able children discussing a particular issue it becomes very evident, from snippets of conversation, that they are clearly aware of the functioning of the group. For example,

> 'Let Brian have a go! You keep stopping him.'
> 'Do shut up, Shinobu! You're doing all the talking.'
> 'We'd better get on a bit faster or Miss K. will be here before we've got anything done.'

This insight into group dynamics is not shared by all children unless specific help and teaching are given.

Clearly the teacher has an important role to play if this insight is to be gained. The rules of discourse need to be taught. Children need to be shown how it is possible to gain a hearing and to recognise that different audiences need different approaches in style; in speech as well as in writing.

Children need to hear recordings of group discussions in which they have taken part, and with the help of their teacher, analyse them and interpret the rules for classroom discourse and communication within the peer group; and most complex these can prove! They vary from situation to situation whether it be preparing for a games lesson, participating in small group scientific explor-ation, discussion taking place within the whole class, working on assignments where cooperation is encouraged, or combining with peers on thematic work. As the children play and replay the recordings, comments should be sought on the part they have played. Their attention should be alerted by skilful questions, for example:

'Did you agree with what . . . said?'
'Could you have supported him/her?' 'How?'
'If you disagreed, what could you have said?'
'Did you think you put your point clearly?'
'How could you have stated it so that everyone would have understood you?'

Children should be encouraged to listen carefully and be somewhat self-critical, but all intervention by the teacher must be most sympathetically undertaken. Great care is necessary to avoid the undermining of the speaker's confidence (in fact every effort should be made to reinforce it). Nevertheless pupils need to be asked to consider whether their talk was too egocentric and, perhaps, boring for the other participants; whether they were domineering or, as is more likely, whether they acceded too readily to others. If they were silent, what were the reasons for their non-contribution? Did they think there were 'fair shares' in the group discussion period?

All of this can be most time-consuming for the teacher, but most rewarding for the child. It is teaching which is totally relevant and which ultimately will result in far greater independence in all areas.

Furthermore these recorded group discussions will prove to be of inestimable value when completing the attainment target records now demanded by the national curriculum; Speaking and Listening.

A real context for talk

The purpose of the talk matters, as does the setting in which it takes place. So, for group discussions to be of value, careful thought must be given to the topics on offer and to the comfort and well-being of the participants. The work programme must ensure that a wide variety of subject matter is introduced, for different stimuli evoke differing types of reaction. At a simple level many pieces of apparatus can be constructed easily and cheaply, as previously discussed.

Question asking is an essential skill, and one way to encourage its development is to have an identical picture on either side of a folding piece of cardboard placed between two children. One child selects a 'hiding place' in the picture, and his/her partner tries to identify his/her secret by questioning. Or again, using two identical pictures the teacher can make slight alterations to one and ask a pair of children to 'Spot the differences'. This can be turned into a far more difficult game by letting each child see only one of the pictures, then by careful description, one to another, locate the alterations. (It is helpful, at the outset, to state the number of differences to be found.) 'Twenty Questions' played with 'Logiblocs' is a further useful aid to the formation of questions.

Interview techniques are of great value for all children, and those who experience difficulties in oracy benefit enormously from learning how to conduct an interview. As a start it is useful to allow them to attempt an interview with any willing adult who has been primed not to give assistance but to answer only the questions asked. These tapes should be analysed – and from this it transpires invariably that some forms of questions beget little or no response, and the children need to work out for themselves the type of query which elicits a reply of more than monosyllabic length. With help and practice they can become quite expert – knowing that any long gap during the interview must be prevented by their own skill in maintaining the flow of the topic. This will assist concentration, for in any appreciable pause, or break, the interviewer must pick up the thread of the theme under discussion and ask further pertinent questions.

Topic themes should develop gradually from the egocentric concerns of the very young school child to the wider interests of the older one, but throughout the importance of talk is paramount; talk of a specific nature too. All children must be allowed to use their own register when they are coming to terms with new knowledge; no teacher should permit him/herself to interrupt the interpretation of expressive thought into spoken words by the correction of grammatical errors or mispronounced vocabulary, the communication of ideas is the essence. However, the teacher should assist when the child fails in clarity, first by pretending not to understand so that the child has to elucidate further, and if this fails, by modelling the explanation for the child to repeat. 'School talk' must develop from 'home talk' and it is during this teacher/child interaction that some formality may be introduced into the discourse in order to help with the written word.

During the recording of so-called research in topic/thematic work too often one sees writing which consists of great chunks of copied text which carry such enigmatic additions as '(see fig. 3)' or '(see accom. diag.)' when nothing of the sort accompanies the written word. It is a plain indication, of course, of a complete lack of comprehension of the books used, not an uncommon phenomenon unfortunately.

There is a cure (which is almost magical!) which teachers can use to help pupils comprehend better the material they are 'researching'. If two children are encouraged to study their books together, reading and discussing, making notes, and collating their material from various sources many difficulties vanish because, working in this way, understanding comes, and with it the need to copy blindly goes.

Grouping

What sort of grouping then holds out the best chance of success? It would be a valuable exercise for the teacher to record various groups in action and analyse the results, not seeking information at this juncture on cognition, or assessing children with regard to 'Levels of Attainment', but trying to answer the all-important question, 'Does this grouping hold out the very best chance of success for every member of the class?' It would be useful to think about:

(a) Distribution of the talk among members of the group:
Does any child dominate the talk?
Do some children take little or no part in the discussion?
Are there fair 'shares'?
(b) What effect does the size of the group have on:
participation
interchange of discourse
success in the alloted task?
(c) What effect does the presence or absence of the teacher have on:
active involvement in the group discussion
collaboration with other members of the group
success in the allotted task?

It will be evident that the type of group participation usually alters when the teacher arrives to join in the discussion. Remarks and comments tend to be directed to her and not across the broad membership of the group, and frequently the children await teacher approval and a lead into further conversation. Also it may become apparent that some children are actually far more likely to offer contributions to the topic in hand when no adult is present. The converse is also true, some children responding far better with their teacher as leading member of the group. The reluctance of some children to speak in the teacher's presence may be a reflection upon his/her teaching style, but this is not necessarily the case. Some children are just far more at ease with their peers than with an adult and it is essential that the teacher does not under-estimate their true ability in this field.

(d) Teachers' questions and their effect upon the quality of the discourse. Are they, in the main, closed-ended questions which have only one acceptable answer? Or are they open-ended questions which do not have a pre-determined answer but which lead to depth of thought and longer utterances?

(e) Collaboration. How well do the members of the group:
work together
support one another
introduce a topic
hold interest by good narrative
elaborate when it is obviously necessary
role-play
ask questions
discuss sensibly
show willing to modify their opinions in the light of further evidence?

In-depth study of recorded tapes can speak volumes about collaboration and, perhaps more importantly, about actual cognition. Indeed it is essential for the keeping of true records and for the completion of assessments and profiles (this will be referred to later).

It will become obvious that no one grouping should be used throughout a year. Yes, on some occasions it will be economic of teaching time for slow learners to be grouped together, but this should not be for a large proportion of the school day. Nor should these children be taken out from the peer group if this can possibly be avoided.

Too much 'remedial work' in a setting removed from the normal routine of the classroom can underline the child's position as an outsider and deny him/her many shared experiences. Too often these losses are not compensated for by the teacher. Children who experience difficulties in learning need the sparkle of ideas from outside themselves. Group formation, if limited to those of like ability, denies those children the stimuli they need, above all others.

So to maximise the benefit of mixed ability grouping, for example when working in science or problem solving in mathematics, children should be asked to 'think aloud' through the problems facing them, mentioning possible strategies and reasoning why these should or should not be adopted, so that other children can gain great insight into logical reasoning of this type.

Unfortunately it may well be that pupils who experience difficulties in learning are not a welcome addition to a group, partly because their conversation is so unrewarding and their contribution to the work in hand often minimal. Therefore, care must be exercised to ensure that these children get no hint of rejection, or at least that such perceived rejection is kept to an acceptable minimum. Many already have feelings of inferiority and the last thing they need is further indication of their unsatisfactory social status. This can only serve to undermine what little confidence they have.

It would be wise to construct a simple sociogram, and even enlist the co-operation of some of the 'star' members of the class, to see that a welcome is extended and that integration is ensured. Nothing leads to failure in oral communication more surely than the feeling of being a social outcast.

Records

It is essential that a meaningful programme is constructed for oracy and to this end the keeping of records is vital. Though the ladder of growth from babyhood-babbling to adult-competency in language is similar in all speakers, there is great variation in the rate of progress. Even by the age of school entry there will be wide differences. So first the teacher needs to assess 'where the child is' on entry to the school. From this moment forward, development must be both systematically planned and recorded; oracy is far too important in our modern world to be left to the discretion of individual teachers. Close monitoring is necessary not only for the recording of progress but for the diagnosis of current use and the identification of an individual's future needs.

In the past the tracking of each individual's development in spoken language was a formidable task; with the advent and common use of tape recorders the detailed analysis of children's talk has become possible, but it must not be just a once-yearly or even once-termly event; continuous assessment is imperative! One needs a keen ear, a somewhat dispassionate approach and a method of recording which indicates the salient features to listen for.

REFERENCES

Charlton, T. and Hoye, L. (1987) in David, K. and Charlton, T. (eds) *The Caring Role of the Primary School*, Basingstoke: Macmillan Education.
Department of Education and Science (1975) *A Language for Life*, London: HMSO.
Tizard, B. and Hughes, M. (1984) *Young Children Learning*, London: Fontana.
Wells, G. (1985) *Language, Learning and Education*, Windsor: NFER/Nelson.

RECOMMENDED FURTHER READING

David, K. and Charlton, T. (1987) *The Caring Role of the Primary School*, Basingstoke: Macmillan Education.
Hutchcroft, D.M.R. (1981) *Making Language Work*, Maidenhead: McGraw Hill.
Ripich, D.N. and Spinelli, F.M. (1985) *School Discourse Problems*, London: Francis Ltd.

Chapter 5

A real context for reading

Helen Arnold

Children are perceived as having special needs in reading earlier and more frequently than in any other curriculum area. There are many possible reasons for this.

Firstly, all parents – and their children – seem to equate schooling with the acquisition of literacy, 'book learning', and have high expectations that teachers will engineer early reading mastery for their children. After his first day at school, Justin was asked how he had got on. 'Not very good,' he said. 'Why not?' 'Didn't learn to read today,' was the reply. Although parents are taking a greater share in helping their children with reading, many still look on its mastery as a skill needing the professional intervention of the teacher. Many children who can read on school entry do not say so, as they think that there is some added magical ingredient which can only be provided by their teacher.

Secondly, until very recently, the teaching of reading in infant classes has been related directly to the reading of text from particular books, which are clearly graded. Extrinsic motivation is therefore built into reading acquisition at school. Not only are books coloured and numbered according to level, but some build in even more obvious 'carrots' – for example, the 'glittering prizes' of 'Silver' and 'Gold' books. Some schemes state categorically 'You cannot go on to the next book until you have finished this one'. These 'special' books are invariably referred to as 'reading' books, which reinforces the idea that 'real' learning to read can only happen with a 'reading book'. One wonders what all the other books in the classroom are for!

Thirdly, the teaching of reading is associated with oral reading from these texts – oral reading being public and therefore competitive. As a result of this the child who is on a 'lower' book than his/her peers, who finds it difficult to articulate words, who does not realise that reading is a problem-solving activity, sees himself or herself as a failure at a very early stage. It does not matter how old s/he is, the sense of failure may seriously affect future performance (see Chapter 2).

Margaret Clark (1987) points out the anomalies which arise from expectation of reading mastery at whatever age children enter school. She comments that:

> We are inclined to assume that children should enter school ready to read, but not too ready. In Britain we tend to assume that five years of age is the appropriate age for starting school, and reading.

She goes on to say that many children are now entering school at the beginning of the year that they reach five and that:

> in many instances there is very quickly a start to the more formalised teaching of reading and writing ... with children previously thought to be too immature!

The First School Survey (HMSO, 1982) stated that young children were being introduced too early to formalised reading schemes and instruction. Margaret Clark points out that in Britain it is often assumed that children should be able to read by seven years of age. She cites other countries which do not start formal schooling until seven with no apparently adverse effects on reading mastery and comments that:

> We should question whether and why failure to learn to read by seven years of age should lead to long-term educational failure. Such may not be inevitable but a consequence of the educational structure of our system and its expectations.

Fourthly, the early diagnosis of failure is underpinned by the almost universal screening by authorities of young children, by the administration of reading tests which produce reading 'ages'. This yet again sets up a false correlation between chronological age and reading ability.

This structure, presently becoming even tighter with the advent of national testing at seven, seems unavoidable in our society. Many children will be labelled as failing readers at seven and, although the teacher is rightly expected to accommodate such children in the 'normal' classroom, the individual support and resources which these children require may not be forthcoming. As they become more disheartened and disaffected, they are likely to be referred for some alternative form of special provision.

What happens then? There is a tremendous variety in the practice of teachers who have a responsibility for special needs, and in advised methods of helping failing readers. The best support teachers set up learning experiences which make the children feel favoured rather than branded. Sadly, however, there are many examples of 'remediation', which are associated with an unexpressed but implicit sense of punishment.

It is important to examine the methodology of remedial teaching, and its effect on the failing reader. There is a vast literature of discussion, even conflict, about possible approaches. Margaret Meek (1973) in 'Achieving Literacy' stands at the extreme of the 'top down' exponents, supporting a philosophy eloquently propounded by Frank Smith (1971) well over fifteen years ago. Meek gives case-studies of teachers struggling alongside older pupils to establish long-lost confidence and faith in themselves, often a long slow haul. (Tony Charlton elaborates further on this aspect in Chapter 2.) The diametrically opposed view is the behaviourists' approach. This is still very prevalent, perhaps because the special needs support services are often administered by educational psychologists, many of whom coming from behaviourist backgrounds of study, seriously believe in carefully stepped reinforcement, with the promise of success in small doses. They find that the cueing system that failing readers are most uncertain with is their skill in using phonics. Failing readers' phonic attack is often confined to first-phoneme matching, and they are unable to decode new words with any degree of success. The obvious answer would seem to be to initiate remediation in that which they are lacking. Remedial programmes therefore become heavily phonically based. This fits in well with the methods of assessment most popularly used – norm referenced tests based on word-recognition with a minimal comprehension element.

This approach is not the only, or perhaps even the best, way to help children whose motivation is low and whose confidence in decoding has been eroded (see also National Curriculum Council, 1989, Para 6.1). We must be careful, however, not to go too far in the other direction, believing that all children will slide into reading if the books are interesting enough to engage them. We should not dismiss phonic training out of hand, and put all our eggs in the basket of 'learning to read by reading'. Bryant and Bradley (1985), in a very fair and closely analytical examination of backwardness in reading, found that one big difference between successful and failing readers was the inability of the latter to locate rhyming words. They came to the conclusion that teaching about rhyme and alliteration facilitated the mastery of reading. 'Children read better after being taught about sounds.'

Children, it seems, need to become aware of all elements involved in reading, and to use the cueing systems in a balanced way. The mistake we have made in the past is perhaps not so much to over-teach phonics, as to teach them as automatic responses, 'barking at print', without any accompanying explanations. Obviously one cannot explain abstract theories to young children. The activities suggested in the rest of this chapter exemplify attempts to demystify reading, to emphasise its day-to-day functions, and to use materials other than specially produced 'reading books'. They may be seen as cunning ways of 'getting in by the back door'. Certainly they embrace the notion of reading being part of the context of ordinary living, and assume that all children in Britain have unconsciously absorbed print in some form since babyhood. They aim to make such children more consciously aware of what they already know and to build on that. This approach is compatible with a number of attainment targets within the national curriculum which, for example, stress the importance of:

- recognising individual words or letters in familiar contexts (English AT2 Level 1)
- reading accurately and understanding straightforward signs, labels and notices. (English AT2 Level 2)

Reading cannot be isolated from other aspects of language. 'Special needs' is a misleading label. The 'special needs' are the same as anybody else's needs – to use language and reading in order to understand and communicate with others, to achieve 'communicative competence'.

'Classroom' language provides the framework for extending and decontext-ualising the competence children already have (see Chapter 4). There is a danger, though, that too early on this language becomes distanced from the home and peer group talk. The terms used in teaching reading, familiar in every classroom, build a web of artificiality round the skill. We have already mentioned the strange term 'reading book'. 'Sound it out' and 'What does it say?' are equally confusing and inaccurate expressions which we all use. Although most children ignore and/or accommodate to such phrases, they may be really confusing for those worrying about the whole learning process.

The following suggestions may help such children come to understanding and awareness in a context of meaning and enjoyment.

Reading without vowels

Children work in pairs. Each member of the pair is given a different piece of text. A couple of sentences is enough, taken from any source which will be within the child's experience, preferably not from a reading scheme. Examples given here are at a fairly high level of readability, in order to engage the present reader!

The children rewrite their texts, *omitting all vowels* (the obvious and simple explanation of vowels being A E I O U). There is no need to leave gaps where the vowels have been missed out.

Whn th nmls hd bn n rth fr sm tm thy grw trd f dmrng th trs, th flwrs, nd th sn. Thy bgn t dmr ch thr, vry nml ws gr t b dmrd, nd spnt prt f ch dy mkng tslf mr btfl.

The pairs then swop their versions and try to read them, at first individually and then later in discussion with their partner.

This simple deletion exercise seems to have remarkable consequences:

1   Children use contextual clues, including looking forward in the text, almost automatically.
2   It becomes apparent that one doesn't really *need* vowels for reading. (Pitman's Shorthand does not transcribe vowels except positionally; Arabic and Hebrew are two languages which do not have written symbols.) Since it is the vowels which cause the trouble in reading, it is comforting to realise that they are largely redundant!

The effect is not to make the readers less aware of vowels, however, but to make them more conscious of what they really do. It is impossible to read the vowel-less words out loud without inserting breath between each consonant. Children thus come to realise that a vowel is merely breath exhaled while changing the position of the organs of speech (tongue, teeth, lips, etc) to get ready to sound the next consonant. Vowels begin to make sense as integral physical components of speech – not as five odd letters picked arbitrarily from the alphabet. Of course, the complexity of explanation will vary according to the age and ability to under-stand. Nevertheless, most children can perceive the difference, especially when experimenting with mirrors, and the expression of delight when they find they can actually read the strange code demonstrates heightened motivation.

Here we are looking at the physical properties of words and the way in which we depict them on paper. But they are not divorced from meaning, and context helps their recognition. Other 'games' to develop this sort of awareness are variations on this initial theme.

Letter 'swapping'

Using the same paired organisation, get the children to rewrite a similar short passage, this time swapping two letters over whenever they occur. The choice of letters can be left to the child. For example:

> Whan tha enimels hed baan on aerth for soma tima thay graw tirad of
> edmiring tha traas, tha flowars, end tha sun.

or:

> When ghe animals had been on eargh for some gime ghay trew gired of
> admirint gle grees, ghe flowers, and ghe sun.

Halfway to Jabberwocky already!

Younger children can be given a simpler approach:

What did you miss?

Give each child a sheet with about two hundred words of text. They have an allotted time (about a minute for this length) to scan their sheet and put a line through a given letter whenever it occurs. When the time is up, children swap sheets and mark any examples of the letter that have been missed in a different colour. Discussion follows, not so much about the number of omissions, but why some letters were missed? For instance, is the silent 'e' often missed? Did partners tend to miss the same letters?

This 'playing with words and letters' can now be extended to embrace a

stronger element of meaning. Almost any word can be made into a picture, signi-
fying its meaning in visual form, for example:

dr oppe d   j um p

p i t   b o r i n g

y a w n   miss ng

distance

S T O P

running

This will help children to look carefully at the word and its spelling while they are
transforming it.

Children can set puzzles for each other to find out how many, and which,
letters of a word can be redundant. For example:

> r e v e r s e

Delete one letter only

rvrse	✓	still comprehensible
everse	✗	does not make sense
rverse	✓	still comprehensible
revese	✗	does not make sense
revere	✗	meaning has changed
revers	✓	still comprehensible

or:

> | k i t c h e n |

itchen	✗	does not make sense
ktchen	✓	still comprehensible
kichen	✓	still comprehensible
kithen	✗	does not make sense
kitchn	✓	still comprehensible
kitche	✗	does not make sense

Cloze procedure

Cloze procedure has become an accepted means of assessing comprehension without tears. Often it is difficult and rather boring. By creating their own cloze experiments, however, children may become aware of redundancy. At what frequency of deletion do some sentences become difficult to comprehend?

Every 10th word?

> When the animals had been on earth for some ----, they grew tired of
> admiring the trees, the flowers, ---- the sun. They began to admire each
> other. Every ---- was eager to be admired, and spent a part ---- every day
> making itself more beautiful.

Every 5th word?

> When ---- animals had been on ---- for some time they ---- tired of
> admiring the ---- , the flowers, and the ----. They began to admire ----
> other. Every animal was eager ---- be admired, and spent ---- part of each
> day ---- itself look more beautiful.

Every 3rd word?

> When the ---- had been ---- earth for ---- time they ---- tired of ---- the
> trees, ---- flowers and ---- sun.

Now it becomes obvious that some words are easier to replace, and some are more 'fixed' than others. We begin to sense the difference between 'content' and 'function' words.

Children can begin to experiment in this way with a partner, with each child having a different passage to delete. Each child will rewrite his/her own passage, omitting all **function** words first (that is, words which do not carry meaning in themselves: e.g. and, but, which, on, because).

> Long ago, world brand new, before animals birds, sun rose sky brought first day.
>
> Flowers jumped stared round astonished. Every side, under leaves behind rocks, flowers began appear.

If the reverse is attempted, one thing becomes self-evident:

> When the was or the in the into the and the. The up and down and then from from and.

Function words link words in a sentence rather like vowels link letters within a word. They do not *need* to be there for content, but it is difficult to read aloud without them. The effect of deleting the function words, however, is quite startling, giving an immediacy to the text which could well lead the children on to certain kinds of poetry writing.

It would be a short and credible step to classify the parts of speech according to function, using their accepted names. For example, function words are usually prepositions, conjunctions, auxiliary verbs.

COMPREHENSION OF DISCOURSE

As they come to longer stretches of text and so become more involved with the comprehension of discourse, children are almost invariably given the time-honoured comprehension exercises, based on the reading of an isolated passage followed by written questions. This is not the place to argue an extensive criticism of such practice, but to suggest that on the whole this is not the way that we as adults approach comprehension tasks in real life. We know what we want to find out, and we go about it the quickest and most appropriate way. We usually have some idea of the organisation and content of the text we select to fulfil our purpose. We never carry out any activity remotely like the comprehension exercise. Some suggestions follow for making children's 'understanding' tasks more appropriate.

Infant teachers often familiarise their pupils with text by introducing the characters and words that they are likely to meet before they read a complete story.

This principle can be used to some effect with older children, including those whose reading ability is professedly poor.

Clustering

Select a number of words from an article or part of a story or poem. Present them in jumbled form. The example below is from an adult text (newspaper article):

security

detectives

£50,000

raiders

bags

van

handgun

bank

alleyway

guards

Islington

mask

burly

1   (Individually). Cluster the words together into small groups as quickly as possible, relying on intuition rather than logic. Maybe like this:

van	burly detective
alleyway	security guards
Islington	

bank	raiders
£50,000	handgun
bags	mask

2   Discuss with a partner whether the groupings are similar. Follow by short class discussion.

3   A 'story' is beginning to emerge. Discussion follows on what might happen in the story. What is going to happen first? Is a detective telling the story? Does the robbery take place in a bank, or is there head-on conflict in an Islington alleyway?

4   The original text is finally distributed for reading. The reading is usually highly-motivated, and will be halfway between a cloze and a skimming activity.

£1.3 MILLION STOLEN FROM SECURITY VAN

Two robbers, described as burly white men, aged about 30, are being hunted by detectives after a £1.3 million raid on a security van in London, disclosed by Scotland Yard yesterday. The raiders intercepted a Group Four armoured vehicle in Caledonian Road, Islington, as it was about to deliver cash to a Midland Bank branch. A blue Mini forced the van to halt and two men, one armed with a handgun, leapt out and made the driver go to an alleyway off Pentonville Road. There the raiders, who wore balaclavas to mask their faces, ordered the three guards to hand over 60 cash bags, then made their escape. The security firm has announced a reward of £50,000 for information leading to the robbers' arrest and conviction.

We discover that it was the thieves who were burly rather than the detectives (naturally – how could we have thought otherwise?), and that £50,000 was a reward, rather than the money stolen.

This activity was tried with three seven-year-olds, who were presented with words from a geography text which seemed on the face of it too difficult for the readers. The boys grouped their words and discussed them with each other and the teacher. The passage was subsequently read aloud to them. What followed had not been envisaged. The children listened to the reading with their eyes glued to their jumbled words. As they heard one of the words, their fingers darted towards it on the page, without anyone suggesting it. This was an added bonus to an already fruitful exercise.

The skills of skimming and scanning follow naturally from such activities. Very few adults seem to have been taught these skills, and they are often deemed 'higher order skills'. For the slow reader, though, the realisation that one does not have to wade through every word on every page may come as a release. Such readers will often need some convincing of this, as the need for accurate reading aloud has become their one goal. Purposes for reading need to be planned carefully in advance, and the idea of letting words 'jump out from the page' explained to the children. Even virtual non-readers can look down a page and quickly find proper names or the names of places. This would be only the beginning. Eventually they will be able to collate two or three pieces of information from different parts of the page, or even different pages.

Whilst skimming involves reading quickly through a passage in order to extract meaning, 'scanning' is looking for specific items from a text which have been predetermined. This means that one does not need to assimilate the whole passage. Speed is important, because slowing up tends to make one forget the original goal and be waylaid by other chunks of, in this case, irrelevant text. Again, although it might be thought that only mature readers could engage in scanning, the slow reader is often engaged by it because it is so different from his/her usual ponderous read.

The scanning game

Duplicate a short passage of an appropriate readability level. The passage below is from a newspaper. Distribute copies, warning readers not to look at the text. At a given signal, turn over the sheets. Ask questions one at a time, and answers can be given orally or in writing. Do not give children any time to read the text first, and allow a minimum time before going on to the next question. The activity should be done in a relaxed manner, but with a sense of urgency.

THE GRAND KNOCKOUT TOURNAMENT (BBC-1, 7.40)

A very royal tournament, this one-off revival of the popular fun-and-games contest, with Prince Edward, Princess Anne, and the Duke and Duchess of York captaining squads of international celebrities. The setting is Alton Towers, the theme a Tudor one, the aim a million pounds for four charities, the games a little more dignified than the old ducking-and-dashing variety, and the event (though not the press conference) already much covered in the media. Of course protocol demands that a line be drawn at princely pitfalls: the royal skippers don't actually compete, leaving the horseplay to a list of champions which reads like a *Who's Who* of showbiz and sport, taking names like Kiri Te Kanawa and Tom Jones, Barry McGuigan and John Travolta, Meatloaf and Nigel Mansell.

Questions:

1 Name three of the royal team captains.
2 What historical period is being copied?

3   Do the royals take part in the games?
4   What programme is this on?
5   Name 3 celebrities taking part.
6   Where does this take place?
7   How much do they hope to raise?
8   Make up a headline for the article.
9   What is your personal reaction to the article?

Skimming is reading a passage quickly in order to grasp the main ideas. This is a more difficult skill for less able readers. Here we suggest a different approach, which incorporates group work on a story rather than information text.

Each group will choose a picture story book. The purpose of the activity is explained first: to make a tape-recording of the story, using sound effects only. When the tape is completed, it is played to an audience, with one member of the group turning over the pages of the book as the sound effects emerge.

The response to narrative should be holistic – a 'total' response, intellectually and emotionally derived, which appreciates the unity of the theme rather than remembering discrete events. The group will 'skim' various books before they choose one. Then they will do a 'close read' in order to select what they are going to back by sound. The use of sound effects emphasises the 'feel' of the story and its underlying atmosphere. Many picture books carry sophisticated messages which lead to deep reading. This activity helps the children to absorb the deeper qualities of the book without abstract discussion. Nor do they feel that they have gone back on to 'baby' books.

We have been trying to show the value of various styles of reading for all children. Equally important is the notion of using all kinds of texts, particularly those with which children are already familiar in ordinary life. Advertisements, notices and labels are examples: the use of labels will be discussed in detail.

Labels

We learn to read 'naturally' by finding out what labels in shops and homes can tell us. Many people seem to have started their reading career on the H.P. Sauce bottle! A whole language curriculum, gradually increasing in complexity, can be built round labels. The attainment targets of the national curriculum recognise their importance. The overall purpose would be to help children to use a variety of clues, some visual, some textual. It is important that real containers and labels should be brought into the classroom, with the children encouraged to make their own contributions. Possible developments are described below:

1 Recognition

The linking of text with previous experience. Discuss a collection of boxes, tins, bottles, etc. Select one to look at in detail:

- What do you think is inside this?
- Are there any other boxes here which have the same sort of thing inside?
- How do we know what is inside?
- What do we do with what is inside?

2 *Diagnosis through linguistic and perceptual discrimination*

- Let's look more carefully at one of the labels.
- Where is the name of the product?
- Does the label tell you anywhere what the product *is*? (its function, not its name).
- Does the label tell you anything about what is inside?
- Can you tell me in your own words what it says?
- Does the label tell you *how much* is inside?

Children can start collecting lists of the different words used on labels to show weight, quantity, capacity etc.

- Does the label tell you *who* made the product?
- Can you find *where* it came from?
- Is there anything else written on the label? What? Why?

Classification

Give each group a collection of labelled containers. Ask the children to group them in any way they choose, giving reasons for their grouping. Other ways of classifying might then be suggested. The classification will, of course, depend on what has been presented. One group might work with, for example, nothing but cleaning materials. They would then be able to classify according to the different cleaning jobs carried out, or the composition of the cleaners (liquid, powder, solid, etc.), or dangerous/safe materials, and so on.

Next ask the children to find all the words which tell how good the products are. Which words do they think are best? Find all the words which sound like the product they are describing. This will often include the name of the product itself. Can the products be classified according to name?

Cut up labels, separating pictures from text and jumble them together. Ask the children to sort them out.

Critical evaluation

1 What would you add to any of the labels to make it better, clearer?
2 Evaluate the pictures on the labels.
3 Would you buy this product? Why?
4 Surveys can be carried out on the popularity of products with family and

friends. Questionnaires may be devised in which interviewees are asked if labels influence them, and in what way.

Creative use of labels

Ask the groups to create new names, mottoes, advertising rhymes for chosen products, and make their own labels for chosen products.

A card game

1   Make one set of cards with labels stuck on, omitting or blanking out the identity of the product, e.g. Nescafé (omit the word 'coffee').
2   Make another set of cards, each bearing the name of a commodity (coffee, crisps, soap powder, etc.).
3   Place Set 1 face down in a pile on the table.
4   Deal out Set 2 to the players. The aim is to get all the cards in the hand down on the table.
5   Each player takes it in turn to pick one card from the central pack. If it matches a card in their hand, the pair may be laid face up on the table.

Although many of the suggestions above may seem contrived and artificial, they do attempt to set up 'realistic' if not 'real' situations, which the English 5–16 documents suggests (HMSO, 1986). What is real for the child does not necessarily mean a reality that can be touched. It means that what he is doing will be real in his mind, that he is able to slot it into his conceptual framework. In summing up, therefore, we are trying to provide real contexts for the 'special needs' child which incorporate:

1   Getting away from the artificial structures and irrelevant content of the conventional reading scheme. Acknowledging that narrative is not the only way into reading.
2   Encouraging children to vary the way they read for different purposes right from the start. Interrupting the 'straight read' so that they can experiment.
3   Making use of all the familiar material which surrounds children in everyday life.
4   Helping failing readers towards cognitive clarity and metalinguistic awareness by involving them in game-like analyses of features of text.
5   Encouraging the sharing of reading and its use for real purposes and audiences. Devising purposes which involve talking, reading and writing.

REFERENCES

Bryant, P. and Bradley, L. (1985) *Children's Reading Problems*, Oxford: Basil Blackwell.
Clark, M. (1987) 'New directions in the study of reading', in Anderson, C. (ed.) *Reading: The a b c and beyond*, London: U.K.R.A. Methuen Education.

Department of Education and Science (1982) *Education 5–9: An illustrative survey of 80 first schools in England,* HMSO.

Department of Education and Science (1986) *Curriculum Matters – English from 5–16,* London: HMSO.

Hughes, T. (1963) *How the Whale Became and Other Stories,* Harmondsworth: Puffin Books.

Meek, M. (1973) *Achieving Literacy,* London: Routledge & Kegan Paul.

National Curriculum Council (1989). *Curriculum Guidance 1: A Framework for the Primary Curriculum,* York: National Curriculum Council.

Smith, F. (1971) *Understanding Reading,* Eastbourne: Holt, Rinehart & Winston.

Chapter 6

Providing for pupils' writing needs
Stuart Dyke

GETTING THE ATTITUDE RIGHT

As a useful first base, let us admit that most adults find any writing composition to be a problematic activity. It requires skills of organisation and an application of thinking, involving effort and perseverance for myself and most of the teachers with whom I have discussed the matter. They will often say that 'they have to be in the mood', or that their schooling somehow destroyed their motivation and confidence. In a few cases it is marvellous to listen to the extracts of personal writing that some teachers have written with their pupils, or written just for their own pleasure of craftsmanship.

If we begin by looking at our own attitudes to the writing process it provides us with useful insights, reflections and the essential empathy needed for addressing the writing needs of children who experience difficulties. Another useful starting place is the attitudes of the pupils themselves. Discussion with children in the primary age-range (as part of early work of the National Writing Project, 1989), provided many fascinating, alarming and enjoyable comments regarding attitudes to the writing curriculum that they are presented with. At the crucial transfer stage of primary to secondary schooling (during the final junior year) many useful insights were gained by project teachers when they were confronted with responses that came straight from the frustration experienced by many pupils. As an illustration, here is just a flavour of some of the verbal comments:

1   When my teacher says today we are going to do some writing I do not feel very well. But sometimes, when I am in a good mood, I can be a good writer.
2   In creative writing there are a lot of interesting things that we could write, but the teacher always picks quite boring stories. It is hard to write down what you feel. The teacher should give us more time so that we can write a good story.
3   When I do writing my arm aches because we do a lot of writing.
4   Writing is a thing most people don't like, but have to do.
5   When I get my book back I feel like I don't want to open it. When I do and

just find a few mistakes, I give a big sigh of relief. Why do I get giggly every
time I get my writing back?

6   When Miss says do writing, I say to myself, 'Oh no! Crappy writing again!'
But then I don't like any school work.

Given a knowledge of the individuals involved in the sharing of attitudes about
writing, it is not difficult to make a match with their actual on-task performances, to consider the validity of their informal comments. The messages are
always clear regarding the importance of developing a positive self-concept, the
need to provide time for a variety of writing opportunities and the sensitivity to
who actually reads the writing and how it is responded to. These key issues, of
how to provide motivating purposes and audiences for young writers, are particularly crucial when we consider the writing curriculum for pupils who are
experiencing confusion and distress with the process and conventions of writing.
The broad principles and difficulties are the same for all children and adults. It is
the nature of the provision that we need to examine carefully if we are to suit
individual needs.

How then do we get the attitude right, to enable progress in writing development to take place? Fortunately, with infants and most lower juniors we have a
valuable starting resource. They want to please teacher! They also recognise that
writing is something deemed as important by the adult world and its acquisition
is 'part of growing-up'. The importance that school attaches to learning to write
can also be part of the problem. The seminal work by Donald Graves (1983),
outlines clearly this desire of children to write before school, and when they come
to school, motivated by the personal desire to 'make one's mark' upon the world,
whether it be on pavements, walls or paper.

This chapter will, therefore, outline the kind of classroom environment that is
conducive to the encouragement of a positive attitude to writing, with a view to
helping those children who experience difficulties when confronted with the
heavy demands of the primary writing curriculum.

CREATING A COMMUNITY OF WRITERS

How writing tasks are established and how teachers structure the responses to
the work is a fundamental issue. The work of the National Writing Project
(1989) offers useful advice in this area when it refers to the need to establish 'a
real community' of writers and readers in the classroom. What is meant by this
attractive notion?

Martin Coles gave some amusing insights as to what it does not mean when
he wrote a 'spoof' on the drafting process in the journal 'Education', as part of a
response to 'English 5–16' (1984). Tongue in cheek he wrote:

Make sure a child knows that his writing must be right first time. Never allow
a child to alter what he has written. It is possible of course for a child to reflect
on what he has written, to change or erase words, to revise the order of things,

to add thoughts, but this only wastes time that could be used to do more important things, like learning about the functions and names of all the main parts of speech.

Of course, we must give children time to organise their ideas through drafting, and allow the opportunities presented by this process to shape the nature of our responses. The opportunity to draft writing also invites comments from trusted peer-group members and the possibility of publication for a real audience at the end of the process.

Not all writing needs to be drafted: this will depend on the purpose of the activity. We should not use drafting as a machine to put pupils endlessly through a set routine of re-writing, editing and publication. But, in its proper place, as a means of finding real readers, all pupils need this regular opportunity of publication. For pupils who experience learning difficulties it is particularly important, as they have often been denied any chance to make the vital connection between the construction of their own messages and the satisfaction of another party being able to read their statement, opinion or story.

OVERCOMING THE DIFFICULTIES

Learning to write, as with learning to read, requires a developing awareness of phonology, syntax and semantics on the part of the language-user. No discussion of the writing process can ignore the central role that structured opportunities for talking and listening play in the development of this conceptual organisation and development. Pupils need to be able to talk through their ideas and think out their messages on to paper. Many children who struggle to write anything have not had time to get organised with the physical demands (the location of the pencils, pens, paper and their manipulation) as well as the thinking demands of the task. Talking with a partner, or small peer group, or with the teacher provides the space and opportunity for this necessary organisation. A chance to draft (re-think) and obtain informal responses from trusted partners (peers and teacher) provides more space and time for the talking-thinking-organisation that is so essential, if any progress is to be made.

But how does this apply to the pupil who experiences writing difficulties, whose readers are unable to respond to the marks the writer has made on the paper? With these pupils the physical aspect of writing is often the main difficulty. The manipulative skills of the writing task need to be considered and developed alongside the conceptual requirements. The poorly coordinated child, with sensory-motor difficulties that hinder the development of fine manipulative skills, will invariably produce early writing that is often described as 'scribble'. Interestingly, so do other early writers at the pre-school and early infant stage. This physical difficulty, therefore, should be seen in its developmental context. The core framework 'English in the National Curriculum' (1989), clearly outlines the significance of this 'level' of development, when in Attainment Target 3 (Writing) it states:

Level 1   Pupils should be able to . . .
use pictures, symbols, or isolated letters, words or phrases to communicate meaning.

and in Attainment Target 5 (Handwriting):

Level 1   Pupils should be able to . . .
begin to form letters but with some control over the size, shape and
orientation of letters or lines of writing.

The following example from the National Writing Project illustrates these Level 1
features:

Illustration 1: The child should be given credit for clearly differentiating writing
and drawing, and for using single letters and clusters of letters to represent whole
words, even though the writing is not interpretable without the teacher's notes
written below the child's attempt.

Whilst the implications for the teaching of handwriting are clear, so also is the
need to respect 'scribble writing' as a valid early level of communicating
messages. It only requires the child to be asked to read his/her own writing, informally to the teacher or on to a tape recorder, for the sense of the message to be

conveyed. It is also useful to note the comment on the example, that 'the child should be given credit for clearly differentiating writing and drawing, and for using single letters and clusters of letters to represent whole words'. Given this perspective and response, a child experiencing manipulative difficulties can be given a sense of achievement and the satisfaction of communicating personal messages through emerging writing. If this level of performance is dismissed as 'mere scribble' then distress for the child (and teacher) is almost inevitable.

One teacher of reception infants, participating in the National Writing Project (Somerset and Wilts. 'Writing to Learn'), monitored the early development of children over their first nine months in school. The stages that were observed are useful as they give a flavour of the rich variety of writing behaviour that can be expected from early writers, and can give a context to identification of levels of achievement for all pupils:

- Some children scribble, some write their name or part of it; others do not attempt anything after they have drawn, but talk about their pictures and let me scribe their story
- Random letters begin to appear – upper and lower case – all over the page
- The letters are ordered in a left to right straight line, often on one, two or more lines
- Some sounds in this stream of letters match the initial sounds of the words of the 'story' the child is recounting
- The number of random letters decreases and every letter has a phonetic function. There may be no spacing between yet
- Words are clearly defined and fluency is developing.

Observations by the teacher are a useful first stage if any provision is to be planned that will be appropriate to individual needs.

INTERVENTION

After observation of pupils' level of writing behaviour, thought needs to be given to provision that can encourage further development. Recently I have been working with teachers in my own Authority (SCEA, 1989) to devise a 'Curriculum-related profile' to give guidance to special needs and classroom teachers, regarding pointers for further development and provision. The work of Marie Clay (1975) and the National Writing Project helped inform the discussion of pupils' work, necessary for the agreement of appropriate criteria. Whilst no profile can do away with the need for teachers to create real purposes and audiences for writing, it can provide a framework to allow informed intervention and constructive responses to take place.

Children of the same chronological age will have had differing experiences and make different assumptions about the writing process and its conventions. But, if we take the time to observe and record this individuality, we deepen our own knowledge and can find more appropriate ways to help each child's development. The implementation of drafting and publication opportunities are not enough, important as they are for all writers. The statements in 'English in the National Curriculum' (1989) are certainly not enough guidance for the classroom teacher. Teachers need specific criteria of observable writing behaviour, that can be used as a basis for informed intervention within the 'community of writers and readers'. Unless teachers are aware of all aspects of children's writing development, how can we discuss with our pupils what they already know and in what areas they require help?

Marie Clay (1975) suggests that we look at three particular aspects of children's writing:

1   *The language level*   How a child handles letters, words, phrases and sentences.
2   *The message quality*   How the child develops initial concepts of print and learns how to use a range of writing functions.
3   *The directional principles*   How a child moves towards orthodox arrangement of text.

Using these three aspects as a guide, the SCEA working party constructed a profile that can be used to:

- monitor and diagnose children's knowledge and progress
- decide where help is most appropriate
- check the suitability and range of writing tasks available
- pass on well documented information to other staff
- form the basis for consultations with pupils, parents and psychologists

The first pre-requisite is that samples of the pupil's writing need to be collected and discussed with other colleagues, to begin the shading-in of the profile at the existing level of writing behaviour and achievement. The most useful record of achievement is a dated collection of samples from each child's work, to offer evidence for the profile indicators. This can be achieved by:

- maintaining individual folders containing regular samples
- pinning individually named packets on the classroom walls, where children can store their drawings and writing
- using personal writing files as the main record, supplemented regularly by other samples.

Whether these or other ways are chosen, it is important that teachers give children a sense of their own development as writers, through discussion of the writing process and their actual achievements with it. The SEN profile (SCEA, 1989) that follows is only useful when placed in this positive context.

The wheel-profile covers children's writing development from reception onwards. This observable assessment of Message Quality is based on language and thinking criteria. The assessing teacher should consider these criteria in terms of what the pupil can rather than cannot do and locate further appropriate

The development of early writing
INSTRUCTIONAL ——————— INDEPENDENT

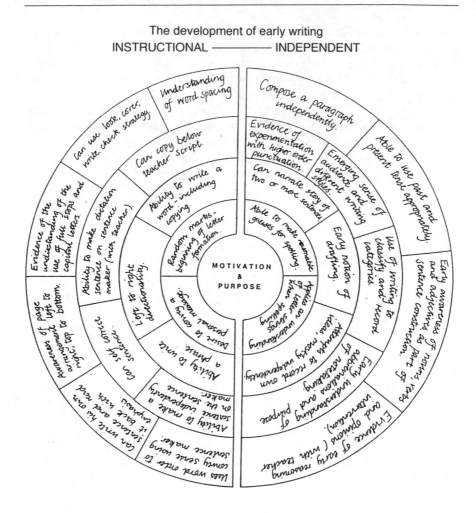

areas to extend the pupil's achievement. The achieved stages can be shaded in. No child is at any one stage at any one time.

Instructional

This is the stage of regular supportive interaction between teacher and child. The development stage of the instructional language level considers the child's early writing in terms of the language-experience approach of *Breakthrough to Literacy* (1978), as well as an alternative approach using 'copy script'. Observation of children suggests that they may operate at more than one level of language at any particular time. Children with learning difficulties, however, need encouragement and support to develop across the stages as they may remain for too long on any one level. They may lack the ability and confidence to experiment with different language levels. This underpins the importance of assessing a child's own particular developmental stage, in order to plan and devise appropriate teaching strategies.

Independent

At this stage a child will have acquired a degree of independence in writing.

We must encourage the development of organisational and thinking skills, in order to achieve successful learning through the writing provision across the curriculum. All children have the ability to reason and it is the teachers's responsibility to help them use and develop this resource. Encouraging children to write for a 'purpose' is likely to help them to develop their planning skills.

All children should be made aware that the process of writing varies with the audience and, as a result, they need to experiment with different styles and drafting techniques.

Towards independence

When one studies the criteria contained within the two sections (Instructional-Independent) of the wheel-diagram, a useful distinction should be made between the 'secretarial' skills and 'composing' skills.

Whilst 'secretarial' skills can be described as 'lower-order', to do with getting the ideas down on paper in a standard comprehensible form (involving handwriting, spelling, punctuation and syntax), they should not be seen as solely 'instructional'. Of course they need to be taught, as part of a structured provision, but they also develop hand-in-hand with emerging independence. They should not be seen as skills that can be taught as a pre-requisite to writing! They are conventions which need to be learnt as part of the writing process, alongside the composing skills.

However, the 'composing' skills are the driving force towards independence from constant teacher involvement, as they involve children in having to think for themselves and make evaluations of the quality of their own drafting attempts. The beginnings of this evaluative thinking can be observed and taught by the encouragement of self-correction.

Self-correction can be seen as a natural early aspect of emergent writing and can also be encouraged by those teachers who use the more structured 'breakthrough to literacy' approach advocated by Mackay, Thompson and Schaub (1978). Criteria pertaining to this approach are included in the profile. This necessitates the teacher viewing 'error' as points for progress.

The 'wheel' design of the SEN profile (in contrast to more conventional listing of criteria) is an attempt to portray the fact that children do not learn about language on any one level of organisation. There is no small-step accumulation of skills through a listed hierarchy. There are developmental pointers, moving out from the centre, beginning with:

Desire to convey a personal message
Random marks – beginning of letter formation

towards . . .

Ability to write a phrase
Early notion of drafting
Attempts to record own ideas, mostly independently

towards . . .

Ability to self-correct sentence
Evidence of experimentation with punctuation
Emerging sense of audience and different writing styles

towards . . .

Evidence of early reasoning and opinions
Early awareness of nouns, verbs and adjectives
Compose a paragraph independently

You will notice how all the selected aspects have secretarial (code learning) and composing (organisation of ideas) elements within them. They can only be pointers and no child follows any definite pathway. The recording on the profile will tend to move outwards, but progress will also occur over the spectrum, if the central respect for motivation is provided for. This motivation is only sustained by the provision of real purposes and a variety of audience-readership, that involves opportunities for actual sharing of publications from one child to another and between classes. (Many schools also include pupils' books as part of the class, year, or school libraries.)

In a classroom where writing is regularly shared, the secretarial and composing aspects are given their proper context as part of the writing community. Children can be shown how the same processes operate within newspaper and publishing offices, as well as when adults write letters and articles at home. The example of the difficulties faced by the teacher, when attempting personal writing, has a similar powerful motivating influence when it is shared with the pupils.

A group of Scottish teachers (Jackson and Michael, 1986) have formulated a list of useful key questions that pupils can be invited to ask themselves. These questions help develop their composing skills and the necessary basic meta-language of writing (DES, 1988) through discussion about the writing process. The questions are a series of invitations to the writer(s) to make decisions about the following:

• Why am I writing?
• What will I select from all I might say, to serve the purpose of the writing?
• What will the people who will read this need to be told, or might want to be told?

- What words and structures will I select that will satisfy me and convey what I have to say clearly and effectively?
- Will the people for whom I am writing expect my piece of writing to be communicated in a particular form?

Obviously, for young writers (in fact, for any writer) these are challenging questions. A positive attitude to 'trial and error', and time given for discussion with other pupils and the teacher, will allow adaptation of the questions to suit the needs of any pupils, when decisions have to be made regarding where the writing should go to next (second draft, writing folder, publication, etc.). When this level of collaborative activity is encouraged, the variety of response and assistance to any one writer is immeasurably increased.

What about spelling?

You will have noticed that several spelling criteria are included within the wheel-profile, as part of overall writing development. It is an important secretarial aspect, but it is evident that a child can be a poor speller and yet still write in a well-organised and imaginative fashion. Equally, good spellers may not necessarily be effective composers and communicators of meanings. There must be, however, a helpful boost to the general confidence and motivation of a writer if his/her spelling ability is steadily improving. Certainly an effective speller draws less criticism from insensitive readers! There has to be a gain to fluency and a cutting-down on proof-reading time, if spelling ability is reasonably accurate.

The recent core curriculum supports this need to teach spelling, with the extra emphasis of a separate attainment target (AT4) within the overall assessment of writing development. *English 5–11* (1988) states:

> The main line of development concerns children's increasing control not simply over correct spelling of individual words, but also over the most frequent sound-letter correspondences and the other principles of English spelling. Despite the undeniable irregularities of English spelling, it is important that teaching and assessing focus on those areas that are systematic . . .

English in the National Curriculum (1990) offers an example of a systematic framework for the teaching and assessment of speaking. Pupils should be able to:

(a) produce a meaningful and recognisable (though not necessarily always correct) spelling of a range of common sight words;
(b) spell correctly, in the course of their own writing, simple monosyllabic words they use regularly, which observe common patterns;
(c) recognise that spelling has patterns and begin to apply their knowledge of those patterns in their attempt to spell a wider range of words;
(d) show knowledge of the names and order of the letters of the alphabet.

The overall approach should be the teaching of helpful strategies, such as 'look-cover-write-check' and the visual remembering of the key letter-strings (Peters and Cripps, 1978), placed in the context of drafting and proof-reading. The provision of structured word-banks and dictionaries, as part of the self-correction of the drafting process, puts the secretarial skill of spelling in its appropriate place as a checking activity demanded by a critical readership.

The following examples, from the work of the National Writing Project, show features that relate to the Levels 1 and 2 of Attainments for Writing and Spelling. They offer some useful indicators for special needs teachers.

Illustration 2   Though the child is further towards the conventional spelling of whole words, and some common spelling patterns are emerging, individual words are not demarcated by spaces.

Illustration 3   is interpretable, with only slight difficulty, without the teacher's help. The child is moving towards level 2, as illustrated by this independently written short piece, consisting of complete sentences (though not punctuated), and showing several main spelling patterns

I am play with smokey
in bed he is miy ted ber
and I play with him a pt
he is miy besd ted ber

By the time the child's development in writing has progressed into more independent composing, it is possible to identify and illustrate an increasing range of writing across the curriculum.

The next example was produced as an unaided first draft by a middle infant girl. This is intuitively a stage further on and illustrates several level 2 features. This is a simple chronological account with a clear story structure, including a conventional beginning, narrative middle and end. The sentences are almost demarcated, though via the graphic, comic-strip layout, and not via capital letters and punctuation. The spelling is almost entirely meaningful and recognisable. In several cases, it shows that the author has correctly grasped the patterns involved, even though the individual spellings are wrong (e.g. trooth, eny, owt, sumthing, cubad). The handwriting occasionally mixes upper and lower case letters, though only at beginnings and ends of words, not at random.

ENCOURAGING THE WRITER

As a summary of the underlying themes of this chapter, the following positive approaches can be encouraging to the pupil who is experiencing difficulties with his/her writing:

- Think about how to encourage a purposeful writing community.
- Listen to children and respond to content first of all.

When I was naughty

It wasa ferw weex Past My birthday wen Me and My sister went to the Kitchen

I went to the Cubad and Clare opnd the cubad and We tuck the crips andWe went uP seris My

daP cort Me and Clare so he said have you tuck Sum thing From the cubad no we said

then My daD Said have you noI.lid are you teling lis no no no I lidagain In the end My daD Mád me tell the trooth

then he Said you naughty gils and sent me and clare to bed with owt eny SuPa And Clare blamd it on Me.

- Tell them what you like about their writing, before discussing a specific area in need of development.
- Give time for drafting and publication opportunities, where appropriate.
- Offer a wide range of purposeful writing activities, that includes poetry as an esteemed medium of expression and reasoning.
- Involve children in self-correction, wherever possible, as a first informal assessment of where the writing should go next.
- Be careful of too much writing, to allow time for oracy and the expressive arts as an integral part of communicating, shaping and comprehending meaning.
- Set up 'response partners', within the peer-group, for further informal assistance to the writer.
- Be wary of short-term exercises, especially their effect on motivation.
- Encourage sharing and display of good examples, wherever possible.
- Ban the use of red biro as a marking instrument.
- Teach handwriting and spelling strategies.
- Try to get hold of tape recorders, a jumbo typewriter and word processor, to give further flexibility and reality to the writing community.
- Record individual achievement and outline one or two new areas for the pupil to focus on next.
- Discuss some of the basic metalanguage of the writing process (e.g. secretarial, composing, publication), where appropriate.
- Occasionally write with the children and share your own difficulties and achievements.
- Build on the natural interest of all children in their own experiences, stories and arguments. Build-in the links with literature and include some of their writing in the class library, alongside the other books.

In essence, a writing community should seek to protect the craftsmanship of the writing process from any association with punishment, mechanical routines and pointless copying. It should celebrate achievement, through sharing and publication, viewing difficulties as growth-points for discussion and further development.

REFERENCES

Clay, M. (1975) *What Did I Write?*, London: Heinemann.
Department of Education and Science (1984) *English 5–16*, London: HMSO.
Department of Education and Science (1988a) *English 5– 11*, London: HMSO.
Department of Education and Science (1989) *English in the National Curriculum*, London: HMSO.
Department of Education and Science (1988b) *Report of the Committee of Inquiry into the Teaching of the English Language*, The 'Kingman' Report, London: HMSO.
Graves, D. (1983) *Writing: Teachers and Children at Work*, London: Heinemann.
Hoffman, M. (1976) *Reading, Writing and Relevance*, Sevenoaks: Hodder & Stoughton.
Jackson, W. and Michael, B. (1986) *Foundations of Writing*, Scottish Curriculum Development Service.

Mackay, D., Thompson, B. and Schaub, B. (1978) *Breakthrough to Literacy*, London: Longman.

National Writing Project materials (1990). About to be published by Nelson.

Perera, K. (1984) *Children's Writing and Reading*, Oxford: Blackwell.

Peters, M. and Cripps, C. (1978) *The Word Bank Project*, Basingstoke: Macmillan.

Service Children's Education Authority (1989) *Curriculum-related profile for SEN*, Teachers' Centre, JHQ-Rheindahlen, BFPO, 40BFPO 140.

Smith, F. (1982) *Writing and the Writer*, London: Heinemann.

Snowling, M. (1985) *Children's Written Language Difficulties*, Windsor: NFER-Nelson.

Wilkinson, A. (1986) *The Writing of Writing*, Milton Keynes: Open University Press.

Wilkinson, A. (1986) *The Quality of Writing*, Milton Keynes: Open University Press.

Chapter 7

Meeting the special needs of mathematical low attainers in the primary school
Derek Haylock

INTRODUCTION

This chapter explores ways of helping pupils who perform poorly in mathematics (compared to their peers), with particular reference to those in the age range 8 to 12 years, the age range with which the author has most experience.

Two approaches are outlined to tackle the special needs of primary school pupils whose attainment in mathematics is low. The first of these is the objectives approach. It is argued that this can be effective provided the target objectives are realistic and appropriate for the particular pupils being considered, and that the emphasis is shifted from the learning of recipes and routines to the development of understanding. An alternative or complementary approach is to seek to identify meaningful and genuinely purposeful situations and activities in which low attaining pupils can develop their mathematical skills.

LOW ATTAINMENT IN MATHEMATICS

The label 'low attainers' is chosen quite deliberately. It implies that the pupils under discussion are precisely those whose attainment is low when compared to other children in their year groups. We are talking about those pupils in an ordinary school who struggle along in the bottom set for mathematics, or those pupils in a mixed ability class, for example, who are still ploughing laboriously through Book 1 of the school's maths scheme when most of the class are on Book 2 or 3. These are pupils whose experience of mathematics has been repeated failure contributing to a sense of frustration and bewilderment.

Other labels have different implications. To refer to 'slow learners' or the 'less able' carries the implication that the basic problem is the pupil's ability, and may limit a teacher's expectations of what the pupils might achieve. It also overlooks the complex interaction of factors which may contribute to poor performance in mathematics (e.g. social, emotional, cognitive, developmental, physical).

To refer to 'low attainers' is to make no judgements about the cause of low attainment, but simply to recognize that the pupils, compared to the peer group, have experienced failure in mathematics and that consequently they may have special needs which must be attended to if they are to get a fair deal and the opportunity for a fresh start during the important years of primary education.

OBJECTIVES FOR NUMERACY

A traditional approach to tackling the problems of low attainers in mathematics, particularly in the USA with reference to arithmetic skills, has been the specification of precise, behavioural target objectives, followed by diagnosis of the pupil's performance against these objectives, and then a programme of remediation. There is clearly some value in an approach which, by making specific objectives explicit, makes success and progress more obvious both for teachers and pupils. The teacher can specify target skills which are currently not attained by pupils, encourage them to commit themselves to its achievement and then, subsequent to an effective learning programme, demonstrate that progress has been made.

But such an approach for mathematical low attainers in the primary or middle school could only be endorsed if the target objectives are worthwhile and realistic: realistic in two senses: (a) being reasonable targets for the pupils concerned to aim for; (b) being related to the real world in which the pupils live. This is particularly relevant to the teaching of methods of doing calculations.

Many pupils' sense of failure at mathematics has been produced by failure to remember and master the different routines which have to be followed in order to carry out abstract calculation by standard, formal written methods. Yet what the teachers are aiming for may well be neither worthwhile nor realistic for the pupils in question. It has been suggested, for example, that there are over sixty different types of mistakes possible in the method of subtraction by decomposition. So if this is set as a target objective, the diagnosis and remediation question becomes quite daunting, particularly for a teacher faced with a class of thirty idiosyncratic children. Furthermore, when a calculation like $100 - 76$ is met in a realistic and meaningful context (such as comparing two purchases priced at £100 and £76, or giving change from a pound), the low attaining pupil often shows a competence which contrasts with his/her performance on the abstract task.

ALGORITHMS, ADHOCORITHMS, AND CALCULATORS

It is in fact quite rare for us to require exact answers to calculations in our everyday lives. Readers are invited to monitor their own behaviour for a week or two and compare the number of times that they find themselves doing exact calculations with the number of times they work out rough estimates or approximate answers to calculations. If we are preparing pupils for the demands of everyday life then we certainly need to put a greater emphasis on numerical estimation and encourage pupils to work out approximate answers by whatever informal methods make sense to them. If the pupils are learning to do their calculations in realistic contexts then we will be more likely to send out the message that good estimates are legitimate and authentic mathematics.

However, there will be times in everyday life when exact calculations are required (when monitoring my own behaviour over a period of four weeks this occurred once, when dealing with my income tax return). In such circumstances there are three ways of responding. The first is to use an algorithm, one of those standard routines which traditionally have been the major emphasis in the teaching of arithmetic: subtraction by decomposition, long multiplication, and so on. The second is to use what I have termed an 'adhocorithm'. This is an informal method which may be carried out mentally, or on paper (or using a combination of the two). But the key factors are that the method makes sense to the person concerned and it is appropriate to the particular numbers, operation and situation.

The third approach is to use a calculator. For example, if you had to find the cost of 16 articles at 25p each you might set out a calculation like this on paper:

$$
\begin{array}{r}
25 \\
\times\ 16 \\
\hline
250 \\
150 \\
\hline
400 \\
\hline
\end{array}
$$

This is the algorithmic approach, with which many people feel comfortable. But there is plenty of evidence that the majority of people in their everyday and working lives rarely use the algorithms which their teachers tried to drill into them at school, preferring instead to use their own adhocorithms, or to turn to their calculators. The reader will find it instructive to think about how they would actually find the answer to the above problem if they encountered it tomorrow in some real situation, say, requiring the cost of 16 articles at 25p each. Some, but certainly not all, may think to themselves: '2 at twenty-five pence makes fifty pence, so that's four to a pound; 16 is 4 fours, giving the answer £4.' This is an example of an adhocorithm. There are, of course, other adhocorithms which could have been used for this problem, depending on which particular number relationships are most readily accessible to the person concerned. And if no informal method leads to a solution then there is always the sensible alternative of entering '25 × 16 =' on a calculator. Just knowing that this is the appropriate calculation to find the cost of 16 articles at 25p each is an important piece of mathematical understanding.

Some 11-year-olds in a bottom mathematics set were playing a small group game called Shopkeeper. In this game each player has a float and makes imaginary sales, taking the money involved in the form of plastic coins from the banker. The sales are generated by turning over cards from two packs, one pack with single digits written on them, the other with items being sold at certain prices. Sean turned over '5' and 'pencils at 16p'. He then said to himself something like this: 'Five 10's make 50p, and five 5's make 25p, that's 75p, and another 5p makes 80p.' On his next turn he had to work out the cost of 6 yoghurts at 17p. After a few minutes thought he turned to his calculator and correctly entered '6 × 17 ='. This seems to me to demonstrate what we should be aiming for with most mathematical low attaining pupils in terms of calculation skills: confidence to tackle calculations by informal methods which make sense to the individual when they are comfortable with the numbers involved, and then knowing what calculation to enter on the calculator when the numbers get too difficult.

RECOGNISING UNDERSTANDING

With low attaining pupils there is a temptation for the teacher to resort to drilling them in the mastery of routine arithmetic processes. The emergence of the calculator has clearly made such an approach untenable, and lends credence to the view that we should be shifting the emphasis in our target behaviours away from the learning of recipes towards understanding.

It is important therefore that we clarify how understanding in mathematics can be recognised. A simple model which enables us to talk about understanding in mathematics is one which views the growth of understanding as the building up of networks of cognitive connections. A brief outline of this model is given here – for a fuller discussion see Haylock and Cockburn (1989). When I encounter some new experience I understand it better if I can connect it to previous experiences (or to a network of previously connected experiences). The more strongly connected the experience, the more I understand it. Learning without making connections is what might be called learning by rote. Such learning is easily confused or forgotten and is of little value in application to real life situations.

When children are engaged in mathematical activity they are involved in manipulating some or all of the following: concrete materials, symbols, language and pictures.

They manipulate concrete materials: for example, moving blocks, rods, counters, fingers, coins. They manipulate symbols: writing digits on pieces of paper, arranging them in the prescribed fashion, copying exercises from the workcard, numbering the questions, crossing out some symbols, carrying one, filling in boxes, pressing keys on their calculator, etc. They manipulate language: reading workcards, processing the teacher's instructions, interpreting word problems, saying out loud the words that go with their recording, discussing procedures with other pupils in a group, and so on. And finally, they manipulate pictures: for example, number lines, set diagrams, arrow pictures and graphs.

It is helpful to think of understanding the concepts of number and number operations (e.g. number, place value, addition, subtraction, multiplication, division, equals) as including the building up of networks of cognitive connections between these four types of experience: concrete experiences, symbols, language and pictures.

As an example, how would we recognise that a child to some extent under-stands the concept of subtraction? The connections framework might lead us to specify a number of important behavioural objectives which could demonstrate some degree of understanding of subtraction. For example, each behaviour stated below indicates a connection between symbols (e.g. 13−8, the keys on a calcu-lator), words (e.g. thirteen subtract eight), concrete situations (e.g. counters or stories), or pictures (e.g. the number line). The child should be able to:

- interpret a subtraction statement written in symbols, or stated in words, by putting out a set of objects and taking some away
- interpret a subtraction statement written in symbols, or stated in words, by putting out two sets of objects and comparing them
- interpret a subtraction statement written in symbols, or stated in words, as a movement on the number line
- know what calculation to enter on a calculator for a problem using the language 'how many more' or 'how many less'
- know what calculation to enter on a calculator for a problem using the language 'what must be added'
- make up a story to fit a given subtraction statement in the context of shopping, using the language of comparison, e.g. 'dearer' or 'cheaper'.

This is just a selection of objectives which might indicate some aspect of under-standing of the concept of subtraction. Targets such as these which emphasise understanding rather than the mastery of abstract routines and recipes should be more prominent in our work with low attainers in mathematics.

DEVELOPING UNDERSTANDING

Having specified realistic targets, the teacher must then design a learning programme aimed at achieving them. If the teacher is aiming for understanding (in the sense outlined above) then the major task will be to devise activities which help the pupils to build up connections, particularly the important connections between symbols, language, concrete situations and pictures.

A small group activity based on this framework has proved to be successful with low attaining pupils in building up their understanding, and therefore their confidence, in handling number operations. In this activity the pupils are given a starting point, for example, a story, and a sequence of swaps: Story – Write in Symbols – Calculator – Base Ten Blocks – Coins – Number Line. The particular sequence is chosen appropriately by the teacher and given to the group as a chal-lenge.

For example, they might start with the story: 'Tom had 28 pens. Mary had 13 pens. How many less than Tom does Mary have?' The group then has to write this story in symbols, i.e. 28−13, enter the corresponding sum on to a calculator, set out some tens and units blocks to show the same calculation, and finally draw a picture on a number line to show the difference between 28 and 13. Having agreed their responses amongst themselves they then demonstrate their sequence to the teacher.

On another occasion, for example, they might start with a calculation written in symbols, and follow the sequence, Symbols – Coins – Calculator – Write a Story – Number Line. Clearly the variations are numerous.

LANGUAGE PROBLEMS

It is frequently the case that pupils whose attainment in mathematics is low have poorly developed language and reading skills. We can draw two obvious conclusions from this, one negative and one positive.

Firstly, it is clearly not appropriate that such pupils still find themselves struggling to learn mathematics through the medium of textbook and workcard schemes. This is inevitably going to be the least efficient way of giving such pupils instruction and explanation. Secondly, teachers working with low attaining pupils must provide activities and experiences specifically designed to develop language in mathematics, particularly in view of the importance of language in the connections model of understanding outlined above. Specific help needs to be provided with getting such words as 'each', 'altogether', 'between' and 'leaves' correctly into important patterns of spoken language.

One useful activity is to provide a small group of pupils with a set of cards with words and phrases such as 'shared between', 'sets of', 'is', 'each', 'altogether', three cards with numbers on (say, 3, 4, and 12), and an appropriate number of counters to manipulate. The challenge is then to make up as many different sentences as possible:

    3 sets of 4 is 12 altogether
    4 sets of 3 is 12 altogether
    12 shared between 4 is 3 each
    12 shared between 3 is 4 each

Make a calculator available and, with a few more phrases and symbols written on cards, other sentences can be added to the list:

    3 times 4 is 12
    4 times 3 is 12
    3 multiplied by 4 is 12
    4 multiplied by 3 is 12
    $3 \times 4 = 12$
    $4 \times 3 = 12$
    12 divided by 3 is 4
    12 divided by 4 is 3
    $12 \div 4 = 3$

One area to be targeted especially is the language of comparison: 'more', 'less', 'longer', 'shorter', 'dearer', 'cheaper', 'heavier', 'lighter', and so on. Many children have difficulty in handling the language patterns associated with these words. Often any word referring to the greater quantity will prompt them to do an addition. For example, 'How many more than 25 is 42?' will be interpreted as '25 + 42'. There is also considerable difficulty involved in constructing sentences using the words which refer to the smaller quantity. For example, many low attaining pupils would struggle to compare their two counters with my five counters and make a sentence such as 'I've got three less than you'. This is hardly surprising since they do not have the three that we are talking about, although I may be wanting the child to say a sentence beginning with the words, 'I've got three ...'. When making a comparison in spoken English of the form, 'The number here (A) is three less than the number here (B)', the language seems to be particularly obscure: A is the subject of the sentence but the three referred to is actually part of B. The same difficulty is built into comparisons of, for example, length (shorter than), weight (lighter than) and cost (cheaper than).

One helpful strategy is always to use the two pieces of language side by side, so that whenever a comparison is made the two equivalent statements are formed. For example, if the pupil has done some weighing and asserts that the book is heavier than the box, he/she should also be encouraged to say that the box is lighter than the book. If they have worked out that the pen costs 10p more than the pencil, they should also observe that the pencil costs 10p less than the pen.

One simple activity specifically designed to help low attaining pupils associate both 'more than' and 'less than' with subtraction statements makes use of a calculator. In the diagram below two packs of cards with various numbers written on then are placed in the boxes A and D. A calculator sits in box B. In box C is a card which says 'more than' on one side and 'less than' on the other.

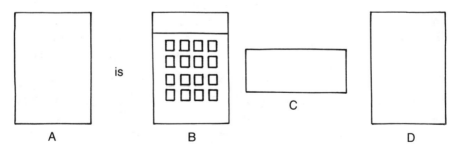

The pupil turns over a card from each of the packs A and D. They then have to decide whether A is more than or less than D, and set the card C to the appropriate words. Next they enter a subtraction onto the calculator in order to find the difference between the two numbers, and the calculator is then placed in box B in order to complete the sentence, as shown in the example below. The completed sentence is then copied into the pupil's book.

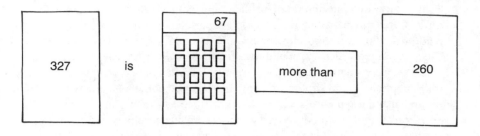

'More than/less than' is a simple game which has been used successfully to help low attainers in mathematics with this problem area of the language of comparison. The game is described here using coins, although a version using Unifix cubes can also be played.

Two pupils each start with the same amount of money, for example, a pound's worth of 1p and 10p plastic token coins, and an empty box. The object of the game is to get as much money as possible into your box. A third pupil acts as the referee. Player A puts down any amount of money. Player B puts down a different amount. The referee then turns over a card from a pack. This card will say either 'more than' or 'less than'. If it says 'more than' then the player who has put down more than the other wins that round. What they actually win is the difference between the two amounts played. This is taken from the larger pile of money, the referee exchanging where necessary, placed in the winning player's box, and the remaining equal piles of coins returned to the two players. If the card turned over shows 'less than', then the player who has played less than the other wins; again, the winnings being the difference between the two amounts. Once again this is taken from the greater amount of money. The game continues with players taking it in turns to go first. The referee should insist on the winning player saying something like, 'My 12p is less than your 18p, so I win the difference, which is 6p', before the winnings are taken. The game ends when each player has 1p left in their pile.

This simple game targets the language of 'more than' and 'less than', and helps pupils connect it with subtraction by finding the difference, when they compare the two amounts, as well as with taking away, when they take away their winnings from the greater amount and put them in their box.

CHOOSING THE OPERATION

One of the fundamental difficulties which pupils face in understanding mathematics, in terms of connecting symbols with concrete situations, is that the same set of mathematical symbols can represent such vastly differing situations. This is particularly the case with the symbols used for number operations.

A subtraction statement, such as $13 - 8$, may be connected, for example, with a comparison situation (how many more than 8 is 13, or, how many less than 13 is 8); a partitioning situation (13 take away 8); a complement of a set (in a set of 13, 8 have some attribute, how many do not); a counting back or reducing situation (start at 13 and count back 8); an inverse of addition situation (what must be added to 8 to make 13), and so on.

Similarly, a division statement, such as $12 \div 4$, must be connected with both 'sharing between' (12 shared between 4, how many each), and grouping (how many groups of 4 are there in a set of 12).

Each number operation can be analysed like this in terms of a number of different models, that is, categories of concrete situations to which the number statements must be connected. The pupil has to learn to connect each operation correctly with the various models. This is a daunting but vital task for the teacher of the low attaining pupil.

Furthermore, each of these models may be encountered in a variety of contexts, such as manipulating sets of objects, money, measuring length, weight, time, temperature, and so on.

In fact, it could be argued that the most basic and important objective for numeracy is precisely this:

> The pupil should be able to state what calculation should be entered on a calculator in order to solve a realistic problem for each of the operations: addition, subtraction, multiplication, division; using any of the models of the operation; and in any appropriate context; and be able to interpret the answer.

So, for example, for subtraction, using the comparison model in the context of money, the pupil should know what to enter on a calculator in order to work out how much more expensive one item is than another. For division (using the grouping model in the context of weighing) the pupil should know what calculation to enter on a calculator to work out how many portions of 25g can be obtained from a bag containing 450g.

The reader will find it instructive to complete the analysis of the operations, and to suggest further examples for each model of each operation in a variety of contexts, such as those given above. The conclusion must be, that if we accept that this is a key objective for numeracy, then we have more than enough to be aiming at with low attaining pupils here, without trying to drill them for mastery of redundant paper-and-pencil algorithms. In the age of the calculator, knowing what sum to do is clearly far more useful and significant than knowing how to do the sum.

PURPOSEFUL ACTIVITIES IN MEANINGFUL CONTEXTS

The basic difficulty which I have with the objectives–diagnosis–remediation approach to teaching mathematics to low attainers is that it tends to focus too much on what the pupil cannot do. My experience convinces me that if only we can find purposeful activities for such pupils in meaningful contexts then they will often surprise us with what they can do.

We might, for example, note that some researcher has determined that a large percentage of low attaining pupils fail at a conservation of weight task, in which they are asked to compare the weight of some joined-up cubes with that of the same cubes separated. But I am sure that I have seen these same pupils happily measuring out 100g of flour when doing cookery at school, transferring it from one container to another, mixing it with other ingredients into their cake mixture, and so on. Am I to believe that in doing all this they might somehow think that the 100g of flour they started with might no longer be 100g after all they have done to it? In the context of this purposeful activity the pupils seem to use the concept of conservation of weight with no difficulty.

I have similarly seen quite young children showing a thorough grasp of the principle of transitivity in the context of weight, when deciding which two of three children should go on the see-saw together. Yet most of them would fail at a purposeless task like arranging three objects in order of heaviness, which purports to determine their grasp of the principle of transitivity.

The sad truth is that most of the tasks pupils are given to do in school mathematics are fairly purposeless. Mathematics is almost always presented in disembedded language, adult language divorced from a meaningful context. The challenge to the teacher of low attainers is to embed mathematical activity in contexts with meaning and purpose for the pupils. For when we do succeed in finding purposeful tasks, then even (or, I should say, especially) low attaining pupils will surprise us with their competence and their determination to succeed.

Consider, for example, the following problem, which sounds like something out of a GCSE examination paper:

> How many bottles of squash must be purchased in order to provide 4 drinks each for 80 players in a football tournament, if one bottle is equivalent to 11 cupfuls, and the squash has to be diluted in the ratio 2 parts of water to 1 part of squash?

A group of low attaining 10-year-olds in a remedial mathematics set actually had to solve this problem – though, of course it was not stated like that – when they were given responsiblity for providing refreshments for an inter-school football tournament. And they did solve it, using their own informal methods which made sense to them in that context. Many other examples of the mathematical skills which pupils show when given responsibility for planning events, such as discos, fetes, sports days, and so on, could be provided.

A low-attaining group of 10 to 12-year-olds were having great difficulty with questions in their mathematics textbooks which involved shading in the coins required to make up certain amounts of money. This was a nice example of a purposeless and disembedded activity. When we threw the textbooks out and gave the pupils more purposeful tasks their competence in handling money emerged immediately! For example, working in groups with plastic token coins, these pupils were challenged to find as many ways as possible of making up 19p.

No doubt the fact that we offered a prize of 19p to the winning group made a difference to their motivation. But it was amazing to see these groups of pupils who fail at most school mathematics finding more than 30 different ways of solving this problem. The same pupils had struggled with the exercises on measuring length in their mathematics textbooks but, when given the challenge of making a box out of card to hold the class set of 25 calculators, quickly mastered the necessary measuring skills, and persisted over several lessons, even carrying on at home, until they had produced a box to their satisfaction.

There is a wide range of activities which pupils will find purposeful, and a number of categories might be suggested. The above examples have been in the categories of planning events, competitions, and construction.

Small group games for many pupils will prove to be purposeful activities, and some examples of such games have been suggested in this chapter already.

An important category of purposeful activities is that of solving real problems. These might often be problems which arise in the school context. For example, one group of pupils tackled the problem of where the school staff should park their cars in the playground. Another group tackled the problem of how to help new children find their way round the school and the local town.

Of course it may not be possible to engage pupils in solving genuine and immediate problems very frequently, so alternatives must be considered. Simulations, particularly using computers, of realistic problems, such as the problems of running a car-wash business or a stall at a fete, are useful alternatives to real problems, which again will prove to be purposeful for many pupils.

Another possibility is that of role-play. Pupils could act out a real situation, such as a family dispute over pocket-money, and then seek to solve the problems which emerge.

Those who work with low attaining pupils in mathematics must face up to the challenge of shifting the emphasis in pupils' experiences of mathematics away from disembedded tasks without purpose, and towards activities with purpose embedded in meaningful contexts.

Alongside the categories of purposeful activities a number of categories of meaningful contexts might be suggested. Teachers may be able to add to this list, but some obvious categories are school organisation, classroom organisation, TV and video, shopping, cooking, travel, sport. Each of these is a context in which pupils are likely to find some meaning.

In the diagram below, each box suggests possible tasks which low attaining pupils might undertake.

For example, the intersection of *travel* and *solving real problems* might suggest that a group of low attainers be given responsibility for travel arrangements for a class trip. The intersection of *cooking* and *construction* might remind teachers of the mathematical skills involved in baking a cake!

The current educational climate in the United Kingdom is one which very much emphasises attainment targets and assessment of progress towards these in

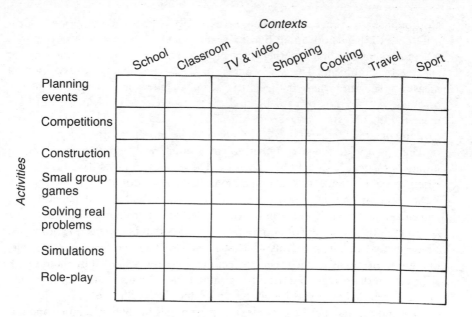

mathematics. With the special needs of low attainers in mind, it is more essential than ever that those who work with such pupils maintain a balance and seek to complement this current emphasis with an equal emphasis on providing those who find progress in mathematics difficult with some purposeful tasks in meaningful contexts.

REFERENCES

Haylock, D. and Cockburn, A. (1989) *Understanding Early Years Mathematics*, Paul Chapman.

Chapter 8

Investigating science and technology
Caroline Dray and Kevin Jones

Many teachers are apprehensive about teaching science and technology to primary aged children, particularly those who 'experience difficulties in learning'. This chapter aims to allay some of those concerns by showing that learning experiences in science and technology can be rewarding for both pupil and teacher alike.

ACCESSIBLE TO ALL?

The term 'providing access to the curriculum for *all* children' has become increasingly familiar to many of us. But what does it mean? Simply letting a child 'with learning difficulties' join a group of others during activities in science and/or technology could be interpreted as 'access', irrespective of the amount of learning which is achieved. If access is defined in that way it is pure tokenism which has little regard for the educational needs of the pupils concerned. At the other end of the spectrum, efforts could be made to ensure that the activity itself is made accessible for a particular child, in order to *optimise learning*. It is towards this latter interpretation that we must strive if we are to ensure that each child receives the curriculum to which s/he is now entitled.

As a core subject in the national curriculum, science is essential for effective learning, both in its own right and within other subject areas. Technology is also given prominence as a foundation subject. The elevated position which these subjects now enjoy emphasises their importance as key areas of learning for *all* children. We can no longer limit our consideration of a child's special educational needs to the area of literacy; to do so is to ignore other equally important areas of learning, in which the child should be able to achieve enjoyment and success.

In order to provide the conditions for optimum learning in science and technology for children with learning difficulties, the teacher will require a good knowledge of:

(a) each child's learning difficulties;
(b) the nature of Science and Technology;

(c) the conceptual demands of the subject areas;

(d) the procedural complexity of activities within those areas; and

(e) the range of outcomes that can be achieved in response to particular tasks.

Each of these issues will now be discussed in turn, and illustrated through an analysis of the special learning needs of one child, John.

LEARNING DIFFICULTIES?

What comes to mind when we think of a child 'with learning difficulties'? We could be excused for thinking that it is a condition which a child has. This line of thought, triggered by the inclusion of the word 'with', in the term '*with* learning difficulties', leads us to consider that the child has either:

(a) *an all-round condition* which prevents learning. For example, on the basis of results from tests of intelligence and/or reading, many children have been labelled 'slow-learner', 'remedial' or 'retarded'. These vague and suspect terms tell us very little about the actual difficulties which these children encounter. If anything, this labelling process hinders attempts to optimise learning, since it brings with it the unfounded expectation that through an innate lack of ability, the child will encounter difficulties in every area of the curriculum.

or

(b) *a specific condition* which causes some difficulty in learning (e.g. poor visual discrimination/auditory memory). It is important to realise that some children experience specific difficulties in learning because of the existence of inherent problems of this kind. If specific learning difficulties are suspected a detailed assessment of their influence upon the child's learning should be carried out. The resultant information should be taken into consideration when planning activities in science and technology (see Chapter 1).

In John's case, visual difficulties had been identified eighteen months previously, when the teacher noticed that he often rubbed his eyes and appeared to have difficulty focusing on the size of print which occurred in most of the written material used in the classroom. A discussion with John's parents and a subsequent referral to an optician led to the prescription of spectacles which John now wears in class.

   Since John had a history of poor vision the teacher decided to assess his visual memory and his ability to discriminate between like shapes/letters/numerals. The results of these tests did not reveal any specific problems.

   Whilst the difficulties which John encountered due to poor vision appeared to have been eradicated once he started wearing spectacles, it is still sensible to maximise the use of his other (stronger) sensory channels (e.g. hearing, touch, taste, smell). For example, an active involvement in investigative work in science would require him to use more than one sensory channel. An approach which is based more heavily upon demonstration, would require him to rely more heavily upon the visual channel.

Whilst it is important to identify and respond to factors which might cause a child to experience specific learning difficulties, a note of caution is necessary at this point. Notably:

(a) if a specific 'condition' is detected, it is not likely to be the only factor which is causing the child to experience difficulties in learning; and

(b) learning difficulties for the majority of children will not be caused by the presence of a specific 'condition'.

The above comments suggest that if we are to understand the causes of learning difficulties we need to look beyond factors 'within the child'. If we are to make activities in science and technology accessible to a particular child, we need to know what difficulties the child actually *experiences* in learning. There is a whole range of factors which can cause a child to experience learning difficulties (see Chapters 1 and 2). We can only begin to plan for optimum learning if we are aware of those factors. Thus, we need to achieve:

(a) a good understanding of the difficulties which the child experiences in other areas of the curriculum; and

(b) a knowledge of the particular difficulties which the child might experience in Science and Technology.

First, let us turn our attention to the difficulties which the child experiences in other areas of the curriculum. We need to know:

(a) in what area(s) of the curriculum the child is experiencing difficulty,

(b) in what particular aspect of that subject(s) the child is experiencing difficulties,

(c) what appears to be causing those difficulties.

The most noticeable difficulty which John experiences is his inability to concentrate upon a task for more than five or ten minutes.

Upon closer examination a lack of concentration occurs when he is involved in written work, or activities which involve a significant amount of reading. During tasks which require very little reading or writing he becomes totally, and profitably, immersed. It is worth noting that a child's distractibility in one area of the curriculum can influence a teacher's perception of that child's learning behaviour during the whole of the school day. John's behaviour, it seemed, was linked to the particular demands of the learning situation.

An analysis of the difficulties which John was experiencing revealed particular difficulties in:

(a) English (AT2 Reading – Level 2). Notably:

using context cues in Reading (English AT2 – Level 2)
predicting what might happen next in stories (English AT2 – Level 2)
reading material with understanding (English AT2 – Level 2)
(b) English (AT4 Spelling – Level 2). Notably:
producing recognisable spellings of a range of common words.

The above analysis of the difficulties which John was experiencing in other areas of the curriculum has several implications for the planning of activities in science and technology:

Firstly, attempts should be made to prevent the above difficulties (reading comprehension and spelling) from causing barriers to learning in science and technology. This can be easily achieved by reducing reading and spelling demands. For example, the recording of results can be achieved by the use of drawings, oral reports, photographs, models, etc.

Secondly, when written work is required, a word-bank of commonly-used words (e.g. 'the', 'was', 'there', 'were', 'then') could be provided, together with those words which are specific to the particular scientific or technological activity which is being undertaken. John could also be encouraged to record his key ideas in written form, whilst temporarily leaving spaces for those words which he could not spell. This technique (Comber, 1985) would allow him to get his main meaning into print without interrupting his thoughts by having to search for correct spellings in dictionaries or word-banks. He could then return to the unknown words at leisure after having written one or two sentences.

Thirdly, reading materials could be adapted in one of three ways:

- the key part of the text could be presented on audio-tape, so that the child could 'read' the text whilst listening to the tape-recording on headphones
- the text could be simplified and supplemented by explanatory diagrams or photographs
- the text could be adapted and matched to John's present reading level and presented in a form which would encourage him to 'read to find out' particular information.

Each of these approaches would provide a context which would help to optimise John's learning in science and technology, whilst helping to provide for his particular needs in literacy. The use of other adult help in the classroom (e.g. parents) can ease the burden which this extra preparation puts on a busy classteacher.

The above account demonstrates that planning for optimum learning in science and technology, depends upon a good knowledge of the learning difficulties which are experienced by a particular pupil, together with an understanding of the factors which appear to be causing those difficulties. It is equally, or even more, important to analyse those areas of the curriculum in which the child is achieving success (see Chapter 1). The clues which we gain from this process provide us with an essential base of information upon which to plan suitable learning experiences. This information can be gained from a process very similar to that used above. We need to know:

(a) in what area(s) of the curriculum the child is achieving success;
(b) in what particular aspect of that subject the child is experiencing success;
(c) what appears to be causing that success?

John was experiencing success in some aspects of: English, Mathematics, Geography, History, Art, Music and P.E. In particular, he showed good progress in the following areas:

- participating in group activities as both a listener and a speaker
- problem solving in mathematics
- investigative work in mathematics, geography and history
- modelling in clay
- practical music making

A closer examination revealed that John's learning was optimised during activities which required:

- active, hands-on learning
- investigations or problem solving
- oral, rather than written responses
- modelling, rather than drawing

Since these factors appeared to optimise learning in so many other areas of the curriculum it seems sensible to suggest that they are also likely to have similar effects in science and technology. Thus, in the planning of activities in science and technology, the above mentioned factors were taken into account.

Having considered the implications of John's specific learning difficulties, and the difficulties and successes which he experiences in other areas of the curriculum, we can now turn our attention to particular difficulties which he might experience in science and technology. An analysis of the nature of the subjects themselves provides a useful starting point.

The nature of science and technology

Recognising the different demands (i.e. different ways of 'thinking') involved in science and technology is another important step in the matching of learning experiences to the particular needs of individual pupils.

Some people (Kite, 1988) suggest that science has particular characteristics which make it accessible to children who experience difficulties in other areas of learning. For example:

- it emphasises first-hand experience, thereby placing less demands upon the literacy skills of pupils
- knowledge and skills can be acquired in small, manageable steps, through practical activity, so helping concentration

- scientific investigations can capture the imagination, thereby enhancing motivation and reducing behavioural problems.

Whilst accepting Kite's point that science, because of its different nature, might be accessible to those children who experience difficulties in other areas of learning, it is also necessary to probe further into the nature of the subjects in order to determine whether their conceptual and procedural demands are likely to cause pupils particular difficulties, which might not occur in other areas of learning.

The *Non-Statutory Guidance in Science* (National Curriculum Council, 1989) provides useful guidance on the nature of these subjects.

- *Science* is distinctive in that it relies more heavily on certain skills than do other areas of human enquiry. Making and testing hypotheses by observation and experimentation are especially characteristic of scientific activity. Scientists are curious, they seek explanations via a variety of methods. Scientists formulate hypotheses, design and carry out experiments, make observations and record results.
- *Technology* is a creative human activity which brings about desired changes by making, controlling and improving the way things work through design and by using relevant knowledge and resources.

The complexity of the demands which are inherent in science and technology means that it would be quite wrong to presume that the subjects will be accessible to children who experience difficulties in other areas of learning (e.g. literacy). The nature of these subjects suggest that children will have, amongst other things, to:

- make hypotheses
- test hypotheses
- observe (under strict conditions)
- experiment
- seek explanations
- record results
- plan changes through design
- control and improve the way things work

If optimum learning is to be achieved in science and technology, teachers will need to 'match' conceptual and procedural demands of particular activities to the past experiences and existing capabilities of their pupils.

A discussion of the implication of matching learning demands to John's past experience and existing capabilities is given after the following two sections which discuss the conceptual demand and 'procedural complexity' of scientific and technological activities.

Level of conceptual demand

Within any group of pupils there will be a wide range of scientific experience, knowledge, skills and understanding which calls for a flexibility of educational provision. The diverse needs of those pupils will only be met if activities are presented at a number of different conceptual and procedural levels which respond to the prior experience of those children. For example, pupils who experience moderate or severe learning difficulties may still need first-hand experience whilst their friends are beginning to cope with secondary materials.

The following chart (Figure 8.1), which was adapted from one presented in the findings of a Project, shows how the level of difficulty of concepts can be judged according to their closeness to the child's experience, complexity, scope and degree of open-endedness.

	Difficulty of concepts	
Criteria	*Easy*	*Difficult*
Distance from child's experience	Direct	Unrelated
Complexity	Can be perceived through senses (tree/house/table)	Related by inference
Scope of concepts	Narrow scope with few concepts subsumed under it (e.g. family, coal)	Broad scope subsuming many concepts (e.g. community, mining)
Open-endedness of concepts	Closed and therefore easy to define (e.g. farm)	Open-ended with vague boundaries and disagreement as to its definition (e.g. democracy)

Figure 8.1

A guide to the level of conceptual demand in various subjects in the national curriculum is indicated in the levels of attainment. For example, in science the conceptual demand is reflected in the various levels of the Knowledge and Understanding attainment targets (National Curriculum Council, 1989). This can be seen in 'Attainment Target 6: Types and uses of materials', in which pupils should develop their knowledge and understanding of the properties of materials and the way properties of materials determine their uses and form the basis for their classification. At

Level 1   pupils should be able to describe familiar and unfamiliar objects in terms of simple properties, for example, shape, colour, texture, and describe how they behave when they are, for example, squashed and stretched.

Level 2   pupils should be able to recognise important similarities and differences, including hardness, flexibility and transparency, in the characteristics of materials.

Procedural complexity

Besides an involvement with the immediate objects and events of scientific interest children should be given the opportunity to practice the processes of science – making hypotheses and considering the evidence for and against a particular idea. Planning simple experiences and investigations is a relatively sophisticated activity, but the experimental method is an important part of science.

Some writers suggest that a greater emphasis needs to be given to the skills which are science based. Richards and Holford (1986) contend that:

> To improve primary science we must focus more attention on the skills which are science based. The most important are: recognition of patterns in observations, explanation of events using science based concepts, use of control in investigations, identifying, checking results and planning experiments.

ATI – Exploration of Science, (National Curriculum Council, 1989) draws together the important and relevant elements of working scientifically and comments that:

> Pupils should develop the intellectual and practical skills that allow them to explore the world of science and to develop a fuller understanding of scientific phenomena and the procedures of scientific exploration and investigation. This work should take place in the context of activities that require a progressively more systematic and qualified approach, which draws upon an increasing knowledge and understanding of science. The activities should encourage the ability to:
> (a)   plan, hypothesise and predict
> (b)   design and carry out investigations
> (c)   interpret results and findings
> (d)   draw inferences
> (e)   communicate exploratory tasks and experiments

The procedural complexity of an activity is indicated by the levels of attainment in ATI. Since these are too exhaustive to list here, the reader is referred to the document *Science in the National Curriculum* (National Curriculum Council, 1989).

On the basis of the above mentioned information concerning:

- the nature of science and technology
- the conceptual demands of activities
- the procedural complexities of scientific and technological tasks

Learning experiences were planned which were matched to John's past experiences and existing capabilities.

The activities which were planned for John were part of the overall provision for a class of 28 children. The advice contained in the document 'Science–Non-Statutory Guidance' (National Curriculum Council, 1989b) provided a useful starting point which led to the differentiation of activities by task, process and outcome. For example, the non-statutory guidance suggested four different ways of approaching a windmill activity:

Approach A

Discussion of task and how to tackle it. Take a sheet of paper cut to the right size with marking on it and instructions of what to do with it – cut, fold, stick, make hole, attach, etc. Explore how to make it rotate (near heater, running in the play ground, holding up high in windiest spot). Oral communication, picture painting.

Approach B

After group discussion of tasks and the variety of papers which could be used, decide which might be used to make a paper windmill similar to the real one; use of a template to cut and then make (using example). Try to rotate in different situation, compare findings with others, consider what makes them move differently. Oral communication, simple tick chart.

Approach C

The group discuss and consider how they might make a paper windmill (no example given), with stimulus of range of materials, including paper cups for example, with opportunity then to try out own ideas, make, modify, remake, gather the resulting models, test in similar ways and compare. Collate and record results in appropriate ways.

Approach D

Making a windmill according to an agreed format, after initial stage of exploration. Identification of variables that may affect the efficiency of the windmill, e.g. size of paper, type of material, number of vanes, means of attaching to rod, etc. Groups to select and test one variable, combine results at the end. Display results graphically, interpret findings, make a generalised statement. Choose the best material, number of vanes, etc, to make a 'super windmill'.

The above approach is presented in greater detail at C11 and C12 in the above mentioned document.

The learning context

Having established a match between John's existing capabilities and the conceptual demands and procedural complexities of activities, it was necessary to give more thought to the context within which he would be expected to learn.

Ditchfield (1987) advises an approach which takes into account a number of different ways of learning. Whilst hands-on investigative approaches are considered to be valuable, Womack (op. cit.) suggests that 'an excessive preoccupation with sense experience can sometimes be a substitute for, rather than a stimulus to, imaginative thinking'.

Womack (op. cit. p. 113) recommends that our concern should be to develop *purposeful* scientific thinking with the 'aim of enriching scientific experiences or extending scientific knowledge'. On the basis of this recommendation Womack presents eight types of activities which should motivate children to learn:

- asking questions
- discussing popular science mysteries
- performing unusual experiments
- investigating the environment
- constructing working models
- studying interesting objects
- making connections
- learning amazing facts

However, to consider that John must pursue these various methods of learning as discrete and unconnected units is as fallacious as believing that investigative work will suffice without recourse to any other approach. Ward (1987) discusses a number of ways in which imaginative and investigatory work can be linked. Ward (op. cit. p. 252) makes reference to a fascinating project which was started after children (7–8 year-olds) complained that their feet were cold (Eastland and Harris, 1983).

> Their teacher told them about a local tramp called Paper Jack, who used to keep warm by wrapping newspapers around himself. The children went outside, to feel the cold of −5 celsius, then returned indoors to 'put newspapers under our jumpers, in our boots and on our head'. Afterwards out again into the freezing weather, the children said they felt nice and warm.

Ward goes on to explain how one child did a fair test by putting newspaper in only one of his wellingtons. Shared experience led to careful work on heat insulators, on the use of thermometers, on the wisdom of putting on winter clothing in layers, on thermos flasks and lagging pipes.

Thus, it was on the basis of an eclectic approach which brought together investigative work with methods of learning that John's experiences were put into a meaningful and purposeful context. The knowledge which the teacher gained about the breadth of his needs (both general and subject-specific) allowed for the provision of learning experiences which were enjoyable and profitable for both teacher and pupil alike.

REFERENCES

Comber, B. (1985) 'Towards "Independence in Spelling"', *British Journal of Special Education*, vol. 12(2), 73–6.

Ditchfield, C. (1987) 'Reviewing developments in science education for young people with learning difficulties', *Support for Learning*, vol. 2(1), 36–40.

Eastland, W. and Harris, R. (1983) 'What to do with the Times Ed?', *ASE Primary Science* 10, Spring.

Kite, J. (1987) 'Developing a scientific approach in children with learning difficulties in the junior school', *Support for Learning*, vol. 2(1), 26–31.

National Curriculum Council (1989) *Science in the National Curriculum*, York: National Curriculum Council.

National Curriculum Council (1989) *Non-Statutory Guidance in Science*, York: National Curriculum Council.

Richards, C. and Holford, M. (1986) *The Teaching of Primary Science: Policy and Practice*, Lewes: Falmer Press.

Ward, A. (1987) 'A sense of wonder: science and technology in primary schools', in Booth, T., Potts, P., and Swann, W. (eds), *Preventing Difficulties in Learning*, Oxford: Blackwell.

Womack, D. (1988) *Developing Mathematical and Scientific Thinking in Young Children*, London: Cassell.

Chapter 9

Providing for movement learning needs
Barbara Brown

INTRODUCTION

Most teachers will be aware of a child in their class who experiences difficulties in any one, or all, of the following aspects of movement:

- a lack of understanding of the requirement of the task
- a distractible manner
- a disposition to be restless and fidgety
- an inability to execute a task in a logical and sequential manner resulting in a movement that is disorganised and inefficient
- a lack of movement co-ordination (sequence, synchrony and rhythm)
- a lack of movement control

In order to provide for the movement learning needs of children, teachers and other professionals will require a good understanding of their individual needs. The adoption and implementation of a developmental approach to the physical curriculum will enable the teacher to meet individual variance in movement skill development. This approach requires an understanding of the development of movement abilities in children, in order that movement experiences can be introduced and developed appropriately. It can help professionals to develop a heightened awareness and sensitivity in the observation of movement strategy, execution and outcomes. The purpose of this approach is to enable the teacher to develop a worthwhile physical educational programme for all children.

The developmental approach can be examined in more detail in the following four sections:

1 Observation of a problem.
2 The nature of the problem.
3 Guidelines for intervention.
4 Movement observation, assessment and recording.

The approach is illustrated by an analysis of the movement learning needs of one child, John.

OBSERVATION OF A PROBLEM

Before proceeding any further let us consider the difficulties which John was experiencing:

To an observer John conveys an aura of untidiness, through his appearance, and exhibits problem behaviours in the areas of movement and expressive language. His clothing is straining to leave his body, and it looks as if it doesn't fit him, his movements are scrambled, and his speech is rushed and often unclear because the words run into one another.

On closer examination his movement behaviour is further aggravated by an excessively fidgety manner, and he is rarely still. He moves impulsively and at a speed that is usually too fast or slow. He has a disposition to trip, bump, knock, drop or fall in the classroom/hall and when moving with others. He seems to move in a different temporal, spatial and effort dimension and causes chaos with objects and people. There is a lack of postural control and so he is unbalanced and looks rather slovenly in the way he sits, stands, walks, runs and moves generally.

John is now eight years old and is tall and well built for a boy of his age. He shows no obvious signs of physical disability (although on closer inspection there is a problem in the sensory, perceptual-cognitive, motor process surrounding movement). He is an only child living in a materially well equipped home, although recently his parents have separated. Quite naturally they find it difficult to manage their son's movement behaviour problem. There is nothing to suggest a lack of care in terms of diet, hygiene and clothing, but like many children he is emotionally affected by parental discord and separation.

An examination of the school records shows that he entered school at four years of age, with a movement behaviour problem. It is apparent in the home and school environment and is evident in his fine and gross movements and his expressive language. Hence his eating, washing, dressing, communicating, playing, drawing, painting, building, modelling and writing skills are all badly affected, which results in his educational progress being severely impaired. He agitates in a movement learning context and his anxious manner is often camouflaged by an over-confidence. His arousal level, as a result, is rarely at optimum (either under or over) which impairs his capacity to learn and perform. He repeatedly seeks attention, reassurance and recognition from the teacher/parent. His attention span and capacity to sustain concentration in a movement context long enough to progress is limited and inadequate. He is easily distracted and will look to disturb others as he skims across diversions.

John's fundamental movement ability in the locomotor stability and manipulative areas is delayed and his performance suggests that there are problems pertaining to perceptual-cognitive dysfunction and dyspraxia (disorganised planning and execution of movement). It is likely that he has grown up through the rudimentary and fundamental phases of movement development (see section

4) with this learning difficulty. This means that he has not established efficient rudimentary movement patterns which will have affected his competency and capacity to progress successfully onto developing sound fundamental movement abilities. This early exposure to repeated failure would account for his behaviour which shows a reluctance to be guided in the learning environment, rather wanting to superficially pursue his own activities. He also stubbornly resists being introduced to learn new activities and sometimes if he cannot quickly grasp the idea becomes disruptive or withdraws within himself and is uncommunicative.

John's affective development has been battered and bruised through repeated failure (see Chapter 2) in a movement context in the home and school. His incapacity to cope in play, social and learning settings has generated significant problems for him in his quest to be a successful person, as movement permeates life. The more he has tried to participate and seek mastery the more he has failed, leading to intense frustration and a sense of hopelessness, lack of self-worth and isolation from his peers, family and teachers. His whole demeanour wreaks of a low self-esteem and he looks at odds with himself and his body.

John is viewed as an aggravating member of the home and class because his mobile manner and uncontrolled movements are disruptive. His movements are in such a tangle that it is difficult for the parents and teachers to know where to start unravelling the mess and how to go about it.

The nature of the problem

John's problems of being disorganised, unco-ordinated and uncontrolled are due to a breakdown in the sensory, perceptual-cognitive and neuro-motor systems, and particularly at the perceptual and effector stages. The outcome results in repeated failure in a movement context which produces high anxiety that also prevents the system from functioning efficiently (see Figure 9.1).

John's attention capacity is reduced because the system is already overloaded with anxiety, therefore he usually fails to focus on the relevant features in the display. He also knows he cannot succeed and so seeks diversions. The high anxiety level also causes him to rush into an activity and creates distortion and confusion at the perceptual stage. It is, therefore, inevitable that a lack of understanding occurs at the decision-making stage, resulting in him having to resort to a guess-work strategy. He does not martial the appropriate information in a sequential order so that he can effect a successful plan of action. Any information he has tends to be scrambled resulting in disorganised movement. It is also unco-ordinated as the temporal, spatial and effort dimensions surrounding his movement are undeveloped due to his movement learning difficulty. There is discord in the 'sequencing', 'synchrony' and 'rhythm' of his movements. His body, space and directional awareness is negligible and the degree of effort applied is either too much or too little. Another feature of his unco-ordinated and uncontrolled movement is the undeveloped kinaesthetic sense which enables him to recognise

System	Process	Outcome
Sensory	Attention Selection	Inattentive Distractible
Perceptual- cognitive	Recognition Interpretation	Distorted Confused
	Decision-making	Lack of understanding Guess-work
Effector	Planning	Lack of organisation
	Ordering	and strategy
Neuro-motor	Executing movement	Disorganised Unco-ordinated Uncontrolled

Figure 9.1

the position and involvement of his body and limbs when moving (co-ordination), as well as monitoring the degree of tension and stretch of the various muscle groups involved in producing controlled movement. The internal feedback system that is alerted to gather movement information via the eyes, ears, body, limbs, muscles and joints is dormant and so is not utilised in the on-going refinement process of learning through trial-error and/or practice of a movement. Hence John, unlike many children of his age (and children from the rudimentary phase of movement development onwards) does not learn through play, practice and incidental movement experiences. Nor does he easily learn through observation in the home, school, play or social environment due to a breakdown in his sensory, perceptual-cognitive, neuro-motor system as has already been described. He also does not retain a good image of a movement in his motor memory because of his lack of movement understanding. The 'feel' and the 'image' of the required movement, if retained, is usually made up of inaccuracies.

The information outlined from the observation and nature of the problem conveys a picture of a child who is a lost cause, but this is *not* so.

GUIDELINES FOR INTERVENTION

Intervention is strengthened if it is of a collaborative nature, as illustrated in the following model (Figure 9.2). A sharing of expertise across professional and personal boundaries should promote an interactive, supportive and progressive programme of help to the benefit of the child.

The discovery, diagnosis and assessment of the possible nature, cause and extent of the problem should be shared across school and home boundaries with

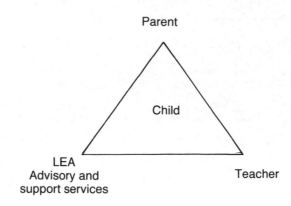

Figure 9.2

support from the education and health services (Figure 9.3), in order that the intervention process is appropriate and incorporates the relevant and required expertise.

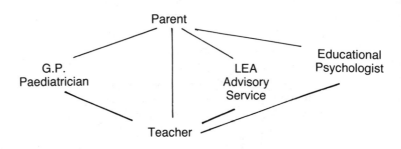

Figure 9.3

Considerations in the intervention process will now be overviewed in terms of the child, teacher/parent, learning environment (school and home), teaching considerations and programme content, development and progression.

Child

- examine the possible nature, cause, extent of the movement learning difficulty in the home, school and play environment
- examine the child's fundamental movement abilities (locomotor, stability, manipulative) – see Section 4
- examine the child's earlier opportunities and experiences for movement learning and development (home, school, play)
- examine the child's movement learning behaviour (anxiety, fear, over-confidence, avoidance, inattentive, disruptive, etc)

Teacher/parent

Examine their role, responsibility and capacity in terms of the following guidelines:

- to convey a sensitive manner that is strengthened by patience, care and kindness
- to enter into a partnership of trust and respect with the child
- to promote and foster an environment that generates movement understanding
- to accept the role of enabler in order to reduce and simplify the demands surrounding movement
- to provide opportunities for successful movement learning and progression relative to the child's phase and stage of movement development

Learning environment

The teacher/parent's capacity to manipulate the variables in the school/home environment should be examined, in order that it can become supportive to meeting the movement learning needs of the child. The teacher/parent should attempt to:

- create an environment that is ordered and organised so the child can understand it and be influenced by this sense of order and organisation
- reduce distractions in the environment in order that the child can learn to focus his/her attention on one task at a time
- create a sense of calm, in order to lower the child's hyper-aroused state which impairs learning and performance
- influence the time structure in the child's movements, in order to develop a sense of sequence, synchrony and rhythm that is an essential feature of unco-ordinated and controlled movement
- increase predictability in the environment and decrease uncertainty, so that the child experiences a feeling of security and learns to recognise and recall information, thereby enabling him to make an appropriate response. This helps to lower the level of fear and anxiety, as well as reduce the risk of an over-bombardment of sensory stimuli.
- introduce the child to movement learning experiences in a stable environment before progressing to the increased demands of an unstable one. This is illustrated in Figure 9.4.
- present experiences so that the child is able to graduate from simple to more complex decision-making tasks in order to build a sound base upon which to build strategies and concepts. This means that initially the teacher/parent presents tasks in such a way that will elicit the correct response in order to stimulate recognition and recall of the appropriate information, as well as promote confidence through success and progression. They can then move on

	Body stable	Body moving
Conditions (stable)	Stand on one leg, knees, side, etc. and limb manipulation. Reach for a stationary object.	Walk, hop, skip and run and limb manipulation. Reach for a stationary object.
Environmental (changing)	Stand on a crash mat, wobble board, and limb manipulation. Reach for/catch moving ball.	Run away from chaser and limb manipulation. Reach for/catch moving ball.

Figure 9.4 A classification of movement tasks
Source: Gentile *et al.* (1975) adapted by Speth-Arnold (1981) in Sugden (1984: 68–9)

to learn how to read a multi-choice display and through a process of recognition and recall, decide upon the most appropriate response.

- gradually alter the environment from 'closed' to 'open' so that the teacher/parent-child relationship changes from a position of child dependence to one of inter-dependence which becomes progressively more interactive.

Teaching considerations

Having considered the learning environment, attention should then focus on teaching within the combined setting of the school and home.

In John's case the over-riding concern is the high degree of distractibility, disorganisation and extraneous movement behaviour that is creating significant learning difficulties for him.

The teacher/parent can promote a child's capacity to *selectively attend*, through the use of task analysis. For example, they can use key words to help a child jump horizontally (see Figure 9.5):

Sequence	Body parts	Action words
Firstly	Knees	Bend
Secondly	Arms	Swing
Thirdly	Feet	Jump

Figure 9.5

This approach can serve to reduce and simplify the task and be matched with the corresponding action in a visual demonstration and/or said by the teacher/parent/child when performing the movement. It also helps to strengthen the order/sequence of the task; which a disorganised child requires much help with, and aids observation, attention and understanding.

To aid perception, a child's arousal level usually needs to be lowered through an ordered and calm environment and approach. The child's capacity to recognise and recall information will develop if the learning cues and teaching approach are consistent. The child will also remember information once s/he begins to order and understand it. The teaching approach and the selection of appropriate incremental movement experiences that are developed via a teaching strategy that promotes attention, understanding and order is crucial.

A structured and explicit teaching approach and environment should provide cues and constancies that enables the child to decide on a movement response and eventually recognise if the decision was correct or not.

The task should be presented in an order with the demands reduced and simplified, so that the child can learn to recognise the sequential steps to achievement, thereby learning to effect a movement plan. It helps the child to effect a progressively ordered approach to movement tasks, and can positively affect his/her movement tempo and rhythm which is normally rushed.

The missing features of co-ordination and control in a disorganised child's movements will slowly develop with a combined approach of 'learning how to learn' and 'how to move' in a context of developmentally appropriate movement experiences. During the *execution stage of a movement* the combination of guidance (tactile, verbal, visual) and the positive manner of the teacher/parent in an ordered environment is conducive to learning.

The child has to learn to recognise his/her progress during the execution of a movement (what s/he is doing, how s/he is doing it) and then be able to make ongoing refinements or corrections. Once completed the child also needs to be able to recognise what s/he has performed and how s/he has performed in the context of the task and situational demands. This process of *movement feedback* is a feature of skilled movement behaviour and is absent in a disorganised child's movements. Children who do not experience movement learning difficulties can exercise and refine this internal-feedback process via play and movement experiences; and increasingly so, from the rudimentary phase, where they appear to learn intuitively, by 'trial and error' and at a later stage via insight. The external feedback process is developed, again, from the rudimentary phase with the help of parents, and in the fundamental phase by teachers and parents, normally without too much difficulty.

The above considerations help the child to recognise, know and feel when there is a mismatch between the intended, expected and the actual movement outcome.

Programme content, development and progression

Since John's disorganised movement behaviour has most likely been a problem to him from the rudimentary phase, he will have experienced failure at a very early age, and is likely to have missed or avoided opportunities for movement development. It also means that he will not have developed good movement patterns during the rudimentary and fundamental movement phase. His movement understanding and strategy will have been severely affected, and therefore the movement programme should take account of these early omissions and difficulties in the development of his movement abilities.

The following model (Figure 9.6) outlines the structure upon which an appropriately devised developmental movement programme should be constructed. It embraces two key aims, namely learning how to learn and how to move, that are central to the purpose of the programme, as well as complement each other.

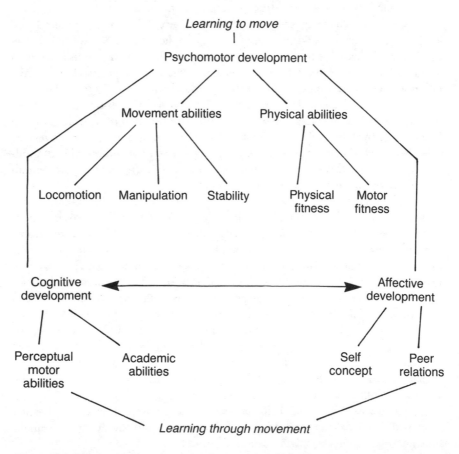

Figure 9.6 The inter-related nature of motor development
Source: Gallahue (1985: 18)

A developmental approach allows the teacher/parent the opportunity to guide the child in order to minimise failure by adopting an incremental approach to movement learning and to commence the programme at an appropriate level. In this case, John should be re-introduced to rudimentary movement understanding, strategy and organisation, so he can form sound basic movement patterns that demonstrate a sense of co-ordination, rhythm and control. This will enable him to utilise these essential features in learning progressively more demanding movements in increasingly complex situations.

The importance of establishing a strong foundation in movement learning at the rudimentary and fundamental phases allows children the opportunity to recognise and enjoy their various capacities and abilities in increasingly more demanding situations. Gallahue (1985 p. 6) illustrates the developmental phases of movement. An example of how selected movement abilities can develop and progress from the rudimentary to the sport-related phase is adapted from Gallahue (1985) and illustrated in Figure 9.7.

Movement observation, assessment and recording

The assessment process should include a comprehensive and in-depth analysis of the child in a variety of situations. It should also include an analysis of the appropriateness of the teaching strategy, learning environment, task and objective and curriculum. The teacher/parent should also be prepared to assess their role, practice and responsibility for the learning environment in order to increase their effectiveness as enablers of learning. Assessment should be a continuous aspect of the teaching-learning process that allows for the gathering and reviewing of methods, in as wide a range of situations as possible, over an extended time period.

There are a variety of ways for observing, assessing and recording movement ability, from a superficial check-list to an in-depth profile. Firstly, the teacher/parent should be clear on why they wish to assess a child's movement behaviour. Secondly, they should decide on what it is they intend to assess; and thirdly, how they intend to assess and record the movement behaviour. When these questions have been answered, the teacher/parent can then select and devise appropriate methods that will enable them to gather and review relevant movement information over a period of time, in various environments (home, school, play and social) in order to provide an appropriate intervention programme that promotes success.

Observation and screening is often necessary, to focus attention more precisely upon those areas in which the child is developing well and those in which there is some cause for concern. The two examples of screening devices (Figures 9.8 and 9.9) presented below display important aspects of 'movement' which should be observed during this focusing stage.

The table on page 138 illustrates the School Entrant Screening (age 4–5) coffee jar test.

Movement abilities	Phases		
Progression → Development ↓	Rudimentary (0–2 years)	Fundamental (2–7 years)	Sport related movement skills general (7–10 years)
Locomotor	Wriggling Crawling Creeping Kneewalking Walking Climbing	Running Jumping Hopping Galloping Skipping Climbing	10m fast pace running Jumping for height and distance Climbing in gymnastic and outdoor adventurous activities
Stability	Static balance Sits Pulls to standing position Stands without hand holds Stands alone	One foot balance	Dodging

Stability (continued)	Dynamic balance		
	Walking	Jumping, Heel-toe walking, Hopping, Rolling	Dodging, Pivoting
	Axial movements		
	Bending	Bending	Bending
	Stretching	Stretching	Stretching
	Twisting	Twisting	Twisting
	Turning	Turning	Turning
Manipulative	Reaching	Throwing	Forehand
		Catching	Backhand
	Grasping	Kicking	Striking
		Striking	Driving
	Releasing	Bouncing	Putting
		Rolling	Chipping
			Lobbing
			Smashing
			Drop
			Throwing
			Catching
			Trapping

Figure 9.7

The School Entrant Screening (age 4–5 yrs) coffee jar test
(The equipment in the coffee jar comprises five one-inch wooden bricks, each with a hole bored through the centre, a reel and a length of stiff nylon lace on which to thread the bricks.)

Test item	Area of development being tested
1. Heel-toe walk across room.	Balance and co-ordination.
2. Come back on tip-toe.	Watch for associated movements of upper limbs.
3. Stand on one leg (8 secs).	Balance and co-ordination.
4. Unscrew lid of jar.	Is possible at 2 years.
5. Build tower of 5 bricks.	Hand–eye co-ordination. Watch for tremor.
6. Build pattern.	Simultaneous movement of both upper limbs.

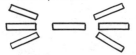

Test item	Area of development being tested
7. Wind lace on reel, right and left.	Manual dexterity. Clumsy child finds this very difficult.
8. Thread bricks on lace.	Hand–eye co-ordination.
9. Replace things in jar and screw on lid.	Is possible at 2½ years.

Figure 9.8
Source: Gordon and McKinlay (1980: 28)

This is a simple screening test for neuro-developmental delay which was designed to be used as part of the routine school medical examination of 4–5 year-old children in the Manchester area.

The Screening Profile provides for a three point assessment of an individual's fundamental movement abilities. Assessment is graded as at:

(a) The initial stage – barely recognisable performance
(b) The elementary stage – recognisable but unpolished performance
(c) The mature stage – a polished performance.

The next part of the assessment process involves a detailed observation of the child in those areas which are causing concern. This can be achieved by using the following pupil profile/skeleton (Figure 9.10), which entails close observation of an individual's body segments whilst performing the skill(s). The teacher/observer completes a profile for the appropriate movement ability (e.g. walking) and compares the child's performance with an explanatory sheet (Figure 9.11). A completed profile (Figure 9.12) illustrates the detailed observations which were made of John's performance in 'walking'.

| Fundamental movement abilities | | | | | |
| Pupil _____ Age ____ Teacher _____ Year ____ | | | | | |

	Initial	Elementary	Mature	Problems	Comments
Locomotor					
1. Walking					
2. Running					
3. Jumping (a) horizontal					
(b) vertical					
(c) from height					
4. Hopping					
5. Galloping and Sliding					
6. Leaping					
7. Skipping					
8. Climbing					
Summary					
Stability					
1. Axial movements					
2. Inverted supports					
3. Body rolling					
4. Dodging					
5. One foot balance					
6. Beam walk					
Summary					
Manipulative					
1. Overhand throwing					
2. Catching					
3. Kicking					
4. Striking					
5. Dribbling					
6. Ball rolling					
7. Trapping					
8. Volleying					
Summary					

Figure 9.9
Source: Brown *et al.* (1989)

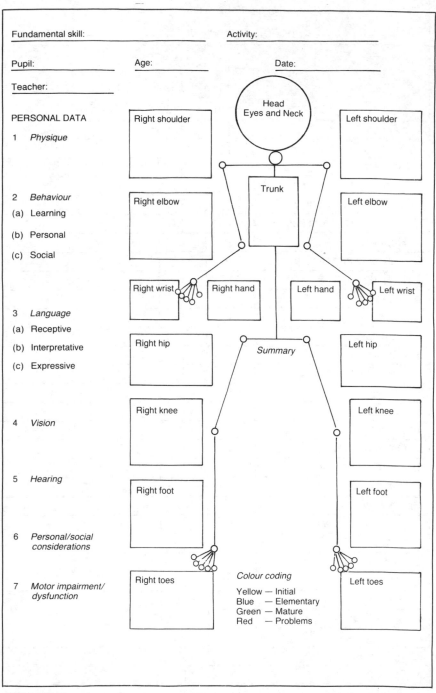

Fundamental skill: Activity:

Pupil: Age: Date:

Teacher:

PERSONAL DATA   Right shoulder   Left shoulder

1   Physique

2   Behaviour   Right elbow   Left elbow
(a) Learning

(b) Personal

(c) Social

Head Eyes and Neck

Trunk

Right wrist   Right hand   Left hand   Left wrist

3   Language
(a) Receptive

(b) Interpretative   Right hip   Summary   Left hip

(c) Expressive

4   Vision   Right knee   Left knee

5   Hearing   Right foot   Left foot

6   Personal/social
     considerations

7   Motor impairment/   Right toes   Left toes
     dysfunction

Colour coding
Yellow — Initial
Blue   — Elementary
Green — Mature
Red   — Problems

Figure 9.10
Source: Brown *et al.* (1989)

Fundamental motor skill: Locomotor			Activity: Walking		Developmental sequence
Body segments		Initial	Elementary	Mature	Common problems
Head eyes					
neck					
Arms shoulders				Reflexive arm swing.	Poor rhythmical co-ordination and alteration of arms and legs.
elbows		Held up for balance.	Arms down to the sides, with limited swing.		
wrists					
hands					
Trunk		Difficulty maintaining upright posture.			Poor posture and body alignment.
Legs hips		Rigid halting leg action. Unpredictable loss of balance.	Increased pelvic tilt. Gradual smoothing out of pattern.	Relaxed elongated gait. Narrow base of support.	Excessive vertical lift. Wide base of support.
knees		Flexed knee out of contact followed by quick leg extension.	Step length increased. Heel-toe contact.	Little vertical lift. Definite heel-toe contact.	Walking on toes. Walking with toes turned in. Walking with toes turned outwards.
ankles		Wide base of support. Short steps.	Base of support within the lateral dimensions of the trunk.		
feet		Flat footed contact. Toes turned out.	Apparent vertical lift. Out toeing reduced or eliminated.		
Supplementary observations					

Figure 9.11
Source: Gallahue (1985) in Brown *et al.* (1989)

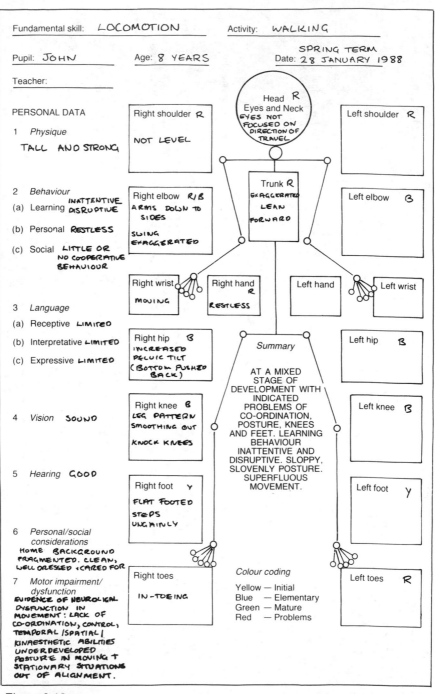

Fundamental skill: LOCOMOTION   Activity: WALKING

Pupil: JOHN   Age: 8 YEARS   SPRING TERM
                                          Date: 28 JANUARY 1988

Teacher:

PERSONAL DATA

1   Physique
    TALL AND STRONG

2   Behaviour
(a) Learning INATTENTIVE DISRUPTIVE
(b) Personal RESTLESS
(c) Social LITTLE OR NO COOPERATIVE BEHAVIOUR

3   Language
(a) Receptive LIMITED
(b) Interpretative LIMITED
(c) Expressive LIMITED

4   Vision SOUND

5   Hearing GOOD

6   Personal/social considerations
    HOME BACKGROUND FRAGMENTED. CLEAN, WELL DRESSED & CARED FOR

7   Motor impairment/ dysfunction
    EVIDENCE OF NEUROLOGICAL DYSFUNCTION IN MOVEMENT: LACK OF CO-ORDINATION, CONTROL, TEMPORAL/SPATIAL/ KINAESTHETIC ABILITIES UNDERDEVELOPED POSTURE IN MOVING + STATIONARY SITUATIONS OUT OF ALIGNMENT.

Right shoulder R
NOT LEVEL

Left shoulder R

Head R
Eyes and Neck
EYES NOT FOCUSED ON DIRECTION OF TRAVEL

Trunk R
EXAGGERATED LEAN FORWARD

Right elbow R/B
ARMS DOWN TO SIDES
SWING EXAGGERATED

Left elbow B

Right wrist
MOVING

Right hand R
RESTLESS

Left hand

Left wrist

Right hip B
INCREASED PELVIC TILT (BOTTOM PUSHED BACK)

Summary

Left hip B

Right knee B
LEG PATTERN SMOOTHING OUT
KNOCK KNEES

AT A MIXED STAGE OF DEVELOPMENT WITH INDICATED PROBLEMS OF CO-ORDINATION, POSTURE, KNEES AND FEET. LEARNING BEHAVIOUR INATTENTIVE AND DISRUPTIVE. SLOPPY, SLOVENLY POSTURE. SUPERFLUOUS MOVEMENT.

Left knee B

Right foot Y
FLAT FOOTED STEPS UNGAINLY

Left foot Y

Right toes
IN-TOEING

Colour coding

Yellow — Initial
Blue — Elementary
Green — Mature
Red — Problems

Left toes R

Figure 9.12
Source: Brown et al. (1989)

REFERENCES

Brown, B. *et al.* (1989) *Movement Observation Manual*, Cheltenham & Gloucester College of Higher Education Publications.

Gallahue, D.L. (1985) *Developmental Movement Experiences for Children*, London: Collier Macmillan.

Gordon, N. and McKinlay, I. (1980) *Helping Clumsy Children*, London: Churchill Livingstone.

Sugden, D.A. (1984) 'Issues in teaching children with movement problems', *British Journal of Physical Education*, vol. 15, no.3. May/June, pp. 68–70.

RECOMMENDED READING

Allonby, J. (1985) 'Children with special educational needs in nursery and reception classes', *British Journal of Physical Education*, vol. 16(2), pp. 47–9.

Arnheim, D.D. and Pestolesi, R.A. (1973) *Developing Motor Behaviour in Children*, St. Louis: The C.V. Mosby Co.

Arnheim, D.D. and Sinclair, W.A. (1975) *The Clumsy Child: A Program of Motor Therapy*, St. Louis: The C.V. Mosby Co.

Brown, A. (1987) *Active Games for Children with Movement Problems*, London: Harper & Row.

Brown, A. (1987) 'The integration of children with movement problems into the mainstream games curriculum', *British Journal of Physical Education*, vol. 18(5), pp. 230–2.

Brown, B.A. (1984) 'Adapted physical education: teaching strategies', *British Journal of Physical Education*, vol. 15(3), pp. 76–8.

Brown, B. and Prideaux, R. (1988) 'Children with movement learning difficulties. A collaborative initiative with 4–5 year old mainstream children and their parents', *British Journal of Physical Education*, vol. 19(4), pp. 186–9.

Cutforth, N.J. (1983) 'Self-concept of the handicapped child in integrated P.E. settings', *British Journal of Physical Education*, vol. 14(4), p. 106.

Cutforth, N. (1986) 'A movement programme for children with special needs in a comprehensive school', *British Journal of Physical Education*, vol. 17(2), pp. 69–70.

Cutforth, N. (1988) 'The underachieving child – implications for physical education', *The Bulletin of Physical Education*, vol. 24(1), pp. 16–25.

Gallagher, M. (1984) 'Children with special needs in the area of motor development', *British Journal of Physical Education*, vol. 15(3), pp. 91–3.

Gallahue, D.L. (1982) *Understanding Motor Development in Children*, Chichester: John Wiley.

Gordon, N.C. and McKinley, I. (1980) *Helping Clumsy Children*, Edinburgh: Churchill Livingstone.

Gordon, N.C. and McKinley, I. (1988) *Children with Neurological Disorders*, Oxford: Blackwell Scientific Publications.

Groves, L. (1985) 'With whom shall children with special needs be physically educated?' *British Journal of Physical Education*, vol. 16(1), pp. 38–9.

Gubby, S.S. (1975) *The Clumsy Child*, London: W.B. Saunders & Co. Ltd.

Henderson, S. (1984) 'The Henderson revision of the test of motor impairment', *British Journal of Physical Education*, vol. 15(3), pp. 72–5.

Higgins, B. (1987) 'Building bridges between mainstream and special schools', *British Journal of Physical Education*, vol. 18(5), pp. 221–2.

Holle, B. (1976) *Motor Development in Children: Normal and Retarded*, Oxford, Blackwell.

Jordon, I. (1987) 'Physical education for slow learners', *British Journal of Phyiscal Education*, vol. 18(5), p. 233.

Keogh, J. and Sugden, D. (1985) *Movement Skill Development*, London: Collier Macmillan.

McClenegham, B.A. (1978) *Fundamental Movement: A development and remedial approach*, Philadelphia: W.B. Saunders.

Meek, G. (1986) 'Awkward performers should not be awkward to teach', *The Bulletin of Physical Education*, vol. 22(2), pp. 39–41.

Miles, A. and Knight, E. (1987) 'The contribution of physical education to the general development of children with special educational needs', *British Journal of Physical Education*, vol. 18(5), pp. 204–6.

Morris, P.R. and Whiting, H.T.A. (1971) *Motor Impairment and Compensatory Education*, Philadelphia: Lea and Febiger.

Paugrazi, R.O. (1981) *Movement in Early Childhood and Primary Education*, Minneapolis: Burgess Pub. Co.

Price, R.J. (1980) *Physical Education and the Physically Handicapped Child*, Lepus Books.

Robertson, M.A. and Halverson, L.E. (1984) *Developing Children – their changing movement – a guide for teachers*. Philadelphia: Lea and Fabiger.

Russell, J.P. (1987) *Graded Activities for Children with Motor Difficulties*, Cambridge: Cambridge University Press.

Stott, D.H. and Moyes, F.A. (1984) *Test of Motor Impairment* (Henderson Revision), Kent: Harcourt, Brace Jovanovich.

Sugden, D.A. (1984) 'Issues in teaching children with movement problems', *British Journal of Physical Education*, vol. 15(3), pp. 68–70.

Tansley, A.E. (1980) *Perceptual Training*, Leeds: E.J. Arnold.

Tansley, A.E. (1980) *Motor Education*, Leeds: E.J. Arnold.

Upton, G. (ed.) (1979) *Physical and Creative Activities for Mentally Handicapped Children*, Cambridge University Press.

Wedell, K. (1975) *Learning and Perceptuo-Motor Disabilities in Children*, London: John Wiley & Sons.

Wickstrom, R.L. (1977) *Fundamental Motor Patterns* (2nd edition), Philadelphia: Lea and Febiger.

Williams, D. (1984) 'Children with special needs', *Bulletin of Physical Education*, vol. 20(2), pp. 43–5.

Williams, H.G. (1983) *Perceptual and Motor Development*, Englewood Cliffs, NJ: Prentice-Hall Inc.

Williamson, D. (1984) 'Student profile and organisational approach to the pupil with special needs', *British Journal of Physical Education*, vol. 15(5), pp. 128–9.

Zaichkowsky, L.D., Zaichkowsky, L.B. and Martinek, T.J. (1980) *Growth and Development: The Child and Physical Activity*, St. Louis: The C.V. Mosby Co.

Chapter 10

Access to humanities

Tim Copeland

A chapter promoting access to humanities could well have been written for any child in the primary school up until the dawning of the national curriculum. As has been widely commented, the humanities (defined here as history and geography) have received very limited coverage in the primary school, being almost non-existent in some establishments, or taught as topic work in the majority of others. If the majority of children are receiving little entitlement to history and geography, then it follows that children who experience difficulties in learning are likely to have even less. This dearth of attention to a major area of knowledge is reflected in the lack of published resources offering advice to teachers in primary schools. In those books which do exist, very little attention is paid to children with special learning needs. The national curriculum might redress the balance, with both history and geography being designated as Foundation Subjects. However, the lowered status of the subjects, in terms of assessment and time available for in-service training courses, causes continuing concern. If we do not carefully reconsider the 'breadth' of educational experiences which our children require we are likely to provide a 'core' heavy curriculum, with more attention being given to the 'basics' to the detriment of the humanities.

A lack of access to history and geography, coupled with a heavy emphasis on the basics, will limit the curricular experiences of children experiencing difficulties in other aspects of their learning. As developing human beings they already have a stock of personal knowledge which enables them to handle many of the concepts that the humanities subjects have isolated. This personal depth of knowledge makes the study of history and geography an area of the curriculum in which they can achieve success and enjoyment, against a background of difficulty in the areas perceived as having higher status in the curriculum – maths and language. A crucial point is that a study of both history and geography can also provide excellent, meaningful contexts within which attainment in other subjects can be enhanced (e.g. the development of 'listening and speaking').

The degree to which children can be given access to the humanities depends upon our attitude towards them and our conception of their special educational needs. Stephen Rowland (1987), whose case study of Ian is re-examined later, states that he is reluctant to describe any child as having special needs as such a description rests on a number of questionable assumptions, the most telling being that someone's special educational needs are most often classified on the basis of their deficiencies rather than their competencies (see Chapter 1). Deficiencies in some areas do not necessarily rule out competencies in others. Teachers rarely assess the special learning needs of children in geography and history, often preferring to base their analysis of special learning needs in humanities upon borrowed assessments of special 'language' or 'mathematical' needs. This often means that some children are excluded from some aspects of history or geography either on the basis of lacking the relevant skills or being incapable of tackling challenging tasks. The following text suggests that this kind of thinking is misguided.

Part of the problem of the teaching of geography and history to pupils who experience difficulties in learning is that the areas have too often been seen as comprising a great deal of 'content' which has to be taught and assessed, rather than as subjects whose main characteristics are 'processes' based upon, and concerned with, problem solving (Bolwell, 1987). The result has often been a proliferation of work sheets with a patronising simplification of ideas and tasks, often under the guise of 'concrete aids to learning', or copying! The wonder of the humanities subjects is that their raw content is available to all, in the present and around them. Children are surrounded by history and geography; it is a question of making it accessible during and after the school day.

What evidence is there that children who experience difficulties in learning can gain access to the humanities? Research is limited, but there are case studies that point to a positive conclusion. The following account of Stephen Rowland's (op. cit.) description of one pupil's involvement with the past provides a good example:

> Ian's learning begins with an examination of past activity (history) in a particular place (geography), although it was not presented to him in that way – it was purely and simply an interesting investigation of a stream in the vicinity of the school. Ian recalls finding leather pieces near the stream which was being studied by his class. He surmises that at one time there must have been buildings near the brook, and that they included a shoe factory. Ian, ten years old and aware of his failure with reading, writing and numeracy, is being an archaeologist. He is using the physical evidence left by human beings from a previous time and he is trying to make some sense of it. Stephen Rowland (the teacher) allows Ian to follow up his interest, putting aside the task of making a model of the stream from its clay. Ian gathers further evidence, a wheel, some pottery, a heel moulder and more leather. Rowland, using open-ended questioning, allows the ownership of the problem of these artefacts to stay with Ian. Ian makes the decision about what he wishes to write and Rowland helps him put the sentence together. Ian concludes; there had been a village, now disappeared; cobblers had worked there; the tools found had been used for burning sole and heel shapes for shoes.

Rowland (op. cit.) analyses Ian's learning in terms of the language he was using, admitting he felt some of Ian's explanations unlikely. However, Ian had discovered evidence from the past that was meaningful to him, attempted to date it, put forward technical explanations for the use of the artefacts, showed an ability to empathise with the user of the tools, and was aware of other sorts of evidence that was available in the guise of his grandfather who used to be a cobbler. Ian was aware that historical change had taken place in his local environment and, with some help, was able to write a report about his findings. Rowland might think that Ian's explanation of the 'heel moulder' as a tool to burn shapes into leather, unlikely; but since we are unable to say exactly what certain artefacts were used for in the past, we can only state possibilities. Ian's explanation, being based on the available evidence, is as likely to be as true as anyone else's. Rowland, to his credit, did not impose his interpretation on Ian.

What can be learned from this episode? Ian achieved a great deal in the process of historical study. He had gone a long way to meeting the proposed attainment targets for the history curriculum:

- AT 1: Knowledge and understanding of history
  Level 3a) describe changes over a period of time.
       b) give a reason for an historical event or development.
  Level 4a) recognise that over time some things changed and others stayed the same.
       c) describe different features of an historical period.
- AT 3: The use of historical sources
  Level 1   communicate information acquired from an historical source.
  Level 2   recognise that historical sources can help answer questions about the past.
  Level 3   make deduction from historical sources.
  Level 4   put together information drawn from different historical sources.

Ian was allowed to achieve; he was allowed to follow an interest; his learning was facilitated by a sensitive teacher; he was dealing with first hand information – historical evidence. It is important to note that Ian was described as experiencing learning difficulties in literacy and numeracy, yet his performance in this area of the humanities was very creditable. His motivation might have been used to draw a map of the place in which he found his evidence, to talk to local people or his local museum, to measure and weigh the objects, to draw them, and to display his findings, all of which would have supported learning in other areas of the curriculum.

Recently, I was working at Kenilworth Castle, in Warwickshire, with two children who experienced similar learning difficulties to Ian. They were reluctant to use the work sheet they had been given. I suggested to the teacher that a work sheet was unnecessary and that observation skills were more important. The teacher retorted that there had to be 'something to show' for the day out of school. We had been following the footsteps of Queen Elizabeth who had visited the castle in 1575, using the documentary evidence of a diary reporting the visit. The group of six children and myself entered John of Gaunt's Hall. Four of the children detached themselves to fill in their work sheet. Kevin and Peter remained with me.

Continuing the Elizabethan theme I asked them how the Queen would have warmed her hands in the hall. The castle structure has lost its first floor paving and the vaulting that held it up. Visitors look up into the shell of the first-floor hall from the medieval cellar. High above us there were two ornate fireplaces, stranded half way up a wall. Kevin thought that there might have been ladders of wood up to the fires. Peter, remembering the full-scale reconstruction of Elizabeth's dress in the Education room, thought that she might have had difficulties in getting up a ladder. Maybe, thought Kevin, the fires would have been big enough to warm people below, but then explained to himself that getting the wood up there would have been difficult. I suggested they looked around for more evidence. They found the stumps of the columns that carried the vault that held the first floor. They suggested that the stones made a pattern down the centre of the floor and that might have been bigger and carried a wooden staircase that would have risen to the fires. Kevin dismissed this, arguing that they might as well have built the fires at ground level. Peter suggested that since there were no windows at our level that explanation was unlikely. This triggered something in his mind. He suggested that they would have had them at ground level if they had wanted and then, eyes bright, said, 'The floor's gone', pointing to the void above us. Kevin looked up and agreed that Peter was right and that the columns had held up a floor. To my surprise Kevin chuckled and said, 'We are in the coal hole. They would have kept the coal down here.' Peter was unsure. How did Queen Elizabeth get up there? This led to a search for a suitable staircase to get access to the now missing first floor.

When the whole group was reassembled Peter promptly put my question about warming hands to the children who had filled in the work sheets. Having prompted the others with some very leading questions and receiving no suitable replies, Peter and Kevin gently explained how the structure worked. The confidence of expert opinion was a joy to see.

The above example illustrates again how children who experience difficulties in learning can make sense out of tangible evidence from the past. Both Peter and Kevin presented their findings at an assembly the following week under the title of 'The Missing Floor'. Drawings, reconstructing the hall with men and women in period costumes, accompanied their explanation and they also put forward a hypothesis about the removal of the paving stones. Since we have some documentary evidence that the stones were put in place in 1350, the boys surmised that they were probably in place until the Civil War when the castle was last used. They were able to work out, with the aid of a calculator, how long the paving had been in place.

So far in this chapter the main response to the problem of giving children

gooey								
muddy								
sandy								
high								
down								
wet								
grassy								
wooded								
see a long way								
bumpy								
watery								
light								
dark								
bushy								

Figure 10.1

access to aspects of the humanities has focused upon the use of evidence of the 'past'. The underpinning of geography is the concept of 'place'. Places surround all children all of the time, and children are constantly trying to make sense of the locations they find themselves in. In its submission to the National Curriculum Working Party for Geography, the Geographical Association listed five enabling questions concerning 'place':

- What is this place like?
- How is it similar or different from other places?
- How is this place changing?
- What would it be like to be in this place?
- How is this place connected with other places?

Rather than using books and maps out of context, the use of these questions in

	Far Marsh	Dry Valley	Willow Marsh	Triangle Field	Long Meadow	South Field	Orchard	The Amphi-theatre
gooey	√		√					√
muddy	√		√					√
sandy		√		√	√			
high	√			√		√		
down		√	√		√	√	√	√
wet	√		√					√
grassy		√	√	√	√	√	√	√
wooded			√	√	√		√	
see a long way				√				
bumpy	√		√			√		
watery	√		√					
light	√		√	√	√	√		
dark							√	√
bushy			√	√		√	√	

Figure 10.2

association with real places (the school, the home, the local environment) gives a lead in to using and making maps as well as to finding a context for using block graphs or other diagrams. The questions can make familiar places 'strange', and they can also make the 'strange' far-off places 'familiar' if the children have enough of a local understanding.

I was lucky to be present in a field study unit in Oxfordshire when a class of local children came for the day. Among the group were a number of children who experienced difficulties in learning, whom the teacher had decided to keep together to work with the warden of the unit. She freely admitted she did not know what they could do that day. The warden took them for a walk around the large, wild site and on their return asked them to think of words that might describe the sort of places that they had seen (What is this place like?). The list grew rapidly: 'gooey, muddy, sandy, high, dry, wet, windy, wooded, see a long way ...', each word being written on a chalkboard. The warden then gave each child a simple matrix, and showed them how to write the given words down the left-hand axis (Figure 10.1).

The children were then taken out again to specific locations. On arrival at each place they put its name at the top of a column on the left axis and put a tick against the words that best described it. This process was repeated in a number of locations (Figure 10.2).

When the children returned to the centre's classroom they were asked to use their data-base to suggest locations for birdboxes, a weather station, some seats and a nature trail that had to include a wide variety of environments (How is this place similar to, or different from, other places? How are these places connected?). The results of the work were impresssive, with some enthusiastic discussion about the criteria for the particular object to be located, and the location itself. On a following visit the warden used the same group to put up birdboxes in the locations they had suggested. On a third visit, the following Spring, the group checked the boxes to see if they had been used. Some of them had.

These children were 'being' geographers and using a geographical technique well. They had tackled three of the five geographical questions listed above and had produced meaningful results. They had used real places for a real purpose.

These examples are not isolated instances. The wider experiences of the writer suggests that the vast majority of children are capable of sustained and serious thinking if:

(a) 'real' and 'meaningful' learning situations can be found;
(b) they are helped to think about and discuss those experiences in a profitable way (see Chapter 4), and
(c) their experiences are not unduly overshadowed by demands which empha-sise those aspects of learning (e.g. written recording) which they may find difficult.

It does take time, thought and particular consideration from the teacher, but it *is* possible.

The stuff of historical and geographical investigations is all around us, can be borrowed from museums, can be visited free through organisations such as English Heritage and can be in the form of local people who can visit the school to describe their early life. Perhaps the most enabling concept we can give the child who experiences difficulties with some aspects of learning is a process to help him/her get what they want from their interests. The above examples have shown how this can be achieved when children *become* geographers and archae-ologists.

However, we must not become complacent. If children are to gain maximum access to geography and history we need to be aware of particular features of those subjects which could, potentially, cause difficulties in learning. Technical vocabulary and graphical representation are two aspects which need particular attention.

Figure 10.3

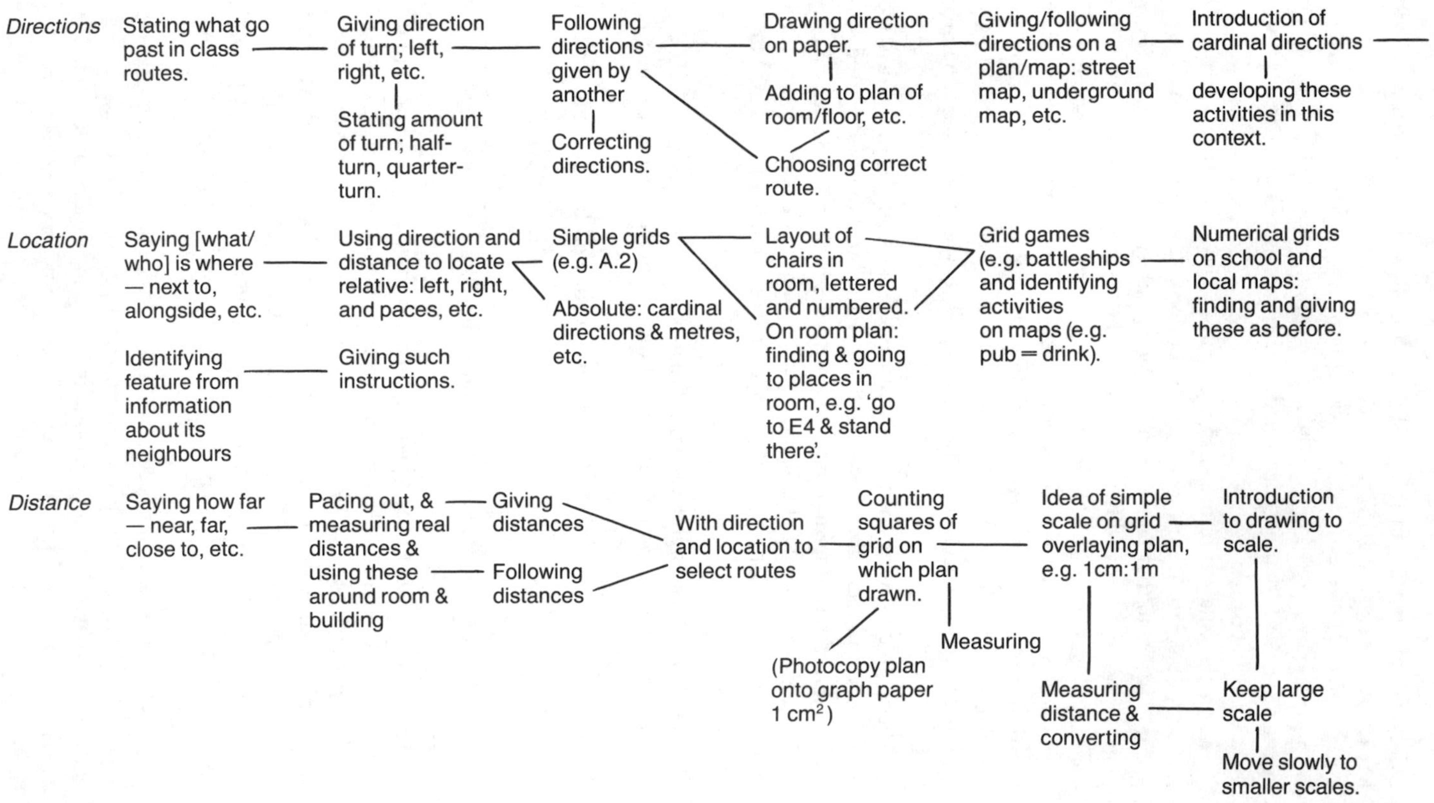

Directions

Stating what go past in class routes. — Giving direction of turn; left, right, etc. — Following directions given by another — Drawing direction on paper. — Giving/following directions on a plan/map: street map, underground map, etc. — Introduction of cardinal directions — developing these activities in this context.

- Stating amount of turn; half-turn, quarter-turn.
- Correcting directions.
- Adding to plan of room/floor, etc.
- Choosing correct route.

Location

Saying [what/who] is where — next to, alongside, etc. — Using direction and distance to locate relative: left, right, and paces, etc. — Simple grids (e.g. A.2) — Layout of chairs in room, lettered and numbered. On room plan: finding & going to places in room, e.g. 'go to E4 & stand there'. — Grid games (e.g. battleships) and identifying activities on maps (e.g. pub = drink). — Numerical grids on school and local maps: finding and giving these as before.

- Identifying feature from information about its neighbours
- Giving such instructions.
- Absolute: cardinal directions & metres, etc.

Distance

Saying how far — near, far, close to, etc. — Pacing out, & measuring real distances & using these around room & building — Giving distances — Following distances — With direction and location to select routes — Counting squares of grid on which plan drawn. — Idea of simple scale on grid overlaying plan, e.g. 1cm:1m — Introduction to drawing to scale.

- (Photocopy plan onto graph paper 1 cm²)
- Measuring
- Measuring distance & converting
- Keep large scale
- Move slowly to smaller scales.

Symbols

Drawing own pictures, symbols on picture/plans. — Discussing what own picture maps show. — Use of agreed 'symbols' (not necessarily conventions, or key needed). — Need for key for others to use plan. — Plans & maps using key agreed by children. — Meeting and using public conventions (rd. to street maps, bus maps OS 1:1,250, 1:2,500 main features), etc. — Exploring range of map types.

Need for common ground to communicate

What shown and how. — Use of Key

Using picture maps and maps from variety of sources.

Plan View

Looking down on common objects. — Model village, street (Lego, balsawood, etc). on base of roads, fields, etc.

Using photos of model from various angles: eye-level to vertical.

Using prepared plan of model to identify features. — Use of model features on overhead projector (Monopoly buildings). — Use of plans of room, floors and school grounds. — Use of plans of local area.

Drawing views including eye-level and vertical.

Tracing outline onto paper and colouring in for feature use, height, etc.

Drawing of own room, floor, ground plans, freehand — Identification on maps and on walks

On squared paper when introducing scale and measuring. — For surveys.

Map Reading

'Cognitive Maps' describing, following routes, verbally and on paper (simple drawings). — Need for drawing maps, e.g. recording walked route or big track route.

Reading the environment: personal knowledge.

home/school, home/shops, etc.

Use of plans of room, models, local area, etc.

— identifying
— surveys
— locating
— routes

Use of 'daily' maps, e.g. bus route, street map, underground, Council Estate maps, 'you are here' map boards, etc.

Other such maps, e.g. postcard maps, maps in adverts and newspapers.

More conventional maps, e.g. OS 1:1,250, 1:2,500, 1:10,000, road maps, tourist brochure maps. etc.

— What is their purpose?
— How do they show things?
— Are they useful?
— What can we find out from them?
— Can we improve them?

Both history and geography have developed a specialist vocabulary that can cause problems for all learners and lead to disenchantment with the subjects. In history, that vocabulary encompasses dates and events, and in geography descriptive items for physical features. Additionally the designation of 'directional' and 'locational' knowledge can be stumbling blocks. The use of a technical term is the final stage in understanding a concept. Much of the 'concept getting' and 'concept using' that underlies final articulation of the concept can be clouded by the use of specialist vocabulary from the outset. Children should be allowed to come to terms with the concepts of history and geography using their own familiar language, no matter how non-standard it might be. Specialist terms for those concepts should only be introduced when the concept has been understood and articulated in their own language.

Graphical representations (i.e. non-numerical and non-verbal) can be powerful aids to learning, whilst presenting others with distinct difficulties. They can form a basis for illustration, discussion and problem solving. Map reading is a more complex skill requiring a good understanding of position, direction, distance and symbols.

The chart on pages 152–3 (Figure 10.3), which was produced by Catlin (1984) provides teachers with a good guide to through activities by which children can develop the relevant concepts which underpin an understanding of material presented graphically.

Other elements of graphicacy; diagrams, flowcharts, networks and graphs, are infinitely adaptable for the child's personal use. Children should be allowed to use them, inventively, for their own purposes in the first instance, before they are introduced to more formal representations. Photographs are also an immense resource for children's learning. The taking of polaroid photographs allows for instant representations to be made which help children to form a bridge between reality and graphical representation (see Harwood, 1984).

The History and Geography National Curriculum Reports address the problems of children with special learning needs. However, their focus is on assessment and facilitating this assessment by allowing the children to use technical aids for recording their learning. It is an important point; but more important is the issue of enabling those children to come face-to-face with the evidence of the past and places near and far; that *is* accessible and meaningful to them. Their own questions, and our open-ended motivating and organising questions lay at the heart of such a process (see Chapter 4). Put simply, children only need to ask:

- What's my question?
- Do I need a place, a person, a thing, or a book to help me?
- Can I find an answer?
- How will I tell others about my findings?

What we do not need is for the failures from other areas of the curriculum to taint possible success in dealing with the 'past' and 'place'. There is an often nauseating strip cartoon character known as Garfield. In one of these cartoons he is seen chasing a dog up a tree. In the second frame both cat and dog sit on the same branch. The final frame shows a boy saying to the dog, 'Odie, dogs can't climb trees.' To which Odie replies, 'It's amazing what you can achieve when you don't know what you can't do.' I think the point is well made.

REFERENCES

Bolwell, L. (1987) 'Rethinking the humanities curriculum' *Support for Learning*, vol. 2, no. 3, pp. 10–15.

Catling, S. (1984) 'Building less able children's map skills', *Remedial Education*, vol. 19(1), pp. 21–7.

Harwood (1984) 'Introducing mapwork to ESN(M) children: stage ONE an approach through the use of aerial photography', *Remedial Education*, vol. 19(2), pp. 65–72.

Rowland, S. (1987) 'Ian and the Shoe Factory' in Booth, T., Potts, P. and Swann, W. (eds) *Preventing Difficulties in Learning*, Oxford: Blackwell.

Chapter 11

Art – a special form of provision
Nigel Furness

Early last spring my son Nicholas, aged 4 years and 7 months, came home from playschool with yet another object of art clutched in his tiny hand. 'This is for Mummy,' he said proudly, then walked off to play with his toys, or watch Super Ted. It wasn't the first time he had brought home something for us that he had made; we already had the spider from pipe cleaners, the caterpillar (a section of egg box inverted and painted green), and a fair assortment of pencil holders and notepads. All of these had been handed over and then forgotten, only ever referred to again if quizzed about their construction, and only then if pushed for answers. Today it was the 'potted plant'.

The 'potted plant' was simply a normal, common-or-garden flower-pot in which were three pipe cleaner stalks, embedded in a ball of plasticine and held in place by a mass of screwed-up brown tissue paper. On the end of each stem was a brightly coloured flower made out of screwed-up tissue paper. I was determined to ascertain how much work my son had put into this latest masterpiece. After a little discussion about the colours and what exactly it was supposed to be, I asked what the flowers were made out of. 'Circles of tissue paper,' I was informed.

'Oh, did you cut out the circles?' I asked, valiantly searching for a justifiable reason for the construction of the 'potted plant'. 'No,' was the reply. 'The teacher only has big scissors and we're not allowed to use those.' My chin dropped, it was worse than I imagined. It transpired that Nicholas' total contribution to the 'potted plant' had been to poke the pipe cleaners into the plasticine and screw-up the tissue paper.

Within this chapter I now intend to examine the artistic development of children during their early school years, stressing the individuality of each child. Teachers will only be able to respond to the special educational needs of particular pupils via a knowledge of the overall development of children's artistic representation. A young infant with special educational needs could well be functioning at the stage of the pre-school child. Mindful of these stages of development, I shall consider the tasks we should be asking children to attempt, making practical suggestions as to how these might be achieved and the materials we need to provide. Conversely, I shall be critical of some of the tasks being undertaken in many of today's primary school classrooms, particularly with those children who experience difficulties in learning; explaining my beliefs that teachers are professional educators, not artistic entertainers. I shall be placing great emphasis on the use of first-hand experience and the local environment in the development of Art and Craft in school.

The role of the teacher is to provide stimulating, exciting and new experiences for children; experiences that will enable them to build upon their existing knowledge, skills and understanding. The early years are crucial in the creative development of young children and the classteacher has a vital role in securing this development. The majority of children in their early years at school seek only to please; they will do all that is asked of them, just to feel that they have pleased. Children have no shop stewards; no one to say, 'Stop! This is boring – we want to be stimulated; we demand to be given exciting things to do – we deserve more than this!'

The onus is firmly on the teachers. Whenever possible, children must work from first hand experiences, from reality, from things that are relevant to where they are and within the stage of development they have reached.

For this chapter, I shall suggest that children's creative development can be thought of in certain stages and propose to use the stages outlined by Lowenfeld (1965). These stages must not be thought of as hard-and-fast entities. Teachers should be aware that children will not all develop at the same pace and indeed, there might be a 9-year-old child still at the Pre-Schematic or even Scribbling Stage. These stages offer a framework within which to work and which will help us to plan and organise classroom activities. These are the suggested stages:

- 2 years to 4 years   The scribbling stage
- 4 years to 7 years   The pre-schematic stage
- 7 years to 9 years   The schematic stage
- 9 years to 12 years   The stage of dawning realism

Before moving on to examine the first two stages, there are two points I would like to make.

ORGANISATION

Once one starts to look at the resources that should be provided and the opportunities which should be made available to enable children to develop creatively, it is inevitable that the question of organisation will arise.

Often teachers work a rotational system, whereby children move, as a group, from activity to activity, from one day to the next, providing the children with a very limited choice (e.g. sand-play today or painting tomorrow). This is equally as confining and restricting as a rigid time-table, whereby art and craft are relegated to Thursday afternoons. The implications of such rigid organisation on creative activity are obvious. There can be no reason for such organisation, other than one of adult convenience. But this begs the question: are classes organised around adults, without due consideration of children and their needs, especially their creative needs?

It is important that young children are given the opportunity to use the medium they require at the moment they need it; if a child is inspired to paint or model, then they should be given the opportunity there and then, not told to wait until tomorrow or Thursday when 'it is your turn'. This delay can destroy the moment and it will be lost forever. Eventually, the child may not even consider representing their thoughts or actions in this way, as they will have become used to being disappointed. Of course, this leads on to a consideration of how a class could best be organised to promote such a philosophy of 'art education'. The answer to this question is not simple and straightforward. Many teachers have faced this problem and found many different solutions. There are no hard and fast rules and I certainly would not want to promote one method of organisation above another. What I would stress, however, is the importance of a permanent art/craft area, stocked and prepared in such a way as to ensure it is always readily available.

There is a further implication from the approach I am advocating – the need for staff to meet regularly and discuss their aims and objectives with reference to the creative development of the children in their care.

ROLE PLAY

I would also like to draw attention to the importance of play in relation to creative development. The first area I would like to touch upon is that of the Wendy house – the home area. For many children this is seen purely as an opportunity for 'free play' (indeed it is commendable that such opportunities are seen to exist). Yet the home area can offer far more in the way of stimulation of the children's creative development. I wonder how often occasions in the home area are structured by adults to lead children into situations through which plays can be acted out? Are adults being given the opportunity to listen to children's conversation in the home area, feeding ideas and suggestions at the appropriate moment? Do adults ever join in the play situation and work alongside the child – as an equal?

Role play is crucial and dressing-up racks should be provided in order to promote and facilitate it. I stress 'rack'; a box of odd bits of clothing is more of a discouragement. Who wants to rummage around in screwed-up pieces of clothing? Far better to keep them on a rack where they can be easily seen, identified and selected. In addition to actual clothing, a large stock of material should be available, as this is far more flexible. I should also like to see a whole variety of old hats for children to trim and make into new designs. It is difficult for an adult, let alone a child, to make a hat from scratch; children need immediate results, and transforming an old hat can provide this more easily.

As with the home area, often the dressing-up rack has been seen as a free activity and once again, whilst one would not want to deprive children of this valuable experience, teachers can inspire the dressing-up with simple but imaginative suggestions involving groups of various sizes. A challenge such as organising a parade of the brightest, or scruffiest, can lead to imaginative creations.

THE SCRIBBLING STAGE

There is a great temptation for the artwork produced by children at this stage in their development to be dismissed as not 'real' art or 'real' creativity, yet it is a vital part of a child's creative development. No parent, or teacher for that matter, would ignore 'pre- reading' or the various early stages of reading development, so why so with art? Indeed, I believe this is the most exciting and interesting stage as children experiment with colour and line; they want to paint, draw, scribble, build, knock down, glue together and they are very excited about what they produce. They 'can do' everything and generally do not mind if it is messy; the important thing is that adults must not mind if it *is* messy (it helps, also, if adults appreciate the developing, and final, product).

For the parent, nursery leader or teacher, these are also very entertaining years, as the work produced is often colourful, imaginative and sometimes quite humorous. Yet as well as being entertaining, it is also extremely important. Children must be given scope and provided with opportunities and materials to develop naturally their artistic skills, without pre-conceived 'adult' ideas. A lack of freedom to develop creativity can lead to a hampering of children's development; their confidence in their ability to create can suffer irreparable damage.

In simple terms, if we as adults impose our own ideas on children, instead of allowing them to experiment with their own scribbles, models or paintings, then they will only think in terms of what we expect and what they should be able to produce from our example. If they are subsequently unable to complete satisfactorily the reproductions of our examples, they may become despondent and view themselves as failures and 'no good at painting'. In such instances they have never been given the opportunity to make their own art and so have missed vital stages in the learning process. People are horrified at the prospect of, for example, a 5-year-old child wrestling with a complex system for adding or subtracting numbers in mathematics without first understanding the nature of the problem; why does this not apply in terms of art and craft?

The Scribbling Stage can itself be divided into four sub-stages:

Disordered scribbling

As the title suggests, this involves nothing more than unrecognisable scribblings; the child is simply experimenting with holding a crayon or pencil and experiencing sheer joy from the freedom of movement around the paper and the making of marks.

Control stage

Hand/eye co-ordination develops and the child now realizes that movements can be controlled. At this early stage, the child tends to repeat the same scribbles.

Naming stage

Although at this stage it would be hard, if not impossible from an observer's position, to recognise any shape drawn or painted, the child can give a running account of his/her imaginative thinking as s/he draws.

Discovery stage

At this stage the child begins to discover relationships between drawing, thinking and the real world. Forms are constantly changed in an effort to represent accurately, or interpret the world. At this stage, the human figure gradually emerges.

These then are the stages of development one can expect during the early part of a child's artistic and creative development, irrespective of the chronological age. *All* children should be given the opportunity to develop through these stages. If children experience difficulties in learning they should be given more, not fewer, opportunities to develop through these stages. To by-pass these crucial stages of development, or to replace them with 'artistic entertainment', would be to deny some children their rights of access to this important area of their education.

Many primary school classrooms are full of smart adult ideas for children to copy; thirty-plus identical caterpillars made from egg cartons, or spiders from pipe cleaners; pictures involving hundreds of pieces of screwed-up tissue paper! Yet from an examination of the stages outlined above, it must be obvious that such things as tracing round templates, copying from the teacher's picture or mindlessly colouring in ready-drawn figures, offers little to the development of the child's creativity or understanding.

Unfortunately this kind of provision is even more frequently arranged for children who experience difficulties in learning. Teachers, with the best of intentions, often try to 'prop up' those children who experience difficulties in learning by producing heavily structured activities in which the children cannot fail. This most often results in a low-level learning experience similar to that experienced by my son in the production of the 'potted plant'.

The television is full of programmes for children (and their parents) containing clever little ideas of 'arty' things to make. These programmes are geared to parents and children, not to teachers or associated professionals. The presenters of these programmes are very good at what they do; they are professionals, but they are not teachers. They are entertainers. We are professionals in our own field and should aim for something more educational; we should not be repeating with our children the kind of 'art' work a well-meaning parent can achieve.

The Scribbling Stage is a stage, above all, where the 'process' is more important than the 'product'; the journey the child makes is far more valuable than the destination s/he reaches. Indeed, apart from possibly assessing progress, the end result is of little consequence to anyone other than the child, and what is important is that the product the child makes or draws from within him/herself is of far greater personal value than any idea copied from a teacher's model.

Once one accepts the importance of the process over the product, then this has certain implications for the materials which need to be made available for children. It is no longer sufficient to provide just the egg-carton, yoghurt-pot or pipe-cleaner required to make a specific 'model'. Children require materials that will help in their creative development, and in establishing their hand–eye relationships. They do not need sophisticated art and craft materials which cost a fortune, but simply those things that make a bright mark or can be moulded easily (materials to which they become attracted and with which they can experiment).

The following suggestions indicate materials that each classroom learning area should hold in order to be able to support the opportunities I have outlined:

- Large sheets of paper of a wide variety of colours: too often we confine young children's work by presenting them with a small piece of paper on which to work.
- Large wax crayons and chalks, for working on playgrounds or pavement, as well as on paper.
- Thick paint in bright colours. Far too often you see bright paints, mixed ready for use, but of a watery consistency. This is of no use to children who want to work quickly; thin paints 'run' down the paper. Commercially prepared paints are ideal, but rather expensive and probably out of the reach of some school budgets. Powder-paint mixed thickly, even with glue if necessary, is just as good.
- Clay, a most important material, is an essential to any early-learning area. Children need to achieve immediate results and nothing provides this better than clay. Certainly it is preferable to plasticine which is more readily available in many schools. That is not to say plasticine should be excluded; indeed it has qualities all of its own, but it does not provide the opportunity for such immediate results, nor does it have the lovely tactile quality of clay. However, it must be remembered that children of this age are not 'potters'. The tasks we are asking must not be those 'adult' conceptions of what can be made in clay. Clay is messy, but that is part of its attraction and there is tremendous value to be gained from giving very young children plenty of opportunity for 'feeling' clay – poking, prodding, squeezing, etc. Here, of course, is the moment for discussion between adult and child. The potential for language development is tremendous during such activities.

A consideration of the value of clay leads us into the whole area of three-dimensional work (one sadly overlooked in many classrooms). Yet this is a crucial area of development, and many reports over the last few years have highlighted the lamentable lack of importance placed upon this area. Children need to be able to 'work big', otherwise later on they will be impeded, almost frightened, by the prospect of being asked to construct or design on a large scale. To this end, schools should have available a wide variety of 'junk', not just the token box of yoghurt pots and egg boxes. Children need excitingly different objects to work with: buttons, beads, clock pieces, cog wheels, odd pieces of machinery, as well as material remnants and a wide assortment of 'odds and ends' (including boxes large enough for children to climb about in).

Clay, plasticine and junk modelling provide children with a valuable opportunity to understand the nature of structures, an understanding they will need in later creative work.

An objection often used when faced with a call for three-dimensional work is – storage space. Many teachers complain that they have nowhere to put the models when they are finished and that clay is too expensive if consumed in large quantities. The answer to that is simply that there should be no need to religiously keep all models that children make; clay and plasticine must be thought of by children as materials that can be re-used.

It is the process, not the product, that should be our concern. As with Duplo, Lego and the numerous other commercially prepared construction kits, children should be encouraged to realize that part of the building process is the 'taking to pieces', the re-cycling for another child to use. Of course you don't break up all models. It would be heart-breaking for children who have spent a long time and put a lot of themselves into a model to see it destroyed; we have to be selective and, above all, we have to encourage the children to be so. Some clay models will, and must, be kept. But there will also be times when, after initial discussion with the child, s/he can go into an activity prepared for the fact that the result will be temporary. In any case, no model should be destroyed without first giving children an opportunity to show and discuss, perhaps even play with their model. Nevertheless, children and parents must be made aware that modelling is not all about keeping.

If children are to be given such materials, then they need the tools and resources to be able to use them. Scissors are an essential component of the class tool box, and left-handed scissors, as well as right-handed ones, must be readily available. Glue will be necessary, but most young children prefer and need 'instant' results. Glue will not give this: staplers and sellotape will. In addition to the all too familiar problem of things falling apart whilst being 'glued', there is the time factor to be considered. Children cannot wait twenty-four hours for the glue to dry before adding the next part; by the following day interest may have waned. The momentum needs to be kept up; sellotape or brown paper sticky tape can do this.

Similarly, teachers need to have available sharp craft knives and large scissors, not for use *by* the children, but for use *with* them. A child needing a large hole cut in a stiff cardboard box cannot be allowed to struggle alone with small scissors, when it can be quickly and easily cut by an adult with the correct tool. It must, of course, be the child who decides where and how a cut should be made; not a well-meaning adult.

THE PRE-SCHEMATIC STAGE

Children start to make their first representational shapes during the Pre-Schematic stage. Having enjoyed the feeling of movement, early squiggles and discussion, they now want to represent their actions or thoughts. Children start to discover relationships between their drawings and the world around them. The human body starts to take shape. Their drawings and paintings are peculiar to themselves; comprising striped skies and bright suns. We must not try to 'train' children to draw or paint pictures that we can understand; we must not expect 'small adult copies'. Children are not miniature adults, and should not be treated as such. If we interfere with the natural process of development and introduce young children to clever adult ideas, they will quickly learn to copy them. The majority of children live to please; if they gain approval by copying our ideas they will continue to do so and their natural development will be interrupted or curtailed.

At the pre-schematic stage, children are very egocentric; they draw what they 'know' and 'see'. Colour has little relationship to nature, they paint as they feel.

During this stage children should own the project, so that it becomes meaningful for them. The inference of this is clear. The child needs to identify with his/her learning experience, and if the child has *real* experience, then it is possible s/he will be able to paint from that experience. Vincent Van Gogh could not paint Cyprus trees without first being in the field with the thunder clouds around him.

A famous authoress, when asked how her latest novel was coming along, replied slowly, 'I'm stuck at the moment because I haven't done my Geology 'O' Level yet.' 'Why do you want an 'O' Level in Geology?' she was asked. 'Because one of my major characters is a geologist,' she replied.

If professionals require such first-hand experiences, then certainly children do too. If it is a frosty morning with cobwebs sparkling on the school fence, then a walk in warm clothes around the school field will kindle the creative powers of the children, presenting an opportune time to paint a frosty morning picture. Similarly, asking a child to paint a picture of 'A day at the seaside', when it is a long time since they visited a beach or played in the sea (or worse still, if they've never been to the sea) is unfair to the child.

It is important, therefore, to capitalise on children's experiences but therein lies a potential danger. If a child feels that every experience at school, every walk, every 'adventure' is followed with an instruction 'now paint me a picture of ...', they will soon learn to dread such experiences.

There is another consideration which we must be mindful of. Exciting things do not happen to children every day! Most days children go home, have tea, 'play out', watch television and go to bed – the number of days when interesting, new, and exciting things happen are certainly few and far between. This is when we, as teachers, should prove ourselves to be the professionals and take the lead.

Teachers must be prepared to stimulate the children in a variety of ways and work hard at doing so by using all the resources at their command, for example:

(a) by telling the children stories within the context of a dramatic situation.

(b) by using the school grounds to their full potential. Often schools go to great trouble to organize visits to places of interest and these are of great value, but a walk around the school fields or playground can provide tremendous scope, especially if the teacher has 'planted' a few surprises beforehand.

(c) many schools now have environmental study or conservation areas and these have obvious potential for 'nature study', but why should it stop there? There is tremendous potential for providing opportunities for the children to develop their powers of creativity, but sadly these are seldom evident. Over the course of the last few years, great store has been set by close observational drawing – class teachers have been encouraged to give children opportunity for study, not only of flowers, beetles, mushrooms or other natural objects, but also shoes, machines, bicycles, etc. This type of innovation has been made partly in response to numerous reports criticising primary schools for their lack of emphasis in this area. Children must be encouraged to look closely at such objects and make careful sensitive drawings or paintings of them, but why does it end there? The children must capitalise on what they have learnt and put this observation to good use. They must apply this newly acquired knowledge in an imaginative and creative way.

Drawing is vitally important, but unfortunately for many schools, it seems to be the 'be all and end all' of art in school. This must not be so. We owe it to our children to be more imaginative in our teaching of art and give them the stimuli that will allow their creative instincts and freedom to grow.

(d) children are great collectors. Displays of these collections should be evident in all infant schools, and these contain potential for the imaginative teacher. With a little creative thought, such objects as shells and stones develop magical qualities to stimulate the child.

(e) dramatic situations are also a crucial aspect of the creative development. If you want the children to paint a tropical jungle, obviously you cannot take them to one. You can, however, after discussion, lead the children through a 'make-believe' jungle, feeling the heat, treading in the swamp and discussing the words that describe the journey. Admittedly this will not actually show them what a jungle is like, but it will help them feel a little of the atmosphere – and set their imagination alight.

(f) an occasion in school, such as a visitor or a travelling theatre group, can excite and interest the children, as can the 'set up' situation (e.g. mysterious creatures tucked away beneath a drain, the strange object inexplicably found in the P.E. store). Special moments – prize giving for the 'best mum in the world', plaque making, hole digging, pond dipping, building, finding – the list is endless. These all have creative potential, which as teachers we need to exploit. If we can lead the children into situations where they begin to actually 'feel' the experience, we have better chances of giving them opportunities for creative development. It isn't easy, in fact it can be really hard work.

CONCLUSION

In this chapter, I have tried to emphasise the crucial role that teachers have in setting the foundations for the development of the creative potential of children who experience difficulties in learning. In order to fulfil this role, teachers must be aware of the stages of creative development young children pass along and, mindful of this, accept their responsibility in stimulating the children in such a fashion that such progress can be made.

I have outlined the stages of development, stressing that children must be allowed to develop naturally through those stages. They must be given freedom to experiment, to experience a range of materials, to get the feel of those materials and become involved in creative work.

One of the key messages I hope to have given, is that the *process* is more important than the *product*. Unfortunately, far too many teachers place too great an emphasis on the finished article. This emphasis stems from our need for the child to take home some proof of their involvement in artistic activity, and the need for that to conform to certain adults' expectations. Having placed such an emphasis on the *process*, I have tried to give a guide to the materials that should be available for children if such a philosophy is to succeed; the need for bright colours, clay to mould, and a variety of 'junk'. Three-dimensional work is sadly overlooked, and in stressing the importance of this area, I have also tried to show that the children will also need the 'tools' if they are to succeed.

I have stressed that as they start to show relationships between their surrounding environment and their representations, so this must be central to the work undertaken by these children. Children must become involved in their activity, if it is to have any meaning for them. This means that emphasis must be placed upon working from first hand experience and not just from the point of good, close observational drawing. Whilst acknowledging the important place this has in the development of the child, I have also tried to make the point that the knowledge gained from such drawings needs to be put to use to extend the child's creative powers. Nor must teachers, whilst giving children opportunities for such drawing, fool themselves into believing that they have fulfilled their obligation to be giving children scope for creative development: far from it. Alongside such drawing, the teacher needs to stimulate the children to think imaginatively, to create; for it is only in these situations that the *real* problem solving will take place.

Stimulating children is hard work and this I have emphasised, but I have also tried to make some suggestions as to the form such stimulations might take. I have emphasised the use of the environment, the role of drama, external stimuli and above all the imagination of the teacher to create moments which will lead to the children giving scope to their own thoughts.

Throughout the chapter I have been highly critical of the common practice of taking ideas from 'crafty' magazines or clever television programmes and reproducing them with every child in the class; particularly those who experience difficulties in learning. I make no apologies for this, as it is central to my concern that such 'tricks' have no relevance to the creative development of our children and cannot therefore be tolerated. Of course children enjoy making jewellery boxes out of matchboxes or tanks for Action Men out of old egg boxes; but they can do that at home. The role of the teacher is about something far more important.

I accept that all I have written has certain implications for the education of children who experience difficulties in learning during the early years. It means that teachers *must* discuss together, very carefully and fully, their aims and objectives and decide whether or not they are fulfilling their obligation to develop 'the whole child'. Most, if not all schools, now have a written list of their aims. Developing the whole child, aesthetically and creatively, is most often included, but I would suggest that, in a number of cases, this just isn't happening!

REFERENCES

Lowenfeld, V. (1965) *The Nature of Creative Activity*, London: Routledge & Kegan Paul.

Chapter 12

Religious education – finding a way

Ted Huddleston

INTRODUCTION

Religious Education may have unique status in law (1988 Education Act), but when it comes to teaching the subject to young children, the pedagogical issues which arise are essentially no different from those found in any other school subject. Whatever difficulty a young child may experience with the subject, it is unlikely to be something which is not experienced elsewhere in the curriculum (Huddlestone, 1990). When young children are struggling with Religious Education what they require, as Bruner said, is simply teaching which 'emphasises the structure' of the subject:

> Good teaching that emphasises the structure of a subject is probably even more valuable for the less able student than for the gifted one, for it is the former rather than the latter who is most easily thrown off the track by poor teaching. (1977)

Emphasising the structure of a subject is a two-fold process. It consists in; first, designing learning activities which reflect the most basic principles of the subject; and secondly, matching them to the different capacities which children exhibit (Bruner, 1977).

THE TROUBLE WITH RELIGION

As Bruner himself admitted, this is not an easy task in any subject, but in Religious Education it seems more troublesome than most. The problem, as those who have tried it have found, is that there is so little agreement as regards what the most basic principles of Religious Education are that it is difficult even to know where to begin.

The controversy is not, generally speaking, about *how* Religious Education should be taught; there is widespread agreement that (apart from in schools run by voluntary bodies) teaching should be conducted in such a way as to respect the rights of individuals to reach their own decisions regarding religion. The trouble lies in the specification of the subject-matter of the subject.

The experience of trying to identify what religion *is* is rather like that of the mathematical creature from the moon who, in Chesterton's allegory, tries to identify what a human being is:

> Suppose some mathematical creature from the moon were to reckon up the human body; he would at once see that the essential thing about it was that it was duplicate. A man is two men, he on the right exactly resembling him on the left. Having noted that there was an arm on the right and one on the left, a leg on the right and one on the left, he might go further still and find on each side the same number of fingers, the same number of toes, twin eyes, twin ears, twin nostrils, and even twin lobes of the brain. At last he would take it as a law; and then, where he found a heart on one side, would deduce that there was another heart on the other. And just then, where he most felt he was right, he would be wrong.
>
> (1961)

Any attempt to emphasise the structure of Religious Education depends ultimately on some understanding of what religion is, so how should it be defined? As a particular type of belief? A particular kind of experience? A particular system of ethics? A particular set of rituals? A particular form of culture? Whatever definition we finally decide upon, there will always be others to argue that our definition is wrong (Smart, 1968).

In other situations this difference of opinion might give little cause for concern, but not so in the case of teaching which is, if nothing else, a practical activity. Different definitions of religion tend to make different, often conflicting, practical demands of those that support them. Depending on how it is defined, you might be expected variously to pray five times a day, or to pick up live snakes, or to have dominion over the earth, or to marry someone you would otherwise never think of marrying, or to refrain from eating meat, or to believe that Christ Jesus dies for your sins, and so on.

The trouble with religion is that, in the near future at least, it seems unlikely that any one definition will gain universal acceptance, with the result that attempts to improve the teaching of Religious Education to young children will remain both isolated and controversial.

AN ALTERNATIVE?

What I wish to argue here is that this need not be the case. That is to say, though we may never be able to land on a definition of religion which will gain universal acceptance, we need not see this as a problem. As Kolakowski (1982) has said, the definition of religion is in principle no different from the definition of any other sphere of the social world. He then contends that:

> In the investigation of human affairs no concepts at our disposal can be defined with perfect precision and in this respect 'religion' is in no worse a

position than 'art', 'society', 'culture', 'history', 'politics', 'science', 'language' and countless other words. Any definition of religion has to be arbitrary to a certain extent, and no matter how scrupulously we try to make it conform to the actual usage of the word in current speech, many people will feel that our definition covers too much or too little or both.

What this suggests is that if the definitions of different aspects of the social world are in principle controversial, then this fact must somehow be incorporated into our understanding of what is involved in teaching them in schools. The plurality of definitions of religion should not be seen as a stumbling-block for good teaching in Religious Education, but as its very basis. We may now consider the implications of this shift in understanding for the planning of Religious Education for primary-aged children, and especially for those who are experiencing learning difficulties in school.

THE SUBJECT-MATTER

Viewed in this way, the subject-matter taught in Religious Education can be anything which is, or has been, described as 'religious' – however defined: beliefs, formulations, creeds, experiences, stories, writings, rules of conduct, language, rituals, buildings, places, dances, art, music, and so on. In principle, at least, no aspect of human life is excluded.

Of course we must recognise that all of these have been shaped by, and continue to exist in the form of, traditions. Traditions often conflict; what is considered as 'religious' in one way may not be considered so in another. No matter. It simply means that the selection of material for use in the design of learning activities in primary schools is bound to be eclectic, maybe even idiosyncratic. All that is required at this stage is that the selection made represents a fair balance of what is available and does not favour unduly any one tradition (1988 Education Act).

THE AIMS

The aim of teaching is to enhance children's awareness and understanding of the subject-matter. Given the logic of the subject-matter as I have outlined it, the kind of understanding aimed for should be practical. Practical understanding is the acquisition of knowledge of something in order to make a practical response to it.

Teaching Religious Education thus means not only providing opportunities for children to learn *about* a selection of things which have been defined as religious, but also to learn *from* them. In other words the subject-matter should be taught in such a way as to enable children to gain some insight, however slight, of the practical difference it might make to their lives.

This is a view of the subject matter which, unlike certain others, does not demand complex reasoning skills of a kind unavailable to many young children. The aim is potentially open to all. To teach Religious Education in this way is simply to create situations in which children are able to encounter materials which others have defined as religious. It is to tell the story of Rama and Sita, to play a recording of a muezzin's call to prayer, to display an icon, to visit a cathedral, to colour in an Islamic pattern, to participate in a short silent meditation, and so on.

ASSESSMENT

'Learning about' is, of course, open to objective assessment – formative, diagnostic, summative or evaluative, but 'learning from' is not. The response which a child makes, or does not make, in an encounter with 'religious' material is ultimately private, individual and unpredictable. In this context we might do well to note Chesterton's (1961) warning that:

> a man may well be less convinced of a philosophy from four books, than from one book, one battle, one landscape, and one old friend.

Similarly we should note Brennan's (1987) tongue-in-cheek remark that 'children of dogmatic atheists tend to become Wesleyan missionaries.'

In this respect the teaching of Religious Education has much in common with that of the creative arts as conceived by Bisner (1975). Starkings (1987) claims that:

> what is desired is not homogeneity of response among students but diversity ... the teacher hopes to provide a situation in which meaning becomes personalized and which children produce products, both theoretical and qualitative, that are as diverse as themselves.

Unlike the creative arts, however, there are no tangible products in Religious Education. The objectives are existential rather than expressive. The products are the children themselves; not simply what they know, nor what they can do, but how they live and what they become, their own 'personal legend'.

PROVIDING FOR CHILDREN WITH LEARNING DIFFICULTIES

As we have already noted, the art of good teaching is to devise learning activities which reflect the basic principles of a subject and to match them to the capacities which children exhibit. This requires, on the one hand, an awareness of the learning characteristics of the children in question; their interests, and their strengths and weaknesses. On the other hand, it also requires a knowledge of the 'pre-requisite skills' demanded by different kinds of learning activities (Clarke and Wrigley, 1988). For example, to gain anything at all from hearing the story of Rama and Sita, it is necessary to be able to sit quietly and listen for a certain period and to be able to follow the chief elements in a plot. A class visit to a cathedral might demand the ability to sit in silence for five minutes or so and find a word which expresses the experience. Colouring in an Islamic pattern requires certain sensori-motor skills and so on. Examples of classroom activities in R.E. for children with special educational needs can be found in Davies (1988), Brown (1987) and Huddlestone (1988).

The golden rule is to ensure that, whatever the learning activity chosen, all children in the class have the necessary pre-requisite skills, with support if needs be, to feel that they are able to participate. A helpful method is to devise a number of different learning activities all relating to a single piece of 'religious' material. This, of course, is the model on which much primary topic work is already based. A useful variant is to make the 'religious' component an element in a topic devised primarily to cover a different area of the curriculum – in a topic on maths (Huddlestone, 1988) for example, or geography and history (Cope, 1987).

Stories are a good start. Christmas has a story; it concerns the wonder of a baby coming from nowhere. Forget the incarnational theology, this is the story of every baby, it can have a personal meaning for all children. Stories can, of course, have many forms: spoken, written, pictorial, dramatic, film or video; so there are many ways to use religious stories to emphasise their personal meaning for children. There are also many stories dealing with religion at the level of a child's personal experience which are not from explicitly religious traditions. Raymond Briggs's *The Snowman* is an example which speaks of love and death, and a world beyond everyday reality. Such stories are equally useful.

Festivals are quite often celebrated by schools. Christmas and Easter are popular and, for some reason, Harvest Festival. Christmas can be experienced as a time of excitement and purpose which gives meaning to life both before it happens and when it is over, in some cases albeit solely in relation to sweets and presents. So, too, may Eid-ul-fitr or Divali, for example. An Eid party or assembly may similarly encapsulate the joy of celebration and its preparation for all its partici-pants, it may widen their knowledge of Islam. For Muslim children, it is the least that can be done in school to value their religious identity. When choosing the festivals to celebrate, the teacher should consider the learning difficulties which are experienced by particular pupils. For children who experience severe diffi-culties in learning, a birthday party includes features remarkably similar to tra-ditional religious festivals; it is the child's *experience* that is important, not the minutiae of a religious tradition.

Artefacts is the usual term given to religious objects. We all have special objects which are infused with their own special meaning peculiar to us; in their own way, they are personal symbols of purpose. Perhaps they start with the child's comforter; is it a coincidence that 'comforter' is an old word for Holy Spirit in Christian terminology? In Religious Education one begins to use artefacts by openly valuing the apparently ordinary things which children find special. This is to take seriously the personal aspect of religion in their lives. If children belong to a religious faith, these might include religious artefacts. When these are introduced into school, children are given the opportunity to have their own experience acknowledged, to see that a school-friend has a similar experience and also that there are objects with special appeal for groups as well as individuals. By extension, artefacts can include other special objects such as food and clothes and so on.

Visits will also emphasise the personal aspect of religion. Forget the nomenclature of the pieces of furniture; the agelessness, harmony and space of a medieval cathedral might feel just like another world. Allow time for them to experience it, remembering of course that the experience will be different for each individual. Allow time, too, for them to express this, for only by so doing can children come to value both their own unique experience and the experience of others. Do the same when a child gives the class a guided tour of his or her own place of worship and a glimmer of what it means to him or her. As in any other educational activity, children are often their own best resources. In common with stories, places not explicitly connected with religious traditions may affect people in a personally religious way. In our culture, it is often nature, in the form of an animal, a waterfall or a wide open space, or perhaps an old building that tends to conjure up feelings of wonder and awe. Being there is best, but you can also simulate the experience with pictures, slides or films. The aim is not so much to trigger 'religious' experiences, even if it were possible, but to acknowledge, value and confirm the experience a child already has.

Finally, school assemblies have traditionally been assumed to be Christian services. This idea has merely been reinforced in the emphasis on 'collective acts of worship' in the 1988 Education Act. However, worship is one thing, teaching another. Perhaps school assemblies can also be regarded as opportunities for religious education. Teachers have always recognised that regular activities can fill a need for order and stability in a child's life, giving shape and meaning to the wider experience of being at school But there is also the unique quality of group experience which such an activity can engender. It makes for a particularly fertile way of dealing with the personal aspect of religion in school; it provides valuable opportunities for children to experience themselves as part of a larger whole, and with a unique part to play in that whole; and it is an activity where a child's own faith can be openly affirmed. Once again, participation is the important thing (Huddlestone, 1987).

GUIDELINES AND CHECKLISTS

The final implication is that it means that school curriculum planning in Religious Education is no longer bedevilled by the (practically impossible) task of compiling intricate lists of skills to be learned and concepts to be developed. A school's guidelines or checklist for the subject is more likely to take the form of 'a bank of well-resourced projects' (Bacon, 1987).

EPILOGUE

Nasrudin tried to get a calf into a pen, but it would not go. So he went to its mother and began to reproach her. 'Why are you shouting at that cow?' someone asked.

'It is all her fault,' said Nasrudin, 'for she should have taught him better.' (Shah, 1985)

REFERENCES

Bacon, E. (1987) 'R.E. across the curriculum in Landsdowne school', *R.E. News and Views*, 4 (3), p. 12.
Bisner, E.W. (1975) 'Instructional and expressional objectives', in Golby, M., Greenwald, J. and West, R. (eds) *Curriculum Design*, London: Croom Helm.
Brown, A.S. (1987) *Religious Education and Pupils with Learning Difficulties*, Cambridge: Cambridge University Press.
Bruner, J.S. (1977) *The Process of Education*, Massachusetts: Harvard University Press.
Chesterton, G.K. (1961) *Orthodoxy*, London: Collins.
Clarke, J. and Wrigley, K. (1988) *Teaching Humanities in the Secondary School*, London: Cassell.
Davies, J. (1988) 'Active learning for children with special needs', *R.E. Today*, 5, 2.
Department of Education and Science (1988) *1988 Education Act*, London: HMSO.
Huddlestone, R.E. (1988) *Practical Approaches: Religious Education for Children with Special Educational Needs*, Exeter: Devon Education Dept. and St. Luke's College Foundation.
Huddlestone, R.E. (1989) *Religious Education for All*, Middlesex/Exeter: C.E.M/ St. Luke's College Foundation.
Huddlestone, R.E. (1990) 'Slow learners' in Hammond, J. *et al.* (eds) *New Methods in R.E. Teaching*, Harlow: Oliver & Boyd.
Pepper, F.S. (1987) *20th Century Quotations*, London: Sphere Books.
Shah, I. (1985) *The Exploits of the Incomparable Mulla Nasrudin*, London: Octagon Press.
Smart, N. (1968) *Secular Education and the Logic of Religion*, London: Faber & Faber.
Starkings, D. (1987) 'How should R.E. change people?', *Westminster Studies in Education*, 10, 58.

Chapter 13

A classroom plan for personal and social education in primary schools

Kenneth David

INTRODUCTION

Primary class teachers, intuitively and through the child-centred primary school ethos, have always had the personal and social development of children in their minds, but this chapter argues for a more planned and purposeful approach by teachers.

Changes in society and new challenges to traditional viewpoints are discussed, as are children's needs, the effects on children of schools and individual teachers, and the varied aims and objectives of teachers and parents.

Definition and outline plans of cross-curricular personal and social education (PSE) are suggested, as is the clear link with national curriculum guidelines. Preparation for adolescence is considered, as are staff preparation and evaluation of the work.

Learning difficulties are presumed to have a clear social and emotional content (see Chapter 2 for an indication of one aspect of this association), and the strong link between learning and PSE is presumed throughout. Much PSE with primary children will be done with emphasis on discussion of varying viewpoints. Children with special needs can be a normal part of the class.

It can reasonably be argued that the relationships between staff and pupils, and between staff and parents, are usually more relaxed and informal in primary classrooms than in secondary schools. Relationships appear to be easier because adults are normally less challenged by children than by adolescents – the parent and child attitude in the home is carried over into the teacher and child relationship in the primary classroom. One can argue that children's expectations of what their primary teachers will provide are slightly less demanding than in later years of schooling, and that teachers are rather more at ease, less obligated to the rigours of subject disciplines, and at least marginally more inclined to give time to individual children and relationships.

Within this less formal setting the class teacher has expected to look to children's personal and social development, and the purpose of PSE has been respected, even if in an informal and unstructured way. Primary teachers have been associated with the dependence of children, as have parents; the independence of children is more emphasised in later years.

This wholesome view of education – that teachers have a relaxed concern with personal as well as learning development – is changing. Public expectations of professional teachers are more demanding and critical, and all teachers are realising increasingly their vulnerability and accountability. Schools are no longer professional fortresses. The local management of schools means that Governors are becoming responsible partners in all aspects of the school's work. The changing nature of family life produces children whose lives are more complicated and whose attitudes are more sophisticated and demanding. The modern 'information explosion' is obliging teachers to realise that the knowledge they deal with is more transitory, the demands of learning are more complicated, and the human skills of communication and relationships are becoming more essential for survival in the future. The relaxed and informal setting of the primary classroom is under challenge and cool critics are watchful not only of the learning skills that children develop, but also of the human skills that teachers have a hand in developing. Professionalism is casting a beady eye on both learning and relationships skills.

Some of this changing attitude is represented in the national curriculum. The National Curriculum Guidance 5 (Health Education) and 8 (Education for Citizenship) contain in the Key Stages 1 and 2 a great deal of the cross curricular area which in this chapter is termed PSE. There are also links with Key Stages 1 and 2 of the Science, Technology, English and Mathematics programmes of study of the national curriculum.

CHILDREN'S NEEDS

What the children in a class need as their priorities for a satisfying life are much the same as those that we adults need. Fundamentals must surely include good health as an early priority, probably joined by security and affection. What else do satisfying future lives require? To be treated as worthwhile, listened to and talked to and respected; having skills of listening, explaining, chatting and generally communicating easily; having some understanding of society's learning and knowledge; being literate and numerate, and accumulating society's measures of qualifications in schooling. It is not difficult to keep adding to this list, but fundamental personal needs – 'survival' needs in the jungle of society – can be kept very simple. They are the needs which instinctively shape parents' care of their child, though inadequacy and selfishness can reduce some parents' abilities. They must underlie what a primary school teacher does with his pupils. Satisfying such needs is the task for families and schools, jointly preparing children for their future, not necessarily our future.

FUTURE NEEDS

The shape of that future can only be guessed: the recent revolution in computing hints at the present speed of change, and forecasts very different concepts of work and career than our generation has held; in 1938 academics told us that 'matter is indestructible', and a few years later the first atomic bomb exploded; the explosion of knowledge in recent decades is illustrated by the vast increase in published books, for example, and points to the concept of obsolescence in knowledge.

Our choices multiply: manufacturing industry and commerce are turned on their traditional heads; family life and marriage are changing fast, with obvious saddening consequences; material comfort and sophisticated entertainment fill the leisure of most people, with near-pornography commonplace; and inflation linked with materialism is changing older financial habits, perhaps with a fresh translation of probity.

There are many other factors in change: a multi-cultural population, growing secularisation, powerful media influence, the lessening of traditional authority; all these provide debate for teachers, for they all affect education.

It would seem that these topics of change form some of the substance of education, and the beginnings of an agenda for PSE in the primary school and the secondary school. Yet our adult background tempts us to keep to what we have known, and to be wary of forecasting the need for change in the way we prepare children for their future. There must also be differing aims for schooling among parents, employers and teachers. All can sincerely argue their views of children's needs, but all can be flawed. Are we educating children for the needs of outdated industry or the needs of jobs not yet thought of; to ways of 'steadfast' or 'tangential' thinking; for a family pattern that is rapidly disappearing; for an individual and mobile life, or for a regional pattern of traditional life that we hope will remain? The curriculum of the primary classroom and the ways in which we teach do have their effect on the way we are preparing children for the future.

Such changes in our society, and the differing views of the future that they develop are well illustrated by, among others, Hopson and Scally (1981), Whitfield (1983) and Stonier (1983). They have affected everyone, including teachers, and presumably should have affected schools and their curriculum and methods. Whether they have is a matter of doubt – I am not convinced that primary schools march with the times.

THE EFFECT OF SCHOOLS

Are schools at one extreme guardians of the dated 'sabre toothed curriculum', at the other irresponsible radicals defying parents' expectations? Where does a sensible balance lie in preparing to live in this changing future society, and are we to be guardians or cynics?

Class teachers still have considerable influence: all of us remember individual teachers and their effect on our personal attitudes; many of us remember poor schools. Habits can be developed, attitudes shaped, values suggested, adult models provided. The curriculum and methodology have their effect, and the 'hidden curriculum' clearly influences through effective rituals, lively leadership, environmental neighbourliness, staff room appearances, and staff personalities and attitudes. It is always interesting to see the range of differing personalities on a staff, and to wonder at the effect on children of differing attitudes to life and work, of differing styles of living, of dress, of speech, of teaching. This variety among a familiar and educated group of adults is an important part of a child's education in relationships.

The one certain thing about the future is that children will need personal competence in communication, whether for family or career satisfaction. Does each primary teacher provide children with:

- language to express clearly what they mean and feel
- knowledge about people and human behaviour
- social competence skills, in developing friendships, for example
- support in living with their own temperament and personality, and with their inadequacies and handicaps
- skills in belonging to groups
- abilities in making decisions?

Whether as part of the formal or informal work of the school, such skills will clearly be part of their future life.

Other factors contribute to the effect of the school.

Rituals need to be studied, for school habits and ways of doing things can be counter-productive – assemblies can be perfunctory and meaningless, and ritualistic questioning or blackboard note copying can be deadening for learning.

Critical incidents occur and can be prepared for to some degree. Bereavements happen, and a teacher will have ways of dealing with this, agreed with his colleagues. Children's ill-discipline and angry parental intrusion over incidents at school can be dealt with in a way agreed by the staff.

Predictability will be balanced with excitement and innovation in the classroom. Many children need a secure and predictable shape to their life in the classroom, perhaps in contrast to their home life. The one thing which should be predictable in an ideal world is the class teacher's patience and humour, for these the child does remember.

Punishments will hopefully be few, prompt, predictable, and constructive.

Counselling presumably will be part of the staff training programme. The likelihood of one-to-one counselling sessions with primary children will be very limited, but counselling opportunities come in many other ways, and counselling skills are a normal and useful addition for every teacher.

Family links hardly need to be emphasised. A class teacher's success in setting attitudes and debating values must be in parallel with explanations to parents, and with a constant enlistment of their help, repeated endlessly even when a teacher is faced with parental apathy.

Staff teamwork. Human perfection comes slowly, but certain standards are part of professionalism, and schools must expect a reasonable agreement among staff in their behaviour in and out of the staff room. We are all vulnerable to children's observation, and it is reasonable to expect certain standards with dress, smoking, lunchtime drinking, and so on. Children are worldly enough to know that teachers cannot be models in all they do, but they should be able to respect what they see.

PERSONAL AND SOCIAL EDUCATION

This general title seems to sum up these competencies that we are seeking to give children – preparing for new attitudes to work, choices and relationships.

Hopson and Scally Personal Skills List

Me and You
Skills I need to relate effectively to you

How to communicate effectively
How to make, keep, and end a relationship
How to give and get help
How to manage conflict
How to give and receive feedback

Me and Others

Skills I need to relate effectively to others

How to be assertive
How to influence people and systems
How to work in groups
How to express feelings constructively
How to build strengths in others

Me
Skills I need to manage and grow

How to read and write
How to achieve basic numeracy
How to find information and resources
How to think and solve problems constructively
How to identify my creative potential and develop it

How to manage time effectively
How to make the most of the present

How to discover my interests
How to discover my values and beliefs
How to set and achieve goals
How to take stock of my life
How to discover what makes me do the things I do
How to be positive about myself

How to cope with and gain from life transitions
How to make effective decisions
How to be proactive
How to manage negative emotions
How to cope with stress
How to achieve and maintain physical well-being
How to manage my sexuality

Other titles can be used. *Health education* is a long established area of work which has been extended into personal relationships; *social education* can mean citizenship education, or it can include activities in social competence, meeting visitors and guests for example, or learning to converse; *family life education* can range widely over child development, relations between parents and children, responsibilities in the home and with the elderly; *personal education* can be interpreted to include group discussion work and activities, and counselling approaches; *education in personal relationships* is another general title.

A wealth of books is available, many directed to secondary school work, a few to primary work. The fact that material is published for potential secondary use does not necessarily exclude its use with younger children, especially when one considers that modern media appears to deny an age of innocence, and sophistication is an expectation of younger age groups.

One example, for discussion on the content of a PSE programme, could be Hopson and Scally (1981) personal skills list, intended for secondary use. Many of these skills can apply in childhood. We can compare such material with the themes suggested by the titles of the booklets in the Teachers' Guides of the *Health Education 5–13* (1977) Project.

All about Me (Early years of schooling 5–8)
Finding out about myself
How did I begin?
What is growing?
What helps me grow?
Looking after yourself
Keeping safe
Knowing about others

Think Well (Middle years of schooling 9–13)
Myself
Food for thought
One of many
From sickness to health
Deadly decisions
Time to spare
Get clean
Skills and spills

It is not difficult to begin building a classroom programme in PSE from such sources, and from other material such as Baldwin and Wells (1979–83), David and Cowley (1980), David and Charlton (1987) and Lang (1988). One can easily make a listing of the topics, activities and skills that would benefit a particular class or school in their personal and social development.

In the infant school health education is very relevant. School routines and practices help with personal habits, a 'home centred' approach reinforces what parents have taught, and care, gentleness, affection and responsibility are part of the atmosphere in any good infant school, and form the groundwork of relationships. Additionally the work can be more demanding; infants are often more capable of intellectual concepts and reasoning than is sometimes allowed, and the fact that health is to do with personal decision-making can be explored more deeply than it often is. The beginnings of sex education can and should be easily dealt with, and infants, who live in an adult world outside the school, are capable of a deeper understanding of human behaviour than is generally acknowledged.

In the junior school classroom the range of topics can be extended and deepened. Family life and caring relationships, the cycle of conception and birth, human growth and development, the understanding of feelings, attitudes and emotions, the effects of the environment on people, safety, community life, and personal habits, all form proper subjects for teaching and discussion. We underestimate children's emotional knowledge, and in turn sometimes forget that intellectual processes will not function without emotional content. It is usually easier to question and discuss human motives and emotions before adolescence.

In forming the agenda for PSE in primary or middle schools what opinions would teachers have on including the following random selection of topics?

- Anger and violence
- Fear
- Deviance and abnormalities of adult behaviour
- Mental illness
- Sex education
- Drugs and alcohol misuse
- Prejudice and racism
- Bereavement and grief
- The handicapped in society

All *can* be discussed with children, all *will* impinge on their families and communities to greater or lesser extent, all *need* explanation at the child's level of development. At what age does a class teacher feel these and many other topics will be acceptable for discussion? Are any of these listed topics better left out? If so, why exactly? There may be good reasons for omitting controversial themes that appear in the child's home newspaper, or on TV programmes in late night watching, or it may be cowardly to avoid them.

We are, I suppose, like parents, attempting to offer and develop knowledge, habits, and attitudes leading to a mature and balanced personality, at stages appropriate to a child's age. Total success is a fantasy, an attempt is our duty. Can we, and will they:

- enjoy and sustain relationships
- live without too much tension in their lives
- be tolerant of other opinions
- accept opposition or criticism
- avoid causing tension in others?

Have we, through the work of the classroom, helped to develop the child's self regard – what the actions of others to you, and your actions to them, have left you willing to believe about yourself? Have we been positive, through lesson planning and classroom activities, in developing different children's positive perceptions about themselves – everyone deserves success, and recording systems and grouping arrangements even may be part of PSE in attaining this. Is there a predisposition to achieve or to fail – that also comes partly from the years a child spends at school.

All this is PSE; it is not only an area of knowledge, it is about the school ethos, interpreted in each classroom, and it is certainly linked with learning abilities.

SELECTION AND CO-ORDINATION

If a school accepts the need for a better planned PSE programme then obvious questions arise. The answers must depend on the school and its setting, and on individual teachers' views and skills.

(a) Is it sufficient to answer children's questions as they arise, and to leave the rest to parents and chance?

(b) Is there to be a selection by the staff, perhaps by parents, even by children, of the topics that need exploration by discussion, by teaching, and by other school and class activities?

(c) On what do we base such a selection of topics: local needs, future needs, crises as they arise?

(d) How do we deal with these topics? Are they to be introduced into general class teaching: special periods of work done weekly, daily, or occasionally by the class teacher; or topic work for all teachers, or (by mutual exchange) by selected or specialist teachers? Is PSE to be implicit in the curriculum or dealt with separately? Many teachers would feel that it is more natural for such work to be part of the general teaching by all teachers, but there may be other considerations in some schools.

(e) How are parents to be fully involved, and persuaded of the mutual benefit of PSE courses and approaches? Might an agreed co-ordinated approach be spelled out as a 'contract' between teacher and family?

(f) What support is needed in the PSE programme from outside the school? What contribution could parents make?

(g) What preparation is needed for teachers? Are most topics capable of being dealt with at the children's level by any educated adult? Which topics involve teachers' attitudes, prejudices, values? Are such topics to be shelved, or dealt with, and by whom?

(h) What degree of confidentiality is required when children talk openly of private family matters, and how will this be managed? What limitations are there to be on searching questions by children? Are any children at risk?

(i) How far do the national curriculum cross-curricular suggestions meet the needs of a planned PSE programme?

A GENERAL SELECTION OF PSE TOPICS

For guidance and discussion the following has been a common selection of themes used without problem in many primary schools. A class teacher could, through discussion with colleagues, map out his or her contribution to such a scheme.

Personal
Personal hygiene
Fitness, exercise and rest
Personal appearance
Dental health
Internal working of the body
Care of feet, ears, hair
Nutrition and diet
Standards of personal behaviour
Growth and development
Understanding ourselves
Decision making
Personal values and attitudes

Community
Cancer education
Diseases
Obesity
Alcohol and alcoholism
Drug taking
Smoking
Health services and public health
Medicines and common illnesses
Handicapped people
First aid
The elderly
Mental health and stress
World health
Food hygiene
Noise
Multi-cultural aspects of health

Environment

Road safety
Safety in the home
Safety at work
Water safety
Conservation
Pollution
Law and order
The mass media

Family life and personal relationships
Feelings, and needs of other people
Tolerance
Friendship
Anxiety and stress
Care of young children
The elderly in the family
Work and leisure and the family
Reproduction and birth
Home-making

Preparation for adolescence

As adults, it is easy to forget our own growth to adolescence, with its confusions, questioning and tentative assertiveness. If we can lead children up towards adolescence – which does not have a clear arrival age – then we can make the transition between childhood and adolescence happier for many.

There are a number of considerations, linking back to our consideration of the content of PSE preparation with the pre-teens age group, probably the 9–12 age group.

(a) Children can be helped to realise the normality of their *growth* towards physical maturity. Clumsiness at the growth spurt age can be humorously explained, as a small example.

(b) There can be help for children in establishing an acceptable understanding of men and women's *sex roles*, and some understanding of the opposite sex.

(c) *Social skills* can be developed – social competence with contemporaries and adults, adding to the impulsive naturalness of childhood. This can be directed towards easing the transition from primary to secondary school.

(d) Explanation can begin to clarify *emotional control and maturity*, and independence.

(e) *Intellectual ability* has to be learned, understood and accepted, and strengths and weaknesses comprehended.

(f) Growing emancipation from home controls, developing into *self control* begins in adolescence.

(g) Hobbies and *leisure* activities are introduced and developed, perhaps giving lifetime pleasures.

(h) *Values and attitudes* can be clarified and alternative views discussed.

Learning to mature is a long process – it goes on all one's life – but the introduction to maturity in adolescence can be properly supported through teachers' work. PSE work is often co-ordinated between secondary schools and their feeder primary schools.

Sex education

Plowden (1976) stated, 'It is not good enough to leave matters vague and open, hoping for the best' in sex education, and the phrase continues to be appropriate. Many years later many primary schools do little or nothing in this educational task. It is only a modest part of PSE, of equal importance with a dozen other topics, but sex education continues rather boringly to demand extra explanation and unwarranted attention. Adult sexuality probably reinterprets and dramatises what youngsters of primary age can accept without great emotional debate. The earlier sophistication and maturity of children, apparently inevitable even when we deplore it, and the pressures on children from society requires that sexuality be interpreted and explained in the primary school years. A majority of parents seem to find it difficult to put over to their children, and value parallel teaching from the school. To learn, as many children do, only from other children must be wrong, for erroneous ideas and selfish exploitive attitudes are commonplace, and these cheapen the happinesses and responsibilities of sexual behaviour. Adolescent lifestyles are set from a child's home and school, sexual behaviour included. It can hardly be intrusive for schools to do something positive in helping parents with their children's sex education. The class teacher's calm, humour and general attitude when dealing with sex education in a setting of family life and caring relationships, must be an integral part of PSE.

Staff preparation

Many school staffs have usefully debated the following exercise intended to begin the clarification of aims and objectives in PSE.

Select and discuss the order of priority that you give to the following:

(a) individually,
(b) then perhaps with a colleague, as a pair,
(c) in groups, or as a staff.

> Which terms cause misunderstanding, and why?
> Which are beyond the competence of the school and its teachers?
> Are these concepts of adulthood, adolescence, or childhood?

Individual self-esteem
Personal codes of behaviour
Order and discipline
Aesthetic awareness
Social competence in groups
Community codes of behaviour
Leisure interests
Group co-operative behaviour
Security
Enjoyment of all types of relationships
Clear individual attitudes
Knowledge
Privacy
Ability to 'chat' easily
Morals
Family values and attitudes
Sensitivity in feelings
A religious background
Ability to listen
Giving and receiving affection
Kindness
Study skills
Clear masculinity or femininity in behaviour
A cynical view of life
Gentleness
Assertiveness

Many primary schools have prepared themselves by a series of such discussions, sometimes with guests giving talks. Some schools plan and prepare with representatives from parents and the local community. Some expenditure on books is needed, and there will be the preparation of materials before a new PSE approach begins. Pictures and newspaper cuttings often provide ample material for discussion with pupils. Staff from voluntary and statutory agencies with a background of groupwork and counselling can be very helpful.

Evaluation

Measuring the effectiveness of a school's or classroom's planned PSE programme is difficult and likely to be largely guesswork. Children and parents should be asked to give their opinions regularly, local people will comment, and there will usually be shrewd comments from advisers and inspectors, as well from other agencies that work regularly with the school. None of this is 'academic' evaluation, but it is all perfectly acceptable, as is the assessment and reaction of experienced teachers.

What exactly can be measured? Knowledge is measurable, and skills can be seen to be progressing – thoughtful behaviour and discussion abilities, for example. Improvements in learning skills can be assessed. Attitudes can not be easily assessed, though changes in attitude sometimes can be seen – a change of views on racial matters, perhaps? Habits can change and be observed – in cleanliness, eating habits and smoking, for example. Assessing changes in tolerance and responsibility, care and sensitivity, are likely to be parental tasks, though experienced class teachers will observe and have views.

CONCLUSION

PSE is already done in every classroom in some degree. Every teacher answers questions, gives opinions, comments on news items, adds daily to their pupils' accumulating evidence about life. Many subject areas deal with topics mentioned in this chapter. National curriculum guidelines are illustrating co-ordinated and cross-curricular approaches. Religious education can be a powerful area of influence. The example of a professional team of teachers can be a lasting model of relationships in children's minds.

What is now needed, one suggests, is:
- plan a little more carefully;
- extend the range of topics;
- co-operate with colleagues in a co-ordinated progression in a school PSE programme;
- prepare rather more in difficult topic areas – prejudice, for example;
- appreciate the need to use the classroom and its curriculum and teaching methods as a preparation for children's demanding future lives, in partnership with parents;
- reflect again on the fact that learning and learning difficulties have a social and emotional content.

- accept that all children have special educational needs in personal relationships.

REFERENCES AND SUGGESTED READING

Baldwin, J. and Wells, H. (1979–83) *Active Tutorial Work*, Oxford: Blackwell.
Central Advisory Council for Education (1967) *Children and their Primary Schools* (The Plowden Report), London: HMSO.
Curriculum Guidance 3 (1990) *The Whole Curriculum*, York: National Curriculum Council.
Curriculum Guidance 5 (1990) *Health Education*, York: National Curriculum Council.
Curriculum Guidance 8 (1990) *Education for Citizenship*, York: National Curriculum Council.
David, K. and Cowley, J. (1980) *Pastoral Care in Schools and Colleges*, London: Longman.
David, K. and Williams, T. (1987) *Health Education in Schools* (2nd Edition) London: Harper & Row.
David, K. and Charlton, T. (1987) *The Caring Role of the Primary School*, Basingstoke: Macmillan Educational.
Hopson, B. and Scally, M. (1981) *Life Skills Teaching*, Maidenhead: McGraw Hill.
Kirby, N. (1981) *Personal Values in Primary Education*, London: Harper & Row.
Lang, P. (1988) *Thinking About Personal and Social Education in the Primary School*, Oxford: Basil Blackwell.
Pringle, K. (1974) *The Needs of Children*, London: Hutchinson.
Schools Council (1977) *Health Education 5–13 Project*, London: Nelson.
Stonier, T. (1983) *The Wealth of Information – a Profile of the Post Industrial Society*, London: Thames/Methuen.
Whitfield, R. (1983) *Family Structures, Lifestyles and the Care of Children*, Aston University: Educational Monograph 9.

Part III

Support for learning within the classroom

Part III examines ways in which children's learning can be supported within their own classroom.

In Chapter 14, Kevin Jones and Tony Charlton examine the responsibilities which must be shared between professionals, participants and parents. The practical use of a simple 'forecasting device' illustrates how members of a team can jointly plan and provide for the special educational needs of primary aged pupils.

The theme of partnership with pupils is developed in Chapter 15, in which Susan Jones emphasises the importance of collaborative enquiry-based learning and training.

Finally, in Chapter 16 Marie Buckland discusses a number of ways in which microtechnology can help children gain access to the breadth of the curriculum within the context of their own classrooms.

Chapter 14

Special educational provision

A shared responsibility

Kevin Jones and Tony Charlton

INTRODUCTION

An acknowledgement of the breadth and depth of a pupil's educational needs (see Chapter 3), together with an understanding of factors which contribute towards that child's successes and difficulties in learning (see Chapters 1 and 2) leads to an acceptance that it is not possible to conduct an in depth assessment of a pupil's special educational needs in a context which is different from the one in which the child functions on a daily basis. Since that learning context (the school and the home) has a big impact upon a child's successes and difficulties, it will have to be changed in certain ways to ensure that the child receives the most appropriate form of educational provision. It has been suggested (Jones *et al.* 1986) that it is the bringing together of key players within that learning environment (teachers, parents, pupils and other professionals) which will make for the most effective planning of educational experiences for those children who encounter difficulties in learning. Thus, it is the skills, knowledge and insights of the classteacher, the perspectives of the special educational needs support teacher, the observations of parents and other professionals, and the views of the pupils themselves, which make for such effective planning.

Hodgson, Clunies-Ross and Hegarty (1984) stressed that the subject-teacher and the specialist-teacher have much to learn from one another, and by working together they can tailor special educational provision to the developing and changing needs of the pupil concerned. They also argue that a high level of collaboration needs to take place from the planning stage when content, materials, and methodologies are first discussed, through the teaching stage (when special resources and support mechanisms are often required) and on to the review and evaluation stage when an evaluation of the pupil's achievements are made.

There is also a considerable body of advice which suggests that teachers and parents can usefully work together in active partnership (DES, 1978, Para 4.29; ILEA, 1985, Ch. 14). It has been suggested that this viewpoint is founded upon the belief that:

> through the sharing of information, advice and practical support, the resultant

assessment of, and subsequent provision for, special educational needs, will reach a level which neither the teacher nor the parent (or other professional) would have been able to achieve on their own.

(Jones *et al.* 1989)

Other commentators and researchers (Widlake and MacLeod, 1984; Wolfendale, 1986) draw attention to considerable advances in the development of effective working relationships between parents and professionals, particularly within the area of reading.

Whilst the above comment stresses the benefits and importance of a sharing of educational responsibility, the complexities of the task must not be overlooked:

* working relationships will need to be developed carefully
* various viewpoints will have to be co-ordinated into a simple, yet effective, plan of action
* time will have to be managed efficiently.

Each of these aspects will now be discussed in turn.

THE DEVELOPMENT OF GOOD WORKING RELATIONSHIPS

The success of any joint planning venture will depend upon the level of co-operation which can be achieved between each key member of the team (e.g. classteacher, special educational needs support teacher, headteacher, welfare assistant, parents, pupil and other professionals).

The extent to which the joint planning process is to be shared will be signalled from the earliest stages. For example, if an educational psychologist, or special educational needs support teacher, presents him/herself as the 'expert' to guide others (e.g. classteacher/parents) this is likely to encourage the 'guided' to assume a more passive role.

Cunningham and Davis (1985) describe three ways of working with parents, each of which gives a good indication of the degree to which a school wishes to incorporate them into the educational process. Cunningham and Davis' models are also applicable to other groups of professionals working together, as discussed below.

In the first model, one member of the team is presented as an expert. For example, a special educational needs support teacher might decide to conduct an assessment of a child's special educational needs outside the classroom, without consulting the classteacher or the child's parents. The results of the tests might then be used as the basis for advice about the best ways of providing for that particular child's needs. The support teacher is clearly assuming the role of 'expert', since neither the classteacher nor the parents were consulted.

A more active form of participation is developed in the transplant model within which certain aspects of one professional's expertise is transferred to others, who might be able to use it. Whilst this model involves other members of the team more actively, it retains a high level of dependence upon the professional who initiates the transformation. Paired reading schemes are a good example of the transformational model. The 'skilled professional' trains other members of the team (e.g. parents/welfare assistants) to use a particular technique whilst reading with children. Whilst this approach can be very successful, it fails to recognise the full potential of those members of the team, who could take a more active part in the planning, implementation and evaluation of the special educational provision.

The acceptance of their 'equivalent expertise' is more evident in the consumer model, where parents, pupils or classteachers, as consumers of a service, are considered to have important contributions to make regarding the educational provision which is made. If this equivalent expertise is acknowledged then a high level of shared responsibility is likely to emerge. This, in turn, will lead to a level of assessment and provision which could not have been achieved by any one member of the team working in isolation.

The first task, then, in developing a positive sharing of educational responsibilities is to create conditions whereby suitably co-operative relationships can emerge. Jones *et al.* (1989) indicate that this can be achieved through four stages:

1   The introductory stage
2   The informative stage
3   The joint provision stage
4   The shared-responsibilities stage

The introductory stage

At the beginning of any new working relationship each member of the team will need to become aware of: the expectations which are being made of them and the benefits which are likely to accrue. Time should be taken to discuss the aims and intentions behind the development of the working relationship. Partners should be introduced to each other in a setting in which they can develop 'a mutual understanding and respect for each other's intentions towards a particular pupil' (Jones *et al.* 1989).

The rationale behind a joint planning approach should be brought out into the open, so that each member of the team understands the reasons for working together. This stage in the development of a shared responsibility is often overlooked.

The informative stage

Once the basis of the working relationship has been established, the focus of attention can shift towards a particular child in whom members of the team have a mutual interest. At this stage, activities can be directed towards the sharing of information about the child. Thus, members of the team can begin to build up a picture of the child's interests, successes and needs and begin to adjust the particular aspects of educational provision for which they are responsible, be that at school or within the home.

The joint-provision stage

The joint-provision stage should flow on naturally from the informative stage, during which each member of the team responded to the collective information about the child's needs in their own way. At the joint-provision stage attempts are made to co-ordinate the various activities. Joint-provision can be made either:

- at class/group/individual level within the school (e.g. with parent/support teacher working alongside the classteacher). Thomas (1986) discusses ways in which classteachers and classroom assistants can work together, or
- for a particular child in their own home (e.g. paired or shared reading).

In each case various members of the team agree upon the provision which is to be made before it is implemented.

The sharing of responsibilities stage

By the time this stage is reached, members of the team will have experienced ways in which educational responsibilities can be shared. The 'sharing of responsibilities' stage attempts to merge roles even further. It is based upon the belief that an adequate assessment of, and provision for, learning difficulties is dependent upon contributions from each member of the team. The main aims should be to:

(a) gather together information about the child's successes and difficulties in learning (see Chapters 1 and 2);
(b) describe the child's special learning needs on the basis of the information gained at (a);
(c) advise each other about the forms of provision which might best meet the child's special learning needs;
(d) support each other in providing the most appropriate learning experiences for the child concerned (see also Chapter 15).

This process has the potential to yield a lot of information about a particular child's special learning needs. It is also likely that a multitude of different approaches will be suggested to provide for those needs. This information will need to be distilled into a simple, manageable, yet appropriate, plan of action.

A relatively simple, yet appropriate, recording format which encourages the joint planning of appropriate educational experiences can be seen in the forecasting device at Figure 14.1 (Jones et al. 1986). A three column format is used so that assessment information can be translated into jointly planned learning

FORECAST   NAME ....

	Small group support	Class based activities	Home
O r a l l a n g			
R e a d i n g			
S p e l l i n g			
M a t h s			
G e o g r a p h y			

Figure 14.1

activities for the child. Notes in the form of *aides-mémoire* about planned learning experiences can be written in each column. The classteacher, support-teacher, parents and other interested parties (e.g. welfare assistants or voluntary helpers) can decide where they can make the most effective input either during classroom work, in small group sessions, or at home.

The three column format also helps to ensure that the work is co-ordinated and that the learning experiences are related to, or part of, the main curriculum. For example, the classteacher will be in a position to inform other members of the team (e.g the special educational needs support teacher) about the 'mainstream' learning experiences which have been planned for the class. Small group support work can then be planned to facilitate access to the mainstream curriculum. 'Remedial work' has often been criticised for being unrelated to, or less stimulating than, the work which is experienced by the majority of pupils (DES, 1983). The process of joint planning, which is supported by the forecast sheet, helps to guard against the recurrence of such unrelated and unstimulating provision.

The forecasting process works most effectively when members of the team:

(a) identify the successes and difficulties encountered by a particular child and clarify the likely causes of those successes and difficulties (see Chapters 1 and 2);

(b) discuss and record notes which summarise the particular needs of the child concerned;

(c) decide upon the most appropriate learning experiences, teaching methods, resources and support strategies in order that the child's needs will be met in the most appropriate way.

The following comments explain the three vertical columns of the forecast sheet in more detail.

Small group support

Small group support can take place in a number of locations, such as in the classroom, a resource base, around the school or locality. Wherever it takes place it should be allied to the mainstream curriculum.

Class based activities

Classteachers have a very useful contribution to make regarding their own intimate knowledge of the child, his or her performance in class, and their own curricular aims and objectives. Their contribution to the planning of special educational provision is vital if the child's access to the breadth of the national curriculum is to be maximised. This level of joint planning also provides an ideal opportunity for staff development.

Home

Parents often have a very good knowledge of their child's strengths, interests and needs. This information can influence the success of special educational provision and should be used in the planning process. Parents can also become actively involved in providing for their child's needs. Webb, Webb and Eccles (1985) showed how parents and classteachers were able to plan and implement an extended, but coherent and effective form of special educational provision.

The forecast can also be divided horizontally according to the areas of the curriculum in which the child is experiencing difficulties. For example, a child might experience particular difficulties in spoken language, reading, spelling, mathematics and geography. The forecast should reflect the child's rights of access to the breadth of the curriculum and not be limited to a consideration of difficulties in the 'basic' subjects.

The forecast can be used to plan for periods of time which will vary according to the severity of a particular child's special educational needs. For some children it may be necessary to forecast on a daily 'precision' basis. For others it may be feasible to provide a forecast on a weekly basis or over an even longer period of time.

An example of a completed forecast sheet (Jones *et al.* 1986) is shown at Figure 14.2. Activities were designed to respond to John's difficulties and success in oral language, reading, writing, maths and emotional/organisational areas. Later forecasts examined difficulties which John experiences in Geography, History and Religious Education.

THE MANAGEMENT OF TIME

Many teachers are frustrated by an apparent lack of time to plan and provide for the special educational needs of children in their classes. The solution, as ironic as it seems, is to find 'time' to save time. Time *must* be built into the working schedule of key members of the team (e.g. support teacher, classteacher and parents) to allow for the planning of special, educational provision. If developed appropriately, the forecasting format encourages a 'sharing' in both the planning and provision. A busy classteacher might not be able to give a labour intensive response to a particular child's difficulties. However, the involvement of parents, voluntary helpers and welfare assistants might help to provide the experiences which are considered important for a child's success.

A sharing of responsibility

The above account emphasises key roles which each member of the team must play in the planning of special educational provision. This chapter concludes by reviewing a whole range of roles which must be shared by members of the team,

Pupil's Name: John

	Small group support	Class based activities	Parents
O r a l	Targeted development of talk connected with reasoning based upon the class topic of space.		Selected activities from *Looking and Thinking. Reading and Thinking.*
	Development of small group stories on to tape (Space Theme).	Selective use of *Concept 7–9 materials.*	With guidance from SEN support teacher.
	Intro, why, because what would you do if? Elements into stories.	Talk to group about aircraft.	
R e a d i n g	Prepared reading activities on tape stressing intonation, and encouraging children to predict outcomes of the story.	Read to find out activities based upon: (a) own readers based on space theme: (b) chosen published reading materials. Paired reading with peers based on class intensive reading project. Use of index and dictionary.	Paired reading as demonstrated by SEN support teacher. Shared reading based upon plays. Read to find out focus.
W r i t i n g d e v	Demonstration of the use of a language-experience approach (basis of *Breakthrough to Literacy* materials). Alternate sentence-writing with teachers.	Variety of real writing purposes using the *Breakthrough* materials and a computer programme (sentence-maker) based upon the space theme. Cartoon book on space. Cloze passages based upon above reading materials, to highlight certain reading clues.	

S **p** **e** **l** **l** **i** **n** **g**	Discussion of look/cover write/check and other aspects of a visual letter-strings approach. Targeting of spelling programme with the child including high-frequency usage words (Ashgate list).	Use of a word-bank approach. Supported by a computer programme and word search activities to facilitate the above writing purposes.
M **a** **t** **h** **s**	Focus upon the concept of monetary exchange and addition to 10.	
	Selected group games based upon the above targets.	Shopping games and making something happen with maths activities, consolidated with selected use of support sheets.
E **m** **o** **t** **i** **o** **n** **a** **l**	Labelled pack of required resources fading to own organization of required items.	Organisation of own resources in class with positive praise for items remembered.
		Self-regulating aspects, e.g. getting out of bed, getting dressed – set targets and rewards.

Figure 14.2

if special educational provision is to fulfil the aim of giving children access to the breadth and the depth of the national curriculum. The roles are presented under the four headings of:

1   The recognition of special education needs
2   Organisation and management
3   Teaching/counselling
4   Liaison

1 The recognition of special educational needs

Class/subject teachers, special educational needs support teachers, pupils, head-teachers, governors, parents and other professionals should consult with regard to:

(a) the identification of children who experience difficulties in learning;
(b) the causes of a child's successes and difficulties in learning;
(c) the relevance of factors within the curriculum as potential contributors to the successes and learning difficulties which children encounter;
(d) the key part to be played by probing discussions with individuals and with groups of pupils when attempting to recognise the cause of a learning difficulty;
(e) the relevance of reading, language, numeracy, conceptual and procedural levels used in various lessons and supportive resources;
(f) the supervision and correct administration of appropriate standardised and non-standardised tests as part of a comprehensive monitoring and screening procedure across the curriculum;
(g) the use of classroom observation procedures in developing an understanding of a pupil's special educational needs;
(h) the diagnostic information to be gleaned from class assignments and assessment exercises;
(i) the monitoring of progress and the maintenance of suitable records;
(j) the transition between various phases of education, year groups and classes for pupils with special educational needs.

2 Organisation and management role

(a) the development of jointly planned teaching approaches, suited to pupils' special educational needs;
(b) supporting pupils with social, physical and behavioural problems;
(c) monitoring arrangements for teaching individuals and groups where the nature of the problem makes it impossible for pupils' needs to be met unsupported within the normal classroom (to include arrangements for pre- and post-lesson teaching);
(d) making arrangements for the short-term educational needs of certain indi-

vidual pupils, who may have returned to school after a long period of illness, family bereavement, or have joined the school from a special school/unit;

(e) managing the involvement of ancillary and voluntary workers within the classroom;

(f) the planning and co-ordination of the curriculum, pastoral arrangements and the allocation of resources in relation to pupils with special educational needs;

(g) guiding pupils, parents and colleagues on the choice of subjects or courses and the design of individualised forms of provision where necessary.

3 Teaching/counselling

It is envisaged that members of the team will be jointly responsible with the special educational needs support teacher for the preparation and implementation of support strategies in all areas of the curriculum in order to facilitate learning. Many of the roles within this section could be carried out within a co-operative teaching situation.

(a) initiating and developing ideas and techniques for the whole range of children with special educational needs;

(b) working co-operatively with colleagues to develop methods of dealing with learning difficulties across and through subject areas;

(c) examining the appropriateness of the curriculum offered to children with special educational needs;

(d) building up an understanding of the range of materials and approaches available to facilitate learning and the associated matching of appropriate resources to children's special learning requirements;

(e) working towards the development of appropriate grouping and setting procedures;

(f) the preparation and implementation of a forecast of learning experiences specifically designed on the basis of an individualised assessment of special educational needs;

(g) supporting children with social, physical and behavioural problems;

(h) offering help regarding the clarification of aspects of language connected with assignments;

(i) working in a preventative way by helping to dissipate feelings of disillusionment and alienation from school, and enable pupils to complete assignments and gain from their relative success.

4 Liaison

(a) liaising with colleagues and convening such groups as necessary within the school to meet the needs of children with special educational needs;

(b) liaising with other schools and with educational support services, such as SEN Advisory and Support services, school psychological services, advisory and para-medical agencies;

(c) liaising with parents, encouraging their equal participation in the educational and general development of their child;

(d) liaising with appropriate professional agencies dealing with social, health, welfare and professional guidance;

(e) liaising with the community at large, drawing on the strengths of individuals and groups to help children with special educational needs;

(f) participating with colleagues in staff development programmes concerned with special educational needs.

REFERENCES

Cunningham, C. and Davis, H. (1985) *Working with Parents: Frameworks for Collaboration*, Milton Keynes: Open University Press.

Department of Education and Science (1978) *Special Educational Needs*, The Warnock Report, London: HMSO.

Hodgson, A., Clunies-Ross, L. and Hegarty, S. (1984) *Learning Together*, Slough: NFER-Nelson.

ILEA (1985) *Educational Opportunities for All*, London: ILEA.

Jones, K. *et al.* (1986) 'Support for learning in service children's schools (North-West Europe)', *Support for Learning*, vol. 1 (4).

Jones, K. *et al.* (1989) 'Working with parents' in Charlton, T. and David, K. (eds) *Managing Misbehaviour*, Basingstoke: Macmillan Education.

Thomas, G. (1986) 'Integrating personnel in order to integrate children', *Support for Learning*, vol. 1, (1).

Webb, M., Webb, T. and Eccles, G. (1985) 'Parental participation in the teaching of reading', *Remedial Education*, vol. 20 (2).

Widlake, P. and McLeod, F. (1984) *Raising Standards. Parental Involvement*, Programmes and the Language Performance of Children, Coventry: Lea Community Education Development Centre.

Wolfendale, S. (1986) 'Involving parents in behavioural management, a whole-school approach', *Support for Learning*, vol. 1, (4) 32–8.

Chapter 15

Collaborative enquiry-based learning and training

Susan Jones

Susan Jones

LIPMAN'S 'PHILOSOPHY FOR CHILDREN' PROGRAMME AND OTHER RECENT EDUCATIONAL INITIATIVES

> Stenhouse argued that if the teacher was serious about promoting decision making then the student must be helped not only to think and enquire *but made to feel that the process was worthwhile because his or her own viewpoint mattered.*
>
> (Tones, 1987a, p. 36, [my italics])

Underpinning this statement is the view that has increasing support today, namely: the most effective way of encouraging individuals to 'think and enquire' is by employing a teaching strategy which makes them 'feel that their own viewpoint mattered'. Such a strategy has variously been called 'equal-footing', 'democratic', 'participatory', 'collaborative, enquiry-based'; and it is vital for nuturing the individual's self-esteem, now generally accepted to be a necessary precondition for promoting academic achievement (see Jones, 1988a, p. 33).

The importance of self-esteem is recognised by Matthew Lipman in his 'philosophy for children' thinking skills programme (Lipman *et al.* 1980). On the surface the programme might be construed as a purely cognitive exercise to increase children's reasoning skills. However, it incorporates a definitive *affective* element which closely parallels the 'equal-footing' approach prescribed by counselling programmes (*c.f.* Cant and Spackman, 1985), which can be summarised as follows:

(a) adopt a non-judgemental, non-authoritarian and anti-doctrinal approach;
(b) encourage the pupils to express their views on what they are interested in rather than impose your views on them;
(c) *listen* to the pupils, and indicate that what they say makes you think (i.e. give importance to what they say, treat them as equals).

(see Lipman *et al.* 1979, pp. i, ii)

This 'counselling' (affective) component is inextricably linked with the programme's 'rationality' (cognitive) element and needs to be so, for how else is 'the learner' effectively to grasp the tools of rational thought (so necessary for the confident handling of concepts and skills in any area of learning) unless the tools are introduced in an environment which promotes their use, i.e. through genuine open enquiry where 'the teacher' interacts with 'the learner' as an equal (see Lane and Lane [Jones], 1986).

In fact, the goal of Lipman's programme is not merely to develop children's formal reasoning ability but, through open 'collaborative' group discussion, to help:

> the child become a reasonable, imaginative and self-critical individual in a democratic society ... if the first is accomplished without the second, the child will have become little more than a piece of reasoning equipment in search of a programmer.
>
> (Lipman, 1985, p. 34)

As well as leading to improvements in formal and informal logic, therefore, the programme has led to statistically significant improvements in reading and mathematics, and to improvements in the broader characteristics of critical thinking, fluency and flexibility of thought, interpersonal relationships and social skills. Also the positive effect of the programme has not been restricted to any particular level or 'ability', but has occurred in a wide spectrum of children, ranging from the 'gifted' to those that are classed as 'learning disabled' for some reason or another. (See, for example, BBC (1990) for a demonstration of the success of Lipman's method for combating severe learning difficulties in the classroom.) It has been claimed that the success of the programme rests on the fact that children come to perceive themselves as thinkers who ought to be taken seriously by adults as well as other children (see Lane and Lane [Jones] 1986, p. 265 for references).

Against a background of various issues of interest and importance to children provided by a series of novels (references in Lane and Lane [Jones], 1986), the programme encourages children to build on one another's ideas; it tries to get children to see the implications of what they say; it tries to get pupils to become aware of their own assumptions; it tries to encourage pupils to find reasons to justify their own beliefs; it encourages the development of alternative modes of thought and imagination, etc. The broad aim of Lipman's 'reasoning skills' programme, therefore, is to promote a general critical awareness and autonomy in children, i.e. independent and rational decision-making skills in a moral, social, and political context. In this it parallels the underlying aims of many other recent educational initiatives. For example, in the area of personal and social education (see Chapter 13) there is the call to give children 'the capacity to come to reasoned judgement ... and the independence in making moral judgements' (Schools Council, 1981, pp. 21, 22); encouraging 'an attitude to authority and to "taken for granted rules" that ... becomes increasingly questioning of the principles behind the rules' (Pring, 1984, pp. 74, 75). In the area of health education one aim is 'to provide individuals with "lifeskills" which will contribute to their belief in their capacity to challenge government and ... with actual competencies – such as political and assertiveness skills – to enable them to do so' (Tones, 1987b, p. 46). Those involved in media studies aim to encourage the pupil 'to posit alternatives; [demonstrating] the importance and strength of group experience; and [considering] the wide range of social, aesthetic, industrial, political and philosophic issues' (Masterman, 1980, p. 12). And, in certain problem-solving programmes the need to use a broad, open-minded, critical, 'equal partners' approach for the development of self-reliance and self-organisation in all spheres of life, is stressed (Brown, 1985).

Lipman's approach also closely coincides with the aims of multicultural education. As the following quote indicates, a key factor in this context is the development of listening skills:

> Listening is not an easy skill for children to learn in an environment where, for the most part, the only person they must listen to is the teacher. And it is not easy for any of us to listen carefully to views that conflict with our own. But it can hardly be denied that, in a multi-racial society which at least pays lip service to toleration, such an ability has the highest importance ...
>
> (Whalley, 1987.)

The traditional 'hierarchy' relationship between teacher and pupil, therefore, militates against a climate of tolerance and consideration towards others. In contrast the overall aim of Lipman's group-discussion programme is to enable what he calls a 'community of inquiry' to evolve, where people learn over time to co-operate with each other, question underlying assumptions, and listen carefully and respectfully to the ways in which other people express how things appear to them from other perspectives (1985, p. 35).

There is then a general agreement between many recent educational initiatives about what the goals of education are. There is also, as has already been referred to, a broad agreement on how these goals might be best achieved, namely, by employing a participatory, 'collaborative, enquiry-based' strategy. As long ago as the 1940s it was demonstrated by Lewin that the autocratic/didactic approach to teaching was much less effective than democratic, group-discussion methods in influencing people's habits, values and attitudes (e.g. Lewin, 1947). From work such as Lewin's it seems that the more an individual participates in the information interchange process, the more likely s/he is to adopt a different and more enlightened outlook, and the more likely s/he is to act upon it. This fact is well encapsulated by Blumberg's claim that 'Participation ... [gratifies] basic human needs for respect, appreciation, responsibility, and autonomy' (1968, p. 130), which provides psychological grounds for the importance of participation in social relations. Hence the need to employ a democratic 'equal-footing' strategy which will make people feel their viewpoint mattered, enhance their self-esteem and their confidence in their ability to question existing situations, and so encourage their participation in the learning/decision-making process.

However, despite the evidence that has been produced since Lewin for the superiority of democratic, group-discussion methods for fostering critical aware-ness and individual autonomy (for examples see Blumberg, 1968); and attempts like Stenhouse's Humanities Curriculum Project to introduce a democratic approach into schools (Schools Council, 1970), such approaches have largely failed to influence educational practice. How, therefore, can the general lip-service that is paid to the importance of participatory, 'child-centred' approaches, be translated into true practice? Consideration of the four main factors responsible for the ineffectualness of democratic strategies up until now, points to one key factor which is paramount to future needs. The four factors are:

1   an imbalance of the 'rationality-counselling' components in the approach used;
2   too late an introduction of the 'collaborative-participatory' approach in schools;
3   external socio-economic pressures on attempts to increase democratic par-ticipation beyond that which exists in society in general;
4   inadequate to no provision for training teachers in collaborative-partici-patory interaction skills.

Factor 1 – The 'rationality-counselling' balance

For many educational initiatives there is a tendency not to give enough attention to exactly how the above-referred to goals are to be achieved by the teacher, much beyond acknowledging the broad need to employ a collaborative-partici-patory approach to enhance pupil self-esteem. Those programmes that do go further and prescribe a definite teaching approach tend to fall short of providing a comprehensive strategy. For example, the admirable group counselling programme of Cant and Spackman referred to earlier (1985), which prescribes the teacher to be 'non-evaluative and non-censorious', and to 'encourage, guide and respond as an equal to pupils' talk', does not indicate how the teacher is to achieve this 'encouraging and guiding'. A pointer to what this might be is provided by Charlton (1985) who has extended the group counselling approach to include the teacher promoting inferential thinking by: (a) encouraging the pupils to identify and discuss which actions lead to particular outcomes, and; (b) asking pupils to suggest, and demonstrate, alternative behaviours which might promote successful outcomes in particular settings.

This coincides with the kind of thinking which Lipman's programme aims to develop, and illustrates how effective counselling requires a 'rationality' (cogni-tive) component – a further indication of the inextricable link between the affec-tive and cognitive domains referred to above (Lane and Lane [Jones], 1986). Also, although counselling programmes stress the need to foster positive affective characteristics in 'the learner', by not spelling out how the teacher is to be 'non-evaluative', 'non-censorious', and 'respond as an equal', they leave open the possibility that the teacher will unintentionally fall back on an unequal, judgemental and censorious approach with pupils. In general, therefore, using Cant and Spackman's work as a model, it can be said that there is a tendency for counselling programmes to fall short in the strategy they prescribe, both in terms of an incomplete affective component and a neglected cognitive component.

Conversely, other programmes prescribe strategies which tend to stress the cognitive at the expense of the affective. Examples of this tendency are problem-solving initiatives (1), Feuerstein's Instrumental Enrichment programme (see Feuerstein, 1980), and de Bono's 'Thinking' programmes (e.g. de Bono, 1976). Feuerstein's programme, for example, although it acknowledges the need for the teacher to increase a pupil's independence and self-confidence, prescribes a model of dialogue to teachers which is more teacher-directed and judgemental than is required to achieve an effective 'counselling' (affective) component (1980, p. 293 ff.). Furthermore, there is a tendency for all three initiatives mentioned to use mainly cognitive exercises which lack moral, social and political content, and which consequently do not relate to the pupils' own personal and social experiences, beliefs and values. Concerning this aspect of Feuerstein's programme Mays comments:

> an individual could learn to master technical skills in a closed society, but he still might not be able to develop an adequate understanding of values, and this would affect his judgement on moral, social and aesthetic questions.
>
> (Mays, 1985, p. 156)

What is different about Lipman's 'philosophy for children' programme is that it recognises the importance of employing a fine balance of affective and cognitive factors, and thereby attempts to provide a comprehensive and coherent strategy for teachers to effectively promote the learner's self-esteem and participation in rational enquiry. It is a strategy, therefore, which is likely to be more effective than less 'balanced' ones for achieving the goals set by the various educational initiatives referred to above. In this way Lipman's programme complements rather than opposes these other initiatives (2); and it follows that the latter would benefit from using teachers who are trained in the 'collaborative, enquiry-based' teacher-pupil interaction skills Lipman's programme prescribes. On this basis, therefore, there are grounds for the provision of teacher training courses in Lipman's technique.

Factors 2 and 3 – Stage of introduction of the 'collaborative-participatory' approach in school and socio-economic pressures

Children's attitudes and beliefs are strongly influenced by social and economic structures within the family and the broader social environment. In the area of political education, for example, White refers to research on children's attitudes to foreign people which indicates that:

> strong political attitudes develop in under-11s in the absence of much political

knowledge ... attitudes which remain firmly embedded in pupils' minds so that attempts at systematic political education in early adolescence have little noticeable affect on them. (1983, p. 111)

Combining this fact with evidence that primary school children are able to operate with political and economic concepts, she goes on to ask why we should not 'try at an earlier stage to marry knowledge and attitudes more rationally?' (p. 111). Indeed it would seem evident that to be effective the deployment of 'collaborative-participatory' methods should not be piecemeal, to be brought in at some particular (and later) stage, but would need to be consistently operative from the inception of the schooling process.

Broad socio-economic pressures also influence the attitudes of parents, teachers, school governors, LEA advisers and the school organisation, and these can work against the effective introduction of democratic-participatory methods in the classroom (see Lane, Lane [Jones] and Pritchard, 1986). In this context Sockett writes: 'One can think of no greater recipe for chaos than a curriculum which celebrates autonomy and a school social structure which inhibits and diminishes it' (1975, p. 43). And similarly White comments:

> In so far as pupils are getting a picture of an indefensible authoritarianism they are being led into an inconsistency. There is *talk* of democratic ideals, practices, etc., but they see that [the organisation of their school is] actually being run on anti-democratic lines. (1983, p. 93)

As was the case for factor (1) above, it will be considered below how this aspect would be alleviated by the provision of effective teacher training in the collaborative-participatory approach.

Factor 4 – The provision of effective teacher training in the 'collaborative-participatory approach'

Teachers are not adequately prepared by present training provision to use an approach in the classroom which does not rely on the traditional authority, knowledge-based model. Consequently, although there has been an outward appearance of a move towards more democratic, child-centred procedures in the form of classroom/lesson arrangement and appropriate verbal allegiance, most teachers do not achieve a true democratic 'equal-footing', collaborative relationship with pupils. The skill required by the teacher to effect a genuine 'participatory' approach should not be underestimated, and accordingly the key to the successful use of such an approach in schools lies in training. Concerning the kind of training required Whalley writes: 'since what is in question is a practical skill – moreover a fairly complex and difficult one, [an important] part of the training must involve actual practice with children' (1987, p. 276). In other words there would be a need to employ a training course which would effectively provide the teacher with a practical skill, and an appropriate vehicle for this is the approach used by Joyce and Showers (1980, p. 380) which contains the following main components:

(a) initial theoretical input – presentation of theory or description of skill or strategy;
(b) practical demonstration in a real situation to follow (a) immediately;
(c) opportunity for students/teachers to practise in a classroom setting;
(d) constructive feedback to (c) with coaching.

Such an approach is necessary because just didactically telling teachers about collaborative-participatory methods – which is essentially the form teacher education takes today – is not likely to influence classroom practice. In addition, there is need to show the relevant approach and give a chance to practise in a classroom situation.

But how each of the components – 'theory', 'practical demonstration' and 'practise with feedback' – is conducted, is also of consequence for the effectiveness of the training. In line with the view that democratic, group-discussion procedures are more likely to influence people's attitudes and behaviour (c.f. Lewin, 1947, referred to above), it would follow that a collaborative, enquiry-based approach to training – a non-evaluative, non-judgemental, equal-footing approach – would be more effective than the traditional evaluative, authority, knowledge-based training model (c.f. Boydell, 1986). In other words, a didactic approach to training is just as likely to fail to impart collaborative-participatory interaction skills to teachers, as it has failed to influence the values, attitudes and behaviour of pupils. Each stage of the training scheme, therefore, would require a collaborative-participatory lecturer-student/teacher relationship in order to be effective. This corresponds to the view of Lipman *et al.* who believe that training will fail unless it uses an identical instructional approach to that which is to be used in the classroom:

> If teachers are expected to conduct dialogues, then they must be provided with opportunities to engage in philosophical dialogues themselves.... If teachers are expected to elicit questioning behaviour on the part of their students, then they must be taught by educators who themselves model such behaviour in the teacher-training sessions. If teachers are expected to teach children how to reason, then they must be given practice in reasoning such as they will expect from their students. (1980, p. 47)

Accordingly, the first stage of the training would need to consist of the students/ teachers experiencing the programme in the same way as the pupils for whom it is designed. In this manner they experience the collaborative, enquiry-based pedagogic approach first hand and thereby are given the opportunity to develop their own critical faculties. This latter point is a crucial and necessary aspect of any effective training course in collaborative-participatory interaction skills. It is recognised, for example, in the area of health education, where it has been pointed out that if educators are to raise 'critical consciousness' they must first become critically aware (see Jones (1988b) for references). Likewise, Klein, in the area of multicultural education maintains:

> The children need to develop their own critical faculties: they need to begin to make their own judgements, to accumulate their own evidence ... *But sometimes it's the teachers that need to learn these things as well.* (1988; my italics)

The collaborative-participatory lecturer-student interaction in the third/fourth 'practice/feedback' phase would be in contrast to the traditional apprenticeship-style of teaching practice supervision, and therefore would require effective training for supervisors. Once again, for the reasons given above, such training would need to be conducted on collaborative-participatory lines (see Boydell, 1986).

A pilot INSET training course which used a participatory 'doing' approach along the above lines proved effective, in a very short time, in empowering the teachers themselves to deploy the 'collaborative' technique with children both within the college and school environment (Jones, 1989 (a), pp. 11, 12). An existing format which would also allow for the deployment of the scheme would be the IT-INSET approach (Ashton *et al.* 1983), where tutors regularly work with small groups of students and teachers in their own classrooms. This approach would be appropriate for effecting 'a [self-critical] community of enquiry' (Lipman *et al.* 1980, p. 45), which could simultaneously involve all the participants in the learning process, namely, pupils, students, teachers, lecturers (and parents). And significantly this would be in line with the aims of critical action research to establish 'self-critical communities of people participating and collaborating in all phases of the research process' (Henry and Kemmis, 1985). Kemmis, in justifying the need for 'action research', maintains that teachers likely to be involved in reform will need to have a coherent social and political perspective, and he sees the role of the teacher as:

> critical curriculum developer and researcher in the context of the school, participating with others in the wider process of educational reform – engaged not only in changing his or her own practices, but also in reforming educational institutions.
>
> (Kemmis, 1986, p. 52)

It can be concluded regarding phase 3, therefore, that teachers and head teachers trained in collaborative-participatory skills in the manner suggested above, will have their own 'critical consciousness' raised, and consequently they will be more equipped to influence the structure of their own schools to accommodate collaborative-participatory relationships with pupils. (See also Jones, 1989 (b), for the underlying importance of this approach to the future viability of teacher education.)

CONCLUSION

Lipman's 'philosophy for children' programme incorporates a 'balanced' and comprehensive affective-cognitive strategy which can be used to enhance self-esteem, critical awareness and autonomy in the learner. Also, and perhaps more importantly, it provides a vehicle for inculcating collaborative-participatory interaction skills in teachers, a necessary precondition for the successful introduction of collaborative, enquiry-based learning into schools. An underlying aim of a training course using this technique would be to raise the reasoning ability and critical consciousness of teachers, where personal concerns and prejudices could be aired, so influencing existing values, attitudes, beliefs and behaviours. It is only through such a training process that educators will achieve the skills of listening, empathy, open-mindedness, tolerance, self-appraisal, and the genuineness necessary for conducting a true collaborative-participatory approach with pupils. And it is only this way that school structures are likely to be changed to accommodate such an approach.

At the end of the 1960s two leading educationists were voicing the following beliefs concerning democratic procedures and training:

> From the outset [the teacher's] efforts must coincide with those of the students to engage in critical thinking and the quest for mutual humanization.... To achieve this, he must be a partner of the students in his relations with them... The students – no longer docile listeners – are now critical co-investigators in dialogue with the teacher.
>
> (Freire, 1970, pp. 49, 54)

> This new pattern of teaching radically changes teacher-pupil relationships and has profound implications for the authority structure of the school. Schools are not likely to succeed in the changeover if they won't face a move from authoritarianism. Teachers are not likely to succeed without some retraining.
>
> (Stenhouse, 1969, p. 128)

And prophetically Stenhouse concludes:

> My own view is that if the financial and institutional support is forthcoming, it will make a lot of difference in the 20 years after the raising of the leaving age in 1971. (p. 128)

Over twenty years on, Lipman's 'philosophy for children' programme represents the same goals and aspirations. Educators cannot afford to continue to ignore these views, and teachers need to seek and request the provision of effective practical skills training in the collaborative-participatory strategy, and head teachers and LEA advisers will need to budget for the general provision of such training, if they are serious about introducing a genuine 'partnership with pupils' in our schools.

NOTES

1. Exceptions to this include the broad-based approach of Brown *et al.* referred to above.
2. This is not so for de Bono's 'Thinking' courses which put strict limits on discussion and its value, in contrast to Lipman's programme which considers dialogue to be central to the learning process.

REFERENCES

Ashton, P.M.E., Henderson, E.S., Herbert, J.E. and Mortimer, D.J. (1938) *Teacher Education in the Classroom: initial and in-service*, Beckenham: Croom Helm.

BBC (1990) *The Transformers – Socrates for 6 Year-Olds*, BBC2, 11th October.

Blumberg, P. (1968) *Industrial Democracy: the sociology of participation*, London: Constable.

Boydell, D. (1986) 'Issues in teaching practice supervision research: a review of the literature', *Journal of Teaching Studies*, vol. 2, no. 1, pp. 115–25.

Brown, C.H. *et al.* (1985) *TVEI-Related In-Service Training* (TRIST), research document, Walsall LEA and West Midlands College of Higher Education.

Cant, R. and Spackman, P. (1985) 'Self-Esteem, counselling and educational achievement', *Educational Research*, Short Report, 27, pp. 68–70.

Charlton, T. (1985) 'Locus of control as a therapeutic strategy for helping children with behaviour and learning problems', *Maladjustment and Therapeutic Education*, 3, pp. 26–32.

de Bono, E. (1976) *Teaching Thinking*, London: Temple Smith.

Feuerstein, R. (1980) *Instrumental Enrichment*, Baltimore: University Park Press.

Freire, P. (1970) *Pedagogy of the Oppressed*, Harmondsworth: Penguin Books.

Henry, C. and Kemmis, S. (1985) 'A point-by-point guide to action research by teachers', *The Australian Administrator*, vol. 6, no. 4, pp. 1–4.

Jones, S.A. (1988a) 'Self-esteem, collaborative learning and Lipman's Philosophy for Children Programme', *Links*, vol. 13, no. 2, pp. 33–6.

Jones, S.A. (1988b) 'The collaborative approach in health education and training', *Journal of the Institute of Health Education*, vol. 26, no. 4, pp. 153–60.

Jones, S.A. (1989a) 'Training teachers by doing', *Education Now*, vol. 1, no. 4, pp. 11, 12.

Jones, S.A. (1989b) 'Quality training in theory and in practice', *New Era in Education*, vol. 70, no. 3, pp. 90–2.

Joyce, B. and Showers, B. (1980) 'Improving in-service training: the message of research', *Educational Leadership*, 37, pp. 379–85.

Kemmis, S. (1986) 'Of tambourines and tumbrils: a response to Rex Gibson's "Critical times for action research"', *Cambridge Journal of Education*, vol. 16, no. 1, pp. 50–2.

Klein, G. (1988) Discussion with Gillian Klein, Editor 'Multicultural Teaching', in *The Education Programme*, BBC 2, 17th March.

Lane, N.R. and Lane [Jones], S.A. (1986) 'Rationality, self-esteem and autonomy through collaborative enquiry', *Oxford Review of Education*, vol. 12, no. 3, pp. 263–75.

Lane, N.R., Lane [Jones], S.A. and Pritchard, M.H. (1986) 'Liberal education and social change, *Educational Philosophy and Theory*, vol. 18, no. 1, pp. 13–24.

Lewin, K. (1947) 'Group decision and social change', in G.E. Swanson *et al.* (eds) *Readings in Social Psychology*, New York: Henry Holt.

Lipman, M. (1985) 'Philosophy and the cultivation of reasoning', *Thinking*, 5, pp. 33–41.

Lipman, M., Sharp, A.M. and Oscanyan, F.S. (1979) *Philosophical Inquiry* (teaching manual), 2nd. edn., Institute for the Advancement of Philosophy for Children, New Jersey.

Lipman, M., Sharp, A.M. and Oscanyan, F.S. (1980) *Philosophy in the Classroom*, 2nd edn. Philadelphia: Temple University Press.

Masterman, L. (1980) *Teaching about Television*, Basingstoke: Macmillan.

Mays, W. (1985) 'Thinking skills programmes: an analysis', *New Ideas Psychology*, 3, 2, pp. 149–63.

Pring, R. (1984) *Personal and Social Education in the Curriculum*, London: Hodder & Stoughton.

Schools Council (1970) *Humanities Curriculum Project*, London: Heinemann.

Schools Council (1981) *The Practical Curriculum* (Schools Council Working Paper 70), London: Methuen Educational.

Sockett, H. (1975) 'Aims and objectives in a social education curriculum', in J. Elliot and R. Pring (eds). *Social Education and Social Understanding*, University of London Press.

Stenhouse, L. (1989) 'Open-minded teaching', *New Society*, 24 July.

Tones, B.K. (1987a) 'Health promotion, affective education and the personal-social development of young people', in K. David and T. Williams, *Health Education in Schools*, 2nd edn, London: Harper & Row.

Tones, B.K. (1987b) 'Health education, PSE and the question of voluntarism', *Journal of the Institute of Health Education*, vol. 25, no. 2, pp. 41–52.

Whalley, M.J. (1987) 'Unexamined Lives: the case for philosophy in schools', *British Journal of Education Studies*, vol. 35, no. 3, pp. 260–80.

White, P. (1983) *Beyond Domination – an essay in the political philosophy of education*, London: Routledge & Kegan Paul.

Chapter 16

Accessing the curriculum with microtechnology

Marie Buckland

Children who fail to achieve expected levels of performance in primary classrooms often have a poor self-image and a negative attitude to their school work (Chapter 2 discusses this relationship in more detail). Many realise they have problems with certain aspects of their work, such as reading and/or writing, and know that they are often unable to perform as well as their peers. They often appear to 'switch off' and show little willingness to attempt new tasks, in the knowledge that they will be exposed to yet another failure situation.

Microtechnology can help to encourage a more positive approach to work, as many teachers have found marked improvements in pupils' concentration, motivation and pattern of work behaviour, when suitable and appropriate use of computers is made (see Jones, 1990). The computer can be a supportive, flexible tool to be used by teachers, when and where they feel it appropriate. The skilled teacher can utilize the power of the computer to help support those pupils who have difficulty with many aspects of the curriculum.

Unfortunately we are still faced with problems of too few computers in schools and too many teachers who lack confidence and experience in their use. Such teachers feel 'de-skilled' when, in fact, with the right software they can put their experience and professional skills to good use. In an ideal situation each classroom would be equipped with at least one computer and teachers would have time to become familiar with using and managing them in their classrooms, with further time being made available for INSET training in the use of software programs. These programs rely upon the skills of the teacher and should be viewed as tools to enhance the style of approach that an experienced teacher already adopts in the classroom. Once teachers have an understanding of the scope and flexibility of these programs, and regular access to a computer, it is possible to create computer-based curricular support material as quickly and easily as any other teacher-made support material. To help bring about this state of awareness, the Department of Education and Science has part funded the services of approximately seven hundred advisory teachers for information technology. These teachers have responsibility for in-service training and the use of computers in classrooms. Some appointments have been made for particular curriculum areas whilst others have assumed responsibilities for cross-phase and cross-curricular work.

THE EQUIPMENT

In this chapter, reference to computers includes the models BBC B, B+ and Master 128, as these are the most commonly found systems in primary education. Others such as the R.M. 380Z, 480Z and Nimbus can be found in secondary schools, although some may be available for use in the primary sector. Many makes of computers have similar styles of software or available programs, but the greatest development in software for special educational needs has been based upon the BBC machine.

For many primary-aged children, especially those who experience learning difficulties, the most successful addition to a computer system (i.e. computer, disk drive, monitor and printer) is a Concept Keyboard. This is a touch sensitive pad that can be attached to one of the ports or sockets on a computer via a long, flat ribbon cable. The Concept Keyboard can be used by the child in place of, or in addition to the keys on the QWERTY keyboard of the computer. A Concept Keyboard is usually available in two sizes, A4 and A3. Many teachers of young children would prefer the A3 size, but it is advisable to look at both before purchasing. For most purposes in the primary classroom, the Concept Keyboard with one hundred and twenty eight individual pressure areas in the form of a grid, is the type to use.

Overlays in the form of specially prepared pieces of A3 or A4 paper are placed over the Concept Keyboard so that when certain programs are loaded into the computer, the child can cause something to happen on the computer screen by simply pressing a particular area on the overlay. Each of the three programs discussed below uses a Concept Keyboard so that ease of use can be offered to children, especially to those who have learning difficulties.

POWERFUL PROGRAMS – THE WORD PROCESSOR

The most successful use of computers has been with the word processor. Word processors vary in their complexity, but they basically offer similar features (i.e. an opportunity to type text on the computer's QWERTY keyboard that can be saved, recalled at a later date, amended and printed out through an attached printer). Those of us who now use word processors as everyday tools for thinking, jotting down notes or composing letters wonder how we managed before the advent of such machines.

With school children, the use of word processors is resulting in marked improvements in the quality and quantity of their written work. A limiting factor has been the availability of computers in classrooms and this has possibly restricted the educational opportunities available to children with learning difficulties.

Word processors are now available to suit the abilities and needs of most children. A very simple, low-cost program is PROMPT/WRITER. The program comes in a package containing a book of helpful documentation, and a number of prepared overlays for both A3 and A4 Concept Keyboards. Three disks accompany the package; the program disk, a utility disk (only needed when creating a new overlay design) and a sample disk which contains a set of sample files to work with the overlays in the pack. PROMPT/WRITER can be used from the QWERTY keyboard and/or a Concept Keyboard. Whole words and phrases can be inserted into writing by one press on the Concept Keyboard. Therefore pupils, who have difficulty producing written work, but can read whole words or recognise pictures, can build up sentences that can be saved onto their work disk, recalled at a later stage, edited with the teacher and eventually printed out in a variety of print sizes.

Pupils, who normally produce poor quality and very little written work, are usually motivated once they receive a professional record of their work in the form of a print-out. If a school does not have a printer to accompany each computer system, the work can be saved onto disk and printed out later.

Using this style of program, the teacher can prepare overlays and files based upon relevant work in the classroom, whether the aim is to support the pupil's reading books, projects or daily activities. The files are easy to create, following instructions from the documentation and menu guidelines on the screen. More skill is needed when designing overlays for the Concept Keyboard. Ordinary A3 and A4 paper can be used and some teachers have made use of pictures, cut-outs and stick-on shapes. The presentation and display on the Concept Keyboard is of paramount importance. This is where the skill and experience of the good, primary class teacher can be utilized. Teachers have always designed sound class-room-based material, and the same principles apply for the designs of Concept Keyboard overlays. Children who experience learning difficulties need a clear, uncluttered presentation of words, phrases and/or pictures. Colour-coding is useful and certain words may need to be linked within a particular area. Once an overlay has been created, the teacher needs to be sure of the words or phrases to be linked with each area of the Concept Keyboard before actually setting about the task of typing in the complete file.

The design and preparation of an overlay and file takes the longest time, but once the procedure has been repeated a few times, it is possible to create new applications fairly quickly. Often when a few teachers within a school decide to work together on a particular project, they create a bank of new files and overlays that are of benefit to many pupils. A group of teachers, in a workshop role, can be a source of inspiration for new applications and can also help to promote continuity within a school.

MATCHING PROGRAMS

Concept Keyboard Match is a very effective but simple program for word, phrase and/or picture matching. Teachers can build up a group of words or phrases in a file, using the utilities disk of Prompt/Writer, that are matched either by word or picture on an overlay. The words are displayed onto the screen and the pupil attempts to match them by pressing the appropriate part of the overlay. With this program, banks of words linked to particular curricular areas can be matched by children. There is an obvious link with supporting reading books and project work, but this program could also be used to support mathematical activities, such as matching numerals to the written word, clock faces to the written time, and so on.

The use of this style of software offers certain benefits to pupils who experience difficulties in learning. There is a lack of 'person' pressure as the pupil is in a non-threatening situation where s/he has control of the progress through the activity.

EXPLORATION

The program Touch Explorer has been available for quite a while. It is an exploration program designed to be used with the Concept Keyboard. The idea is to present the pupil with a blank overlay and, through exploration by pressing the Concept Keyboard keys, written messages appear on the screen to gradually reveal an overlay picture. The disk comes with a few files and with simple instructions on how to make new files. Applications for this program have been endless. It has been used successfully to help children understand contour lines on maps, coordinates and to support mathematical activities.

The author recently designed many outline mathematical overlays with sample files for use on a school-based INSET course. The mathematical topics involved sets, time, money, sequences, patterns and logical reasoning. The material in this INSET Pack (Mathematics and children with learning difficulties – NCET (MESU) Publications) was designed to help support mathematical topics and the files and overlays are suggested starting points for teachers to adopt, amend and extend so that they become more suitable for their particular group of pupils.

The pack was trialled with a number of teachers who have since produced applications of their own. Carol Jarvis of Oxfordshire extended the sequence theme with a file that required her special class group of top junior and 1st year secondary pupils to reveal a Christmas tree picture and message on a gridded overlay. Certain parts of the grid had been left blank so that the pupils had to 'guess' what should have been there. To help the pupils perform the task they needed to understand coordinates; Carol reports that this was mastered in a very short space of time. The advisory teachers of computers and special needs will have knowledge of this material and of other INSET packs.

A new program Touch Explorer Plus has recently become available offering far more facilities than the original Touch Explorer. Whereas the earlier program offered the user a single exploration, Touch Explorer Plus can link together up to six single levels of exploration into a group that can be explored through a single overlay. A number of sample overlays and files come with the package and in order to appreciate the facility of this program, a description of the Time Tunnel group of files and linked overlay might be helpful.

The Time Tunnel overlay shows a line drawing of a particular street in Blackburn. The user is invited to explore the buildings lining the street to find out what each unit was used for. At the top of the overlay are a number of dates; 1874, 1894, 1915, 1939, 1960 and 1988. On pressing each date, the user can discover what the property was used for in that particular year. Thus a picture can be built up of how property changed throughout the years.

An additional feature is a Notepad – a simple word processor that can be used by pupils during the exploration. There is a Print-out option for the Notepad and to record the sequence of exploration.

This package offers a good deal of versatility and great scope for teachers to develop materials to help support many areas of the curriculum. It is more complex to use initially than the other programs referred to and INSET will probably be needed for training and awareness, followed by workshops to nurture ideas for good applications of this powerful resource.

OTHER STYLES OF USE

Within this chapter there has been no reference to programs structured to one particular mode of use. These are sometimes referred to as 'subject specific', and they address particular areas such as spelling, art or mathematics. These programs can be suitable for many pupils with special needs, especially if they offer a flexible style of use in the form of a comprehensive menu system, so that the teacher can personalize the style of activity to suit the child's individual needs.

The aim of this chapter is to show how the curriculum can be made more accessible for children with learning difficulties through the use of a few powerful, flexible programs. Once teachers are familiar with these programs and have the time and confidence to apply their ideas, curriculum support material may be generated and perhaps circulated to help others find a way of helping pupils with learning difficulties. All too often, good teaching ideas remain locked within classroom walls. Teachers tend to be modest or reserved about their own achievements, thinking that they are of no value to others.

News of computer applications that have proved of benefit to pupils with learning difficulties must be made known to other professionals, for the sake of so many pupils who face continual failure.

REFERENCES

Concept Keyboard, AB European Marketing, Cardiff.
Concept Keyboard Match, Blue File software from LEAs and Bristol SEMERC.
Inset packs, NCET (MESU) Publications.
Prompt/Writer, NCET (MESU) Publications.
Touch Explorer, Blue File software from LEAs and Bristol SEMERC.
Touch Explorer Plus, NCET (MESU) Publications.

ADDRESSES

Bristol SEMERC,
School of Education,
Bristol Polytechnic,
Redland Hill,
Bristol,
BS6 6UZ

NCET (MESU) Publications,
Advanced Technology Building,
Science Park,
University of Warwick,
Coventry,
CV4 7EZ

Index

acceptance 32
access: to humanities 145–55; to national curriculum 25,30–1, 38; to science and technology 115–16
active learning 49
'adhocorithms' 105–6
adolescence, preparation for 182–3
advisory teachers 212
affective problems 26–9, 30
algorithms 105–6
Allington School, Chippenham 50, 53–4
all-round needs 8–10
analysing problems 37
analytical model of assessment 17–20
art 156–66; organisation 157–8; pre-schematic stage 163–5; role play 158–9; scribbling stage 159–63
art/craft area 158
art materials 161–2
artefacts 171–2
assemblies, school 172
assessment 44, 46; models for learning difficulties 15–22; movement 135–42; religious education 170; school policy 53; talk 71–2; writing 92–4
Aston Index/Portfolio 16–17
attainment targets: history 147; relevant to reading 75; relevant to writing 90–1, 97–8; science and technology 121–2, 122
attitudes to writing 88–9

behavioural objectives approach 18–20, 75; to maths 104–11
Bell, P. 50–1
Boyd, J. 45
brainstorming 64

Brophy, J.E. 29
Bruner, J.S. 167
Bullock Committee 61

calculation, methods of 104–6
calculators 105–6, 109
Cant, R. 34, 204
card game (with labels) 86
care 54
chalks 161
changing society 175–6
Charlton, T. 24, 35, 36, 204
Chesterton, G.K. 168
child/children: education centred on 41; and movement intervention 130; needs 175; own perception of needs 8–9; 'philosophy for' 201–3, 205; relationship with teachers 174–5
Clark, M. 73–4
class based activities 193, 194, 196–7
classification activity 85
classroom discourse 62–3; promoting 63–6; see also talk
classroom environment 52
classroom organisation 66; for art 157–8
Clay, M. 93
clay 161
cloze procedure 79–80
Clunies-Ross, L. 189
clustering 81–3
coffee jar test 135–8
cognitive connections, networks of 106–8
Coles, M. 89–90
collaborative-participatory approach 201–9; Lipman's 'philosophy for children' 201–3; rationality-counselling balance 204–5;

socio-economic pressures 205–6; stage
    of introducing 205–6; teacher training
    in 206–8
collections 164
communication competence 177
community of inquiry 203
community topics in PSE 182
community of writers 89–90, 101
comparison, language of 108–10
competitions 112–13, 114
'composing' writing skills 95–6
computers 212–16; equipment 213;
    exploration 215–16; matching
    programs 214–15; subject-specific
    programs 216; word processor 213–14
Concept Keyboard 213, 214
Concept Keyboard Match 214–15
conceptual demands 121–2
connections framework 106–8
conservation of weight 112
construction 113, 114
consumer model of partnerships 191
content, emphasis on 146
context, learning see learning context
control, locus of 33, 34–7, 37, 39
controlled scribbling 160
core national curriculum 47–8
Coulby, D. 47–8
counselling: collaborative-participatory
    approach 201–2, 204–5; improving
    self-image 31–4, 36; shared
    responsibility 199; training for teachers
    177
creative development, stages of 157,
    159–65
critical consciousness 207–8, 209
critical evaluation 85–6
critical incidents 177
Croll, P. 14–15
curriculum, national see national
    curriculum
curriculum audit 45
curriculum development 45–6

democatic strategies 201, 204, 209; see
    also collaborative-participatory
    approach
developmental approach to movement
    126, 135, 136–7
directional principles of writing 93
directions 152
discovery stage of scribbling 160
disordered scribbling 159.

distance 152
draft writing 90
drama 64–6, 164
drawing 164
dressing-up racks 158–9

ecological mapping 11–14
education, goals of 56, 202–3
Education Act (1981) 6, 43, 44
Education Reform Act (1988) 1, 169, 172;
    entitlement 10, 38, 44
educational needs 10–11; special see
    special educational needs
emotional problems 26–9, 30; see also
    self-image
empathy 32
encouragement for writers 99–101
entitlement 1, 38, 44
environment: learning 52, 131–2; topics
    in PSE 182
'equal-footing' strategy 201; see also
    collaborative-participatory approach
experience: first-hand and art 163–5; 165;
    learning by 124–5; talking about 63–4
'expert' model of partnerships 190
exploration 215–16
expression, skills in 18

failure experiences: and affective problems
    27–9, 35–6, 37–8; in maths 103–4,
    104; movement 128; in reading 73–4
family life education 179, 182; see also
    parents; personal and social education
fantasy-related drama 64–6
feedback, movement 133
festivals 171
Feuerstein, R. 205
field study unit 150–1
first-hand experiences 163–5, 165
forecasting process 192–5, 196–7
'fortunately-unfortunately' stories 65–6
Freire, P. 209
function words 80
functional integration 43
fundamental movement phase 136–7, 139
future needs 175–6

Gallahue, D.L. 135
games, using 63, 83–4, 86, 110
genuineness 32
geography 14, 149–51; see also
    humanities

glue 162
Good, T.L. 29
graphical representation 151, 152–3, 154
group counselling 204–5
groups: dynamics 67–8; grouping 69–71;
    rejection by peer 66–7, 71

Hanson, D. 53
health education 179, 179–80, 202–3,
    207–8; *see also* personal and social
    education
hearing loss indicators 15–16
Hegarty, S. 189
Her Majesty's Inspectorate (HMI) 48, 54;
    1991 annual report 55–6
history 14, 146–9; *see also* humanities
Hodgson, A. 189
Holford, M. 122
home: discourse compared with school
    62–3; environment and movement
    130, 131–2; forecasting process 193,
    195, 196–7; *see also* parents
home area 158
Hughes, M. 62–3
humanities 14, 145–55

independence in writing 95–7
informal calculative methods 105–6
inquiry, community of 203
INSET (in-service training) 208, 215
instructional language level 94–5
instrumental enrichment programme 205
integration: children with learning
    difficulties 42–3; curriculum 48–9
interactive teaching 48
interview techniques 68–9
investigative work 124–5
IT-INSET 208

Jacobsen, L.L. 37
James, J. 33
Jarvis, C. 215
Jones, K. 24, 189–90, 191
junk modelling 162

Kemmis, S. 208
Kenilworth Castle 147–8
knowledge 61–2, 145
Kolakowski, 168–9

labels 84–6
language: level of writing 93, 94–5; maths

and 106, 108–10; oral 17–18; *see also*
    reading; talk; writing
Lawrence, D. 32–3, 38
learning 26; active 49; by experience
    124–5; optimising 115–16
learning context 9; meaningful for maths
    103, 111–14; science and technology
    124–5
learning difficulties: assessment models
    15–22; recognising 5–22, 117–19;
    specific 116–19; *see also* special
    educational needs
learning environment 52, 131–2
learning successes 11–14, 119
letter 'swapping' 77
letters, missing 77
liaison role 199–200
linguistic discrimination 85
Lipman, M. 201–3, 205, 207
listening: facilities 36; skills 18
LEAs (local education authorities) 43–4
location 152
locational integration 43
locomotor skills 134, 136, 139
locus of control theory 33, 34–7, 37,
    39

management roles 198–9
manipulative skills 90–2, 134, 137, 139
map reading 153
matching programs 214–15
mathematics 103–14; choosing the
    operation 110–11; developing
    understanding 107–8; language
    problems 108–10; low attainment in
    103–4; methods of calculation 104–6;
    objectives approach 104–11;
    purposeful activities in meaningful
    contexts 111–14; recognising
    understanding 106–7
Mays, W. 205
meaningful learning contexts 103, 111–14
media studies 203
Meek, M. 74
message quality 93
microtechnology *see* computers
modelling 161–2
'more than/less than' game 110
Moses, D. 14–15
movement 126–42; assessment and
    recording 135–42; developmental
    approach 126, 135, 136–7; guide-lines
    for intervention 129–35; nature of

problem 128–9; observation of
    problem 127–8
movement feedback 133
movement tasks 131–2, 132–3
multicultural education 203, 208

naming stage of scribbling 160
national curriculum 10, 30–1, 38, 175;
    attainment targets see attainment
    targets; humanities 145; provision for
    special educational needs 44–56;
    reading and accessing 25; science and
    technology 120, 121–2, 122–4;
    spelling 97–8
National Writing Project 89, 92, 98–9
needs: all-round 8–10; children's 175;
    educational 10–11; future 175–6;
    special educational see special
    educational needs; unmet 21–2
networks of cognitive connections 106–8
neuro-motor system 128–9
Notepad 216
number operations 110–11
numeracy, objectives for 104, 111

objectives see behavioural objectives
observation of movement 135–42
observational drawing 164
operations, number 110–11
oral language 17–18; see also talk
oral reading 73
organisation role 198–9
overlays 214

paint 161
paper 161
parents: classroom discourse 62–3;
    movement intervention 130, 131;
    partnership with teachers 189–200;
    relationships with teachers 174, 177–8
participation 203–4; see also
    collaborative-participatory approach
peer counselling 33–4
peer group rejection 66–7, 71
perceptual discrimination 85
personal education 179; see also personal
    and social education
personal relationships 182
personal and social education (PSE)
    174–85, 202; children's needs 175;
    effect of schools 176–8; evaluation
    185; future needs 175–6; preparation

for adolescence 182–3; selection and
    coordination 181; selection of topics
    182; sex education 183; staff
    preparation 184–5
personal topics in PSE 182
perceptual-cognitive system 128–9
'philosophy for children' 201–3, 205
phonics 75
pictures, word 78
plan views 153
planning events 112, 114
plasticine 161
play 158–9
playschool, art in 156
Plowden Report 41–2, 183
political attitudes 205–6
positive reinforcements 36
Practical Issues in Primary Education
    (PIPE) 49
predictability 177
pre-schematic stage 157, 163–5
problem-solving 203; real 113, 114
problems, analysing 37
procedural complexity 122–4
process, art and 161, 162, 165
PROMPT/WRITER 213–14
provision for special educational needs
    41–56
psychomotor development 134
publication 90
punishments 177
pupil profiles: movement 138–42; writing
    93–6
purposeful activities 103, 111–14
puzzles, word 78–9

question asking 68

rationality see reasoning skills
reading 24–39, 73–86; accessing national
    curriculum 25; age and ability 73–4;
    cloze procedure 79–80; clustering
    81–3; comprehension of discourse
    80–4; difficulties 25–6, 117–18;
    emotional problems 26–9; improved by
    enhanced self-image 31–7; labels
    84–6; letter 'swapping' 77; missing
    letters 77; positive influences on
    standards 26; puzzles 78–9; remedial
    teaching 31–2, 74–5; scanning game
    83–4; without vowels 76–7; word
    pictures 78

'reading books' 73
reasoning skills 201–3; balance with counselling 204–5
receptive skills 18
recognition model of assessment 20–2
recognition of special educational needs 11–22, 198
recognition of text 84–5
recording/records 45–6; forecasting process 192–5,196–7; movement 135–42; talk 71–2
Records of Achievement 44, 49–50, 54
rejection by peer group 66–7, 71
religious education 10, 167–73; aims 169–70; assessment 170; defining religion 167–9; emphasising structure of subject 167; providing for children with learning difficulties 170–2; subject matter 169
remedial reading 31–2, 74–5
report, annual 44
rhyme 75
Richards, C. 122
rituals 177
Rogers, C. 34
role-play 113, 114, 158–9
Rosenthal, R.R. 37
rotational system 157–8
routines, arithmetical 104, 106
Rowland, S. 9, 145–6, 146–7
rudimentary movement phase 136–7

samples, writing 93
scanning 83; game 83–4
schemes of work 51
school assemblies 172
school development plan 45, 51
School Entrant Screening coffee jar test 135–8
school grounds 164
schools: effect of 176–8; special educational needs policy 44–6, 53–5
science and technology 115–25; access for all 115–16; learning context 124–5; learning difficulties 116–19; level of conceptual demand 121–2; nature of 119–20; procedural complexity 122–4
scissors 162, 162–3
screening, movement 135–8, 139
'scribble writing' 90–2
scribbling stage 157, 159–63
'secretarial' writing skills 95–6
self-correction 95

self-image 30, 31, 47; enhancing 31–9; 'equal-footing' strategy 201; low and reading problems 28–9
sellotape 162
sensory system 128–9
sequencing 65
sex education 183
shared responsibility see working relationships
simulations 113, 114
skimming 83, 84
small group support 193, 194, 196–7
social education 179; see also personal and social education
social integration 43
social learning paradigm 34–7
society, changing 175–6
socio-economic pressures 205–6
Spackman, P. 34, 204
special educational needs: balance 7–8; provision for 41–56; recognising 11–22, 198; teachers' perceptions of 6; wheel-profile for writing 93–6
specialist vocabulary 151, 154
specific learning difficulties 116–19
spelling 97–9, 118
sport-related movement skills 136–7
stability 134, 137, 139
Starkings, D. 170
Stenhouse, L. 201, 209
stimulating children 164–5, 165–6
stories 65–6, 171
subject-specific computer programs 216
subtraction 107
symbols 106, 153

talk 18, 61–72, 90; classroom discourse 62–3; involving all children 66–71; promoting in classrooms 63–6; records 71–2; vital 61–2
task analysis 132–3
teachers: advisory 212; autonomy 45; effect on group discussion 70; enhancing pupils' self-image 34, 36–7, 38, 39; INSET 208, 215; and movement intervention 130, 131; partnership with parents 189–200; perception of special needs 6; PSE 174–5, 176–7, 178, 184–5; role in art 157; training in collaborative-participatory approach 206–8, 209
teaching/counselling role 199
technical vocabulary 151, 154

technology *see* science and technology
three-dimensional art work 161–2
time management 195
Time Tunnel 215–16
Tizard, B. 62–3
'top down' remedial teaching 74–5
topic/thematic work 69
Touch Explorer 215
Touch Explorer Plus 215–16
training for teachers 206–8, 209, 215
transplant model of partnerships 190–1

unmet needs 21–2

values 55
visits 172
visual difficulties 16, 116–17
vocabulary, specialist 151, 154
vowels, reading without 76–7

Ward, A. 124
Ward, S. 47–8
Warnock Report 42–3, 56
wax crayons 161

weight, conservation of 112
Wells, G. 61
Wendy house 158
Whalley, M.J. 203
wheel-profile 93–6
White, P. 205–6
whole class tuition 66
windmill activity 123–4
Womack, D. 124
word-banks 118
word pictures 78
word processors 213–14
work, schemes of 51
working relationships 189–200;
    informative stage 191–2; introductory
    stage 191; joint provision stage 192;
    roles 195–200; sharing of
    responsibilities stage 192–5; time
    management 195
writing 88–101, 117–18; attitudes to
    88–9; community of writers 89–90,
    101; encouragement 99–101;
    intervention 92–7; overcoming
    difficulties 90–2; SEN profile 93–6;
    spelling 97–9

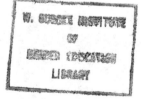